MW01291770

Other Books and Writings by Rhuddlwm Gawr:
Courses
Duienith Cymmry Correspondence Course — "The Thirteen
Treasures" (13 lessons) $10.95 each lesson
An Advanced Correspondence Course — "The Path of the An-
cients" (23 lessons) $12.95 each lesson ("The Thirteen Trea-
sures" Course must be completed first)
Pagan Primer Series
    Celtic Rituals and Festivals
    Nature, Magic and Psychic Healing
    *Human Awakening: Woman, Man, and Paganism
    *Dream Magic: Interpretation and Programming
    Initiation Into the Celtic Tradition
    Sexual Energy in the Old Religion
    *Celtic Astrology - The Twelve Keys
    *A Pagan Herbal
    *Relinking: Cooperating With Nature Spirits
    Pagan Mysteries
    Psychic Development Exercises
    *Celtic Meditation
    *Celtic Mythology
    *Celtic Divination
    Celtic Crystal Magic
    *Earth Energy: Dowsing, Ley Lines and Power Points
Y Tylwyth Teg Series
    The Quest: The Search for the Grail of Immortality
    The Way: The Discovery of the Grail of Immortality
    *The Pentacle and the Sword: The Story of the American
    Wicca Movement
    The Nine Levels
    The Triads: Welsh Wisdom
    *Taliesin of the Radiant Brow
    The Thirteen Mystical Treasures of Wales
* Forthcoming Publications - Not Yet in Print

For Further Information Write:
    Camelot Press, Ltd.
    P.O. Box 674884,
    Marietta, GA 30006-0006
    e-mail camgroup@tylwythteg.com

the way

A Discovery of the Grail of Immortality
Welsh Witchcraft and the Old Religion

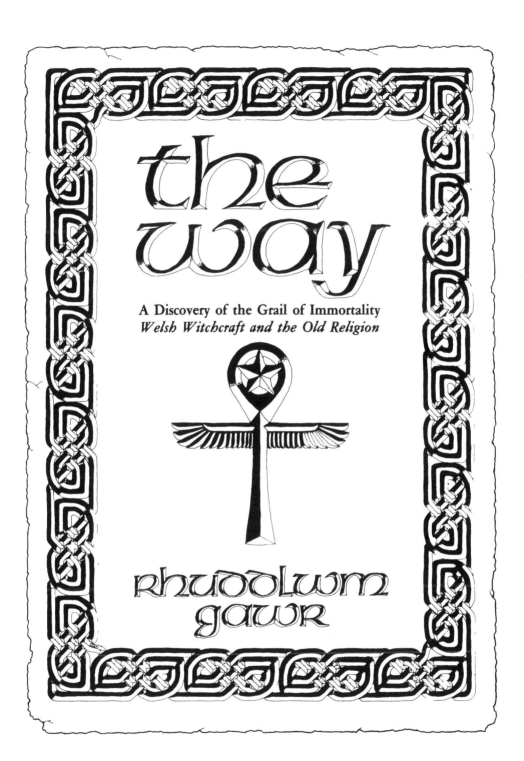

the way

A Discovery of the Grail of Immortality
Welsh Witchcraft and the Old Religion

Rhuddlwm Gawr

Authors Choice Press

San Jose New York Lincoln Shanghai

The Way
A Discovery of the Grail of Immortality Welsh Witchcraft and the Old Religion

All Rights Reserved © 1986, 2002 by William Wheeler

No part of this book may be reproduced or transmitted in
any form or by any means, graphic, electronic, or mechanical,
including photocopying, recording, taping, or by any
information storage or retrieval system, without the
permission in writing from the publisher.

Authors Choice Press
an imprint of iUniverse, Inc.

For information address:
iUniverse, Inc.
5220 S. 16th St., Suite 200
Lincoln, NE 68512
www.iuniverse.com

Originally published by Camelot Press

(The material in Chapters 7, 8, 9, 10, and 12 appeared in course
lessons published by Y Tylwyth Teg in 1970.)

Inside Illustrations: Rhuddlwm Gawr, Janis Ramsey, George Bain
Cover Illustration: Ron Lindahn

ISBN: 0-595-23125-X

Printed in the United States of America

DEDICATION

This book is dedicated to a wonderful and beautiful human being— Diana. She is representative of all that is right and good in humanity. She is always there when she is needed, and she treats everyone with love and respect. Camelot-of-the-Wood, the future home of our tribe, is hers and will be there when she is ready. She deserves the title of Lady if anyone does. Thank you lovely Diana—We love you.

Rhuddlwm ap Gawr

ACKNOWLEDGEMENT:

This book acknowledges the many people who made it possible: To my mother who gave birth to me, Thanks, Mom. To my wife, Mary Sue, who married me, lived with me and put up with me, I love you. To my teacher and guide, Sarah, who showed me the path, there are no words, only tears of happiness. To my high priestess, who stayed loyal to me during the bad times as well as the good, thank you, Branwen. To my students and friends who supported me on my journey, Elise White, Carol Barnes, Jim Carney, Dawn Kramer, Lugh Miller, Ashara, Jim, Valarie, Janice, Sunny and all the rest, I love you all, without you this book would only by an idea.

Rhuddlwm ap Gawr

CONTENTS

INTRODUCTION

There is a magical movement flowing over America. This movement is the result of one primary, overriding force: the coming purification of the earth.

Every ten to twenty thousand years or so the earth goes through a periodic cleansing that must occur before the people of this world are allowed to go on into the next great age. To guide the true *"children of the light,"* the children of nature, through this time of devastation and trouble, the great lords of the planes have sent teachers to the earth to gather together those souls who are following the great plan and will themselves become teachers. These guides are in every country, but for the most part remain hidden from the general population by necessity. They would be hounded, or worse, killed, by those so-called *"children of the true god,"* *"good Christians,"* *"saints,"* *"good Moslems,"* *"good Hindus,"* or other misguided fanatics who are largely responsible for humankind's ills today. Some say Rhuddlwm Gawr is such a guide. He has come out in the open for the first time because of the necessity for haste.

The trying times will soon be here!

Earthquakes, wars, floods, plagues, volcanoes and anarchy — these are just a sample of what is in store for the human race over the next nineteen years. This book is not only the story of Rhuddlwm and his discovery of the Grail of Immortality, it is a guide book to show you "the way" to your own spiritual freedom. This book is not a "how-to-do-it" book, it is a what-to-do road map that leads you to an understanding of the ancient mysteries of Atlantis and how to survive the coming cataclysm.

11

Rhuddlwm Gawr was initiated into the Welsh tradition of Gwiddion, or witchcraft in the 60s. This tradition is a direct descendant of the ancient Atlantean priesthood and is the origin of the Celtic druidic mysteries. He brought this tradition to the United States and began teaching in Washington, DC in 1966.

From the beginning and throughout the early 70s Rhuddlwm taught the ancient secrets of energy movement, healing and magic, but his road was not an easy one. For every true student and seeker of knowledge there were many who were learning Wicca for the wrong reasons: to feed their ego, to use people, and for monetary gain.

Unfortunately, there are greedy individuals who see a religious movement as a chance to make easy money or gain power. Besides charging exorbitant fees for their religious services or products, they sometimes publish newsletters and preach spirituality; but instead of trying to help spread the word, they use their organization for their own selfish ends. "They" teach paganism or Wicca, therefore others cannot advertise courses in their newsletters; "they" are the only group that is "right", therefore others are wrong.

Because of the failure of these groups, Rhuddlwm began receiving more and more requests from seekers to teach classes in the Atlantean Mysteries. Soon there were hundreds who had attended his classes. In 1973 he met a seeker who was to become a future high priestess. Lady Branwen was the equalizing force behind his search for a home for his tribe. The result was the establishment of Camelot-of-the-Woods, a community of elders in northeast Georgia. In 1982 it was decided that there would be several locations for the home of Dynion Mwyn: The first would be near Athens, Georgia. It can be found in the direction of the son. The second is in the north Georgia mountains: an "L" shapes its name; a "bird" finishes the game.

As these centers for esoteric study were established, many seekers came forward. But because of the stringent requirements for membership in Y Tylwyth Teg, many students failed to satisfy those standards and left, starting their own eclectic traditions.

Y Tylwyth Teg teaches the way, but few stay long enough to learn it. In fact, most of the Pagan/Wiccan groups in Atlanta are the direct and indirect result of Rhuddlwm's work in the late seventies.

As more and more seekers have become attuned to the stirring forces of nature, Y Tylwyth Teg as a religious tradition has grown by leaps and bounds, forming groves in California, Florida, New York, Illinois, and Tennessee. As the students grew in numbers problems arose due to the seekers' trying to start groves in areas where conservative fundamentalist Christians live. Members were harassed by "saviours of the faith" and local governments threw stumbling blocks in Y Tylwyth Teg's path as land was being purchased in the church's name. So in 1974 Rhuddlwm applied to the Internal Revenue Service for a group tax exemption. It took three years to obtain it, but in March of 1977 the IRS issued Y Tylwyth Teg the first, and until the present, the only group tax exemption for a pagan organization in the United States, allowing bona fide pagan groves and other religious groups who join the Association of Cymmry Wicca to automatically be tax exempt.

As this book is being written, U.S. Senator Jesse Helms made the first assault on our tax exemption. On behalf of the national pagan community we are fighting for our legal existence. Lady Branwen has done a great deal to inform the pagan community and she deserves a great deal of credit for contacting everyone. Jesse's amendment was defeated in committee, but it is only the first battle. There will be many more.

On Candlemas, February 2, 1977 Rhuddlwm obtained an organizational charter from the State of Georgia declaring that the Church of Y Tylwyth Teg, Incorporated, is a religious organization, to be considered a true religion in every sense of the word.

Rhuddlwm has been working behind the scenes for years using his influence in state and federal governments to slowly create a legal precedent for the complete recognition of pagan groups and Wicca as a true religious movement in the United States. He organized, planned and directed the first "Gathering of the Tribes" in Georgia in the late 1970s and has continued to be involved with many important pagan projects throughout the years.

This book is the result of Rhuddlwm's desire to bring the religion of Y Tylwyth Teg to the largest number of people in the shortest amount of time. His first book, The Quest, a pagan bestseller, described his discovery of the path of Y Tylwyth Teg and his search for the grail of immortality. It was met with bitter accusations from his elders in Wales, and criticism by some in the pagan community. It was too close to the truth! Since writing The Quest, Rhuddlwm has become a seventh level elder in the tradition of Y Tylwyth Teg and determines what should or should not be revealed to the general public in the US. He has written several books and Wicca courses and is currently in the process of publishing more.

In May of 1976 Rhuddlwm experienced a religious and mystical vision of such magnitude that his life was completely transformed and his spiritual path became clear. A being appeared to Rhuddlwm and revealed the true meaning of the ancient Atlantean grail mysteries.

The revelation of these mysteries so amazed Rhuddlwm that for months afterwards he couldn't believe how simple the concepts were, but also how complex. He discovered that the grail legends and the creator myths were really reflections of the true meaning of life — and a secret source of power. They also revealed how a seeker could obtain riches beyond her wildest dreams, happiness only the gods could know, and knowledge, love and power, the keys to the mysteries.

Rhuddlwm has contacted his Spiritual Guides several times since, and each time has received a message. One such message concerns *"The Keys."*

Have you ever thought you were a special person? "A starchild"? Have you ever had the feeling that the earth was headed for an impending disaster? Has your life been filled with coincidences beyond pure chance? Have you been more than a little interested in survival in the last few years? Have you been more in tune with nature than in our dehumanizing society? Do you have an interest in astrology? Are you interested in psychic phenomena? If you are then you too may be one of those special human beings whose soul is one of the "keys". You too may be one of Y Tylwyth Teg, the beautiful family.

We are of Y Tylwyth Teg, one of the five mystical clans of Dynion Mwyn, "the gentle folk" of Wales, and were chosen eons ago to carry the grail, the secret tradition, forward through time until humanity needed spiritual and magical guidance once again.

That time has arrived, and you have picked up this book not by chance but by design. This book has been created for one purpose only — to help certain individuals take the next step of spiritual awareness and join the other "Keys" who are even now working and studying in preparation of the time when they too will take their place in history. We are a race of guides and warriors who are once again reincarnating onto this plane to lead humanity to the gates of Gwlad Yr Hav, the Summerland, paradise. Y Tylwyth Teg teaches by allegory and We manipulate reality by magic. We also heal the mind, body and spirit of those in need.

In The Quest, Rhuddlwm presented for the first time a simple Book of Shadows for the Welsh tradition of "Gwiddon" or witchcraft (Wicca, if you are anglo-saxon). He revealed the basic teachings, mysteries, rituals and mythology which is relevant to all Welsh oriented tradi-

14

tions. In The Way Rhuddlwm continues his journey of enlightenment and expands the Book of Shadows. He tells of his visions of the future: the coming age of earthquakes, anarchy, and famine.

The Way sets down a plan for spiritual as well as physical survival during this coming age of purification and takes the reader into the realm of initiation and advancement on the planes. In The Way, Rhuddlum reveals some of the "Mysteries".

Some will hate him for it, they would keep the knowledge from you — they know little.

Some will mock him for it; they would feed their egos at your expense — they understand little.

Some will lie about it; they would fear exposure as frauds — they care little.

But some will be profoundly affected by it, they would accept the truth and find *"The Way"*.

My life has been totally changed by my contact with this man. He is totally involved with the spiritual advancement of humankind and has shown me The Way to my religion. **Y Tylwyth Teg.**

Every day he writes, teaches, plans and spends his own money and a great deal of time on his religion and asks for nothing in return. He does it out of love for his students and the rest of humanity and without concern for his ego or reputation.

I am profoundly humbled. Every day I see people who claim to teach *"Witchcraft," "Enlightenment,"* or *"Spiritual Advancement,"* for a fee. But here is a man who is quietly teaching the truth as he knows it, without compensation. He has difficulty accepting payment for his expenses or the thousands of lessons that he has published with his own money. I have read *"The Way."* I believe it is one of the most important books that you will ever read.

Blessed Be
Rhiannon

George Bain.

CHAPTER 1

THE MESSAGE

A Vision of the Future

It happened in 1976. It was a foggy and wet May eve, a typical south Georgia spring night. I had decided that I was not going to Atlanta for the Pagan festival and I also *"wasn't going to take it any longer."* I had had it with my wife, my kids, my job, and the craft — everyone and everything. I didn't want to teach any more, I didn't want to be hassled by egotistical witches any more, I was tired of *"witch queens"* who were threatened if they weren't the center of attention. I was glad that we had moved from Atlanta to South Georgia.

Even though this was the *"bible belt,"* there were many benefits to living near Americus — it was quiet, there were forests everywhere, and even though most people were rednecks — they were friendly up to a point.

I drove leisurely toward Lake Blackshear — as I said, it was foggy, and I couldn't see more than fifty yards in front of me. The windshield wipers clicked back and forth as the mist swirled past the car. There was a long bridge across the narrow part of the lake and you could see patches of clearness as the fog thinned and thickened, always moving. I drove across and began looking for the entrance to Veterans State Park. It took me several minutes to find it but when I did the entrance was blocked, so I parked my car and got out.

The walk into the park was long and wet, but it was also quiet and peaceful. I could hear the crickets chirping and the frogs croaking their little song. I found a place on the beach next to some cattails and reeds that looked inviting and sat down, thinking back.

17

The last few years since leaving Wales had been lonely and frustrating. I had worked for NASA on the Apollo Space Program, and I was there when the first man landed on the moon. I had also been there when the recession hit in the 70s and ten thousand engineers lost their jobs. Had I done the right thing going back to the university and getting my degree? And here it was 1976 and I was in another recession, only this time into the housing industry, and I've got a landscape architecture degree! Just my luck. Always the wrong time and the wrong place. I was really feeling sorry for myself. I was making only $8,000 a year as a rural planner in south Georgia. I had trouble at home, trouble with my job, and trouble with my spirituality. I was supposedly someone who was spiritually advanced, yet I was so caught up in materialism that it meant more to me to advance in my job than to advance in my spirit. It was a very low point in my life. That's when the fog over the lake spoke to me.

"Rhuddlwm!!!"

It was like an explosion in my brain without sound. Startled, my reverie was broken and my eyes darted back and forth looking for the source of the voice. And then my body froze where I sat. A face was materializing over the water even as I stared, unable to move.

The voice continued. *"You must not resist. There is too little time to waste it needlessly. The time will soon come when you will be shaken to your knees with the movement of the earth. The sky will darken, the earth will open, and fire will rain down as the molten rock flows everywhere."*

I was totally terrified ! My mind raced in a thousand different directions. What was happening to me !

"Your time has come, Rhuddlwm, the time that was prophesied by the old ones. The young god came to your people almost 4,000 years ago bringing the message of love and light, but his followers misunderstood and kept his word secret. He came again 2,000 years ago, but again the people misunderstood and spread their own words of ignorance and hate. Today you still live in this world of illusion. It is time that your people view the real world, the world that must cleanse itself of lies and deceit. You are one of the elders, Rhuddlwm, a leader who shall appear for a time affecting many and then disappear into the mist, but your words will live on."

I wasn't as frightened now. Curiosity was rearing its head.

"You will publish a book, Rhuddlwm, first by your own hand, and then with the help of others. And more books shall be created by your

18

ties with us, for we are your guides. Just as you teach others and are yourself taught, so shall you be taught by us and teach us. All is one."

More and more interesting; I always wanted to write a book. But how ? I really can't afford it.

"You will soon begin the creation of a hidden community within an open society. This shall be known as Dynion Mwyn, or 'the gentle folk', the home of Y Tylwyth Teg — the fair family. Around this hidden community and protecting it, a visible society shall be created, 'Camelot-of-the-Wood' and 'Bangor' — a school of nature. These institutions shall appear and grow as the first buds to appear in spring, and they shall be planted in the north Georgia hills to flourish and change as the demands of the eternal plan of the Great Spirit. I, Gwydion — give to you, Rhuddlwm, the power to change those things that can be changed."

A misty hand reached out to me and touched me on the forehead, and a blinding pain burst in my mind, blinding me for what seemed like an eternity. When my vision cleared the face was still there, but the voice had changed, now more feminine. But what was it saying about a community and a school ?

"Rhuddlwm, we haven't much time, the hour grows short and the doorway will soon close. You must do your best to teach as many seekers as possible in the next eight years, planting the seeds of Dynion Mwyn wherever you travel. The money will come and you will begin to build 'Camelot' by the year 1987. The number 23 shall guide you, thus putting you in contact with the matrix of fourteen keys. You yourself are one of those keys, looking for thirteen others. You will soon meet those who will help you, some of whom you will call soul mates. You will begin by 'gathering' the many tribes of the people together who are appearing even now on the borders of this land.

"Rhuddlwm, show others the truth as you know it, but above all else watch for the signs as they appear. To prove the things we say to you, look you toward Italy on the 8th of May as well as to Russia. Then look toward the island of New Guinea and Mexico City on the 5th of June. During this year will be many more earthquakes than ever before, but look you to the year 1985 as the beginning of the earth changes that will change the face of the world. Between the year 1986 and the year 2007 the following shall occur:

"Three days of darkness shall pass over the face of the world; The west coast of California shall be devastated; Charleston, South Carolina will fall; The Great Lakes will empty into the Gulf of Mexico and

the earth's pole will begin to shift; Japan will be changed as in the blinking of an eye; and Europe will undergo many rapid earth changes. As these events transpire they will cause many people to wonder at the reality of this world. Some will see the events as the second coming of Christ. There will be a great upsurge in membership in many churches and a great panic. You must not accept refugees at Dynion Mwyn just because they wish to be saved from the coming cataclysm. Choose only those who have the courage to survive and not just the desire.''

My brain seemed to go into overload. What did all this mean? What was this about earthquakes and darkness ? This was like a bad dream. What was happening to me !

"You must make a concerted effort to create Camelot-of-the-Wood as soon as possible, for many people will soon begin to seek you out as a haven from danger and a school of wisdom. When again you visit Wales much of this will be shown to you. Even now your teachers are preparing for your coming. You are one of the fourteen — One of the Keys.

"Soon you will understand the prophecy: 'He that was born of man shall come in many ways in many words — he that was born of the spirit shall come to teach and enlighten. He that was born of mid-summer shall bring the key.'

Although I thought I had learned basic Psychic knowledge when I first visited Wales in 1966, as I listened to the voice, everything I had studied, everything I had been taught by my teachers began to make much more sense to me; but I still refused to believe that a dis-embodied voice was telling me these things! Even though I have been there and I had been born on midsummer day, I couldn't be the per-son the voice was talking about! What and who were the fourteen keys!!?

"Rhuddlwm, I will come to you again ten years from today.'' The face lost its form, changing into swirls of clouds.

"Wait,'' I cried. Too late. I couldn't even ask a question. I didn't know what to ask. I was very disturbed to say the least. As I finally got up off the bank I was shaking and frightened. I walked back to my car slowly and carefully, and even as I began to think this was all a dream the voice again sounded in my ear.

"As you drive home look for a white rabbit. It will give you the answer you need.''

I decided then and there I was a candidate for a mental institution.

I thought of the old movie "Harvey" and the man who claimed white rabbits talked to him. As I drove home I pondered all that I had witnessed. But had I? It all seemed hazy, as if I had been dreaming. I was approaching the cutoff back to Americus when it happened. Several cars were rapidly overtaking me from behind as I slowed down to make the turn.

Suddenly a white figure appeared in front of me and I swerved off the road! As I skidded to a stop a large tanker truck roared over the top of the hill. It was on my side of the road! If I had not swerved I would now be spattered all over the countryside!

The other cars behind me had seen me skid to a stop and slowed enough to get out of the truck's way. One girl in her late teens stopped by the side of the road and ran over to see how I was.

"It all happened so fast. Are you all right!? Wow, if we hadn't slowed down we would all be dead by now! How did you know that truck was coming!?"

"I don't know," I replied, still seeing the image of a large white rabbit in the middle of the road, its eyes telling me to stop!

CHAPTER 2

THE FOURTEEN KEYS

The Watchers and Why They Are Here

It was several years later after much research and meditation that I began to understand the meaning of the fourteen keys. My memory turned to that night long ago. The face over the lake was speaking. *"Before each major change in this solar system, the spirit world and the astral become clouded with teachers waiting to reincarnate. These teachers have come to show the worthy seekers of this plane the path to the future for only a select few will survive the coming devastation.*

"Rhuddlwm, true teachers come to the earth in groups of fourteen, seven males and seven females, Soulmates with each other to find each other. Through the finding comes a recognition and a realization of The Power. This is the Way to the future age of peace and love and the way of true enlightenment.

"These Keys experience both the lower vibrations of physical desire as well as the higher forms of the vibration — what many call Spiritual Love — the basis for a true Soulmate relationship

"Most people have been taught that when two people meet and fall in love, they must mate for life. This 'Law' was invented by men as a means of keeping what they felt was rightfully theirs and as a means of preventing disharmony within society. This occurs when a loved one turns his or her affections toward another, or when two or more people desire to physically love the same member of the opposite sex. Love at this level becomes mingled with many other physical emotions and desires.

"This was not always so. There was a time on Earth when physical bodies were of a much higher vibration, and therefore much closer

23

to the higher spiritual realms from which all souls come. Souls during that time operated in the physical world at a much higher level of existence and were free to love other beings without the lower emotions of possessiveness, jealousy and guilt. Life was more open and less complicated than it is now. When you hear people talking about free love or a freer type of love, they are unconsciously remembering the distant past and how it once was, and looking for it again.

"There is such thing as a spiritual marriage, the marriage between two or more souls (but always in pairs or groups of pairs). This marriage took place on the higher spiritual planes in the distant past.

"Each soul is different. Some are dependent, some are independent; some have very high spiritual purposes and some are still learning. There are also those who have chosen to grow and learn as part of a group of Keys — a team — Soulmates. These Soulmates are always spiritually united and cannot be separated. If they do not meet their counterpart during an incarnation, they feel incomplete even though they may be physically married to another."

This idea of soul mates was interesting. I was wondering if I had really met mine.

"They search constantly for their Soulmates, not consciously realizing who they are searching for. When they do meet, they feel complete for the first time in their life.

"Soulmates sometimes try to establish a permanent union with someone other than their partners. Those keys who are part of such a union are constantly searching for 'true love' and never finding it in their relationships. It is essential that these people understand why they feel as they do.

"Seven male soul 'Keys' are created together. These seven gravitate toward each other, a duality of three plus three and a leader. They are attracted to a group of seven female soul 'Keys'. These fourteen souls represent union and seldom know they are part of a group of fourteen keys.

"The fourteen souls are attracted to one another and any of the seven males is a perfect soulmate to any of the seven females as well as being attuned to the other thirteen members of this 'Sacred' Family.

Why were there fourteen souls in a family? This was very confusing and the ideas seemed to form in my brain so fast that I was having a very hard time keeping up with the concepts.

"Each of the fourteen souls is a 'Key.' But not every soul is a key — only those souls that have reached a higher level of advancement

24

to allow them to recognize the other keys. They are special souls. The rest of the souls that reincarnate on this earth are here to learn needed lessons and to advance spiritually. Unfortunately few are ready for advancement on this earth today.

"Each Sacred Family is a nucleus of teachers who are responsible for certain seekers. These teachers are building Camelot-of-the-Wood, a tribal community that will survive the coming cataclysm.

"Each family unit is responsible for its own advancement and training, at the direction of a Master — a Guide.

"Each Sacred Key is a teacher and a guide, responsible for the instruction of ordinary souls onto the path of enlightenment. Each key may only teach three individual seekers of the opposite sex at one time if they are teaching individuals, or two groups of fourteen seekers.

"When Hu Gadarn established our tribe and gave us the duty of helping humankind through the coming cataclysm thousands of years ago, he gave us the technique of training the "Sacred Keys:" "Always see every action in life as a learning opportunity and a way to help others find The Way.' He said. As each Master establishes a Sacred Family, they dedicate themselves to the service of the Great Spirit and the philosophy of Hu Gadarn."

Now here was a name that I knew, Hu Gadarn. He was in one of the Welsh Triads that I had copied down when I was in Wales.!

"There is total honesty within a Sacred Family, There is no possessiveness and no jealousy, because all insecurity disappears as love and caring take their place. Everything within a sacred family belongs to all."

This was crazy; how in the hell can you have any kind of relationship if there was no jealousy ? In every relationship I had ever heard of, if there was no jealousy or possessiveness, the people really weren't in love.

"Living together in a Sacred Family is the ideal. Each person is supported by the other members. Each child born within the family is considered to be a child of all, as well as a child of Soulmates. This allows each member to become complete and whole, supported by an extended family of people who love each other and care for each other.

"Souls born from the year 1929 to the present are part of a group of souls that were together in ancient Atlantis. Many of these souls built the Egyptian and Atlantian cultures.

"Each of these souls has the choice of becoming a greatly developed

25

soul while fulfilling important roles in their service to humanity or they can choose to bring turmoil and strife to others. Some of these groups of souls are keys, some are not; some are destined to realize their importance and some will never realize anything.

"You will help others find their Soulmates, Rhuddlwm, and recognize their place in the coming new world.

This was sounding like too much work ! What am I going to get out of this ! What about MY happiness ?!

"As each new seeker becomes connected with his or her Soulmate, they will discover their true purpose. But many will not find their Soulmate until they reach Camelot, for the lessons that their soul must learn are individual in nature.

"Rhuddlwm, be kind, for seekers are like children, they will let their emotions govern their minds at first and these emotions are selfish in nature. Have patience with them for they are future teachers of The Way.

"You will find the thirteen other keys, Rhuddlwm," the being said out of the mist. *"They will be your energy and your strength. Those keys will be the nucleus of your community. They will be different, yet the same; and once together it will be this force that creates the knowledge movement that transports the sacred mysteries into the next century.*

"Rhuddlwm, you have met some of the keys during your life. They are important. Don't lose them. A key is a part of the whole, a cog in a machine, the most important concept in your tradition. How else are you to transmit the mysteries into the next century? You will know them by their auras, you will know them by their desire to survive, you will know them by their thirst for knowledge, you will know them by the way they think, and you will know them by their acts. Some will try to convince you that they are keys. Some will try to become keys. Stay to your course. You will know the keys. The knowledge will come from within."

He finished.

I have searched and searched and found a few but there are still keys to be discovered. They are all sizes and ages. Some are young, some are tall, some are spiritual, some are business people, some are pagans, all are part of a group soul cycle.

Even though this chapter is one of the shortest ones in the book, it is the most important. There are several groups of fourteen keys out in the world. They must join together. Begin searching out your soul mates, your spiritual brothers and sisters. Learn to merge completely with them. I have found that a soul mate can be easy to find, but hard to connect with. Soul mates will be found near to your everyday life, but unless they also believe as you do it will be very difficult for you. But if you will open your heart and let your feelings become apparent, your soul mate will be attracted to you.

We are building **Camelot-of-the-Wood** here in the North Georgia hills. Those of you who feel that these ideas are familiar and tug at your mind like a long forgotten memory, you may be one of us. If there is no such feeling that drives you, that consumes you with loneliness for those of your own kind, please put this book down; it is not for you. It is only meant for those who feel a depth of emotion which identifies them with our way — The Way of Love — Knowledge — and Power.

Blessed be.

Rhuddlwm

CHAPTER 3

THE SPIRITUAL REALMS

The Great Spirit and the Planes

I had been thinking all day about what the being in the mist had said. It was really strange because I seemed to be able to remember everything verbatim, as though it was recorded for all time in my brain. Now I could compare the Ideas and concepts with the knowledge that I had received from my teachers in Wales. My mind again drifted back to those days long past.

The Welsh Master was speaking. *"The ancient way after the soul was well established in the human animal, was to send messengers into this dimension or world. The purpose of these messengers was to guide humanity into the light. The messenger was sent by the Great Spirit, who is the life force which inhabits all dimensions of reality."*

Colored lights and swirls of sound seem to envelop my brain as these ideas were being made part of my philosophy.

"Each dimension has access to all dimensions if the gates are open. The dimension that the Great Spirit inhabits surrounds this one, but it is also far away. It is a part of the Great Spirit as this dimension is part of the Great Spirit. This seemingly confusing description of where the Great Spirit is is only one part of the whole. Physical laws do not apply outside of this plane — this dimension.

"Humanity is a physical, mental and spiritual being. Each of us has a physical body, a mental body, and a spiritual body, which is the soul. Each soul's mission on this earth is based on previous incar-

29

The Priest
And Master

nations on this and other planes of existence. In each incarnation there are negative influences due to indecision and engaging in the wrong activity. There are also positive influences due to unselfishness.

"Each body that exists in the physical world has a soul. There is one soul for each and every body. The mission of the soul is to do what is 'right'. This is based on the following seven criteria: keep your path straight; do for others as you would have them do for you; love the Great Spirit and the God and the Goddess; reject evil; look with good humor at life's setbacks; whatever you do in this world, do it well; and show love and patience with others.

"The knowledge is not secret, but can only be understood by those who are ready. When the earth was created by the Great Spirit the universe was already old. The universe is the Great Spirit — every atom, every neutron, every proton, every subatomic particle is part of the thoughts of the Great Spirit. Everything has an electromagnetic field, including humans, animals, plants and rocks.

"The Hermetic tradition states that 'as above, so below.' As the Great Spirit thinks, so thinks a human. The Judaic tradition states that humankind was created in God's image,' male and female were they created in our image.'

"We were created as part of the life force of the Great Spirit, which means that it is true that the Great Spirit knows all and sees all. Each galaxy has a life force, each solar system has a life force, each sun has a life force, each planet has a life force, each person has a life force, each animal, bird, snake and reptile has a life force, each insect has a life force, each tree and plant has a life force, each mountain and stone has a life force, each grain of sand has a life force. Each thing has a life force or soul.

"There is also a group soul of this earth, the Great Mother. There is a soul of the sun, the sun god, the father. There is a soul of a tree, a dryad. There is a soul of the forest, Pan, the nature spirit. There are souls of flowers and plants, fairies.

"This means that everything adds to everything else and everything encompasses everything. All the combined souls equal the Great Spirit. Each person is in his own orbit as each planet is, doing his own thing. As long as you don't interfere with other people's orbits, you are on your path. But if you interfere with other souls' paths, you change the balance. Human beings are definitely different from other animals and/or other forms of life. We can decide to do something based on our concept and not just instinct. Every thought that travels through

31

the nerves of the human being has its complement in the energy pathways of all life and all matters. Every soul is eternal.

"All matter is really energy. All substance is really a wave form rather than a solid. All matter is an illusion. This is Quantum Physics as it relates to religion. This means that most religions have some truth and all religions are trying to say the same thing in different ways," he said as he finished.

This made sense! In my studies of Quantum Mechanics the one thing I had to learn to accept over all other things was that there was no such thing as a real solid, and that everything was really a 'force field!'

"The horned god and the earth goddess are the personification of nature as reflected in your eyes — truth! There is a Great Spirit that exists and created all things — the first cause — truth!

"When a human being prays, he is trying to communicate with a particular identity of the Great Spirit, a god, a goddess, a dryad, a gnome, or a spirit. When a Wiccan does ritual he or she is attempting to influence the actions of nature for his or her benefit — magick. As part of this philosophy, polarity is a means a combining the wills of two or more people to cause action — magick. Such a polarity is the strongest means of accomplishing magick."

"What about time, the fourth dimension?" I asked.

"Time exists only in your mind. If you look back into the past, 'a thing' happened, but it still exists as a fact, a truth. If you look forward, it also exists as a fact, a truth. Possibilities are nothing more than different dimensions, parallel universes existing beside each other.

"Every legend, every myth, is trying to say something very simple. All is one. But how can I, convey to you this concept of 'as above, so below'? You will have to experience it. These are the greater and lesser mysteries." He finished.

In all confidence I can say that some of you will find it completely impossible to understand the last few pages and what they really mean. This is because a mystery must be revealed. The truth must be understood. Your mind must make certain deductions and reason properly in order to understand truth. The mysteries are suddenly understood only in a complex process of revelation. This means that you must make that quantum leap from understanding the operation of a wheel to the operation of the automobile in one step.

But is this really true? Is there only one step involved? A man lives all his life asking the meaning of life. When he is sixty years old suddenly he is driving a car or eating a meal or dictating a letter; he stops dead still, he stares off into space, a look of wonder comes over his face, he says, "I'll be damned!" softly, as he suddenly understands the meaning of life. He turns to the friend beside him and tries to explain what has just happened. He can't. The friend may hear the words but they don't fit. His thought processes have not made that quantum leap and he is not concerned with the meaning of life.

Only a few readers are ready to make that quantum leap. This chapter is for you. It will be a catalyst and a key to allow you to find us and become as we are, enlightened human beings, Y Tylwyth Teg. The others will simply be entertained, and led down a blind alley. That is the great thing about true knowledge; it can only be understood by the few. For you, the masses, put this book away. It is not for you at the present time. Pick it up later, it will mean more.

My mind turned back again to that night long ago. The female voice is speaking. *"In this dimension there are gods and goddesses which reside both on the astral and on this plane simultaneously. These gods and goddesses are group representations of life forms. There is a goddess, a female aspect, and a god, a male aspect, of humans. There is a deva, a spirit of plant and animal groups of each. These devas can be influenced by humans, but not controlled by them, in the same way that god does not control us, it influences us.*

"Hu is the Welsh name given to the Great Spirit of all. Lugh is the Welsh name given to one of the male gods. Danu is the Welsh name given to one of the female goddesses. Pan and Cerunnos are the names given to the male nature deva who rules this planet. Diana and Cerridwen are the Welsh names given to the female nature deva who rules this planet.

"Why are we here? The Great Spirit is a perfected entity and is much like us except he/she is androgynous, is both male and female and fills up the universe. The Great Spirit is keeper of the law over this universe. He/she is governor over billions of souls who have been created to populate this particular solar system. Their purpose is to learn to be perfected as the Great Spirit is perfected and become companions to the Great Spirit.

"The Plan calls for each soul to live on the earth for a time of learning, then on the astral, the mental, and finally the spiritual planes. After a certain length of time each soul chooses its own path up the spiral or back down the spiral toward spirituality or toward the physical. The spiral is involution, the genetic helix, the orbit around the sun, life.

"The Universal Consciousness rules all of space and time. This is the universal law, alpha and omega, the beginning and the end. The galaxy is ruled by the powers of the combined consciousness of the many souls and the Great Spirit.

"Everything attempts to achieve balance, but is designed not to balance. Perfect balance is death. Seeking for balance is life. The Oak King and the Holly King are the human personification of the Great Spirit and are solar in nature. The mother goddess is the human personification of the true ruler of the earth, Cerridwen, the mother, the earth goddess; they seek balance.

"There are entities who are evil. They are against The Plan, attempting to delay it as long as possible. These entities started the churches which exist on the earth today. The original Christ was a messenger from the Great Spirit who came to establish a school of teachers. But the teachings have been perverted and used for the gain of certain human spirits on this earth who mean to delay the learning process of all spirits for their own benefits. They would rather have illusionary power here on earth, than true enlightenment.

"Your duty is to help each spirit gain the knowledge of the one true deity, the Great Spirit of this solar system, that each of you may be perfected and made true. This duty may be performed by meditation and prayer for those who are trapped between the worlds, who are lost and have not found the way to an incarnation. They are on the lower astral.

"The lower astral is close to the physical plane and the physical world. We sometimes see or feel its presence. It is the place where all go who are rebellious of the plan and wish to delay it. The upper astral is that which some call the Summerland, heaven, paradise. The solar system is a birthplace of souls. Some are harvested. Others travel elsewhere, all have free will. Those souls called evil, feed upon humans. They are like tumors or parasites. The lower astral can influence weak, earthbound humans because of its relative closeness to the world of reality.

"Why was the universe created? Only the Great Spirit knows. Why was the solar system created? To be a breeding ground for souls. Why was the fall? The original spirits which governed the solar system became attached to the physical world and created human bodies.

"We are here to help each other. We are here to become as perfected as we can under the circumstances. Identifying with the god and/or the goddess, we take on some of the characteristics of the perfected being, the Great Spirit.

34

"Why must humanity learn the lessons of life? There is within each human soul a seed which is planted by the Great Spirit. This is called light or logos. Each of us can be likened to the light, the word, and can be good, if we listen to that part, that inner voice. Many messengers have come: Buddha, Christ, and many more. They come in cycles of approximately 1,058 years. The cycles are governed by the number 23.

"Rhuddlwm, there have been a number of civilizations or cultures upon this earth since humanity was created. Some advanced to the heights only to fall into the depths. But at each falling, humanity has gained a little more goodness.

"The answer to all questions is that humanity is searching for happiness, goodness, god. Once all human souls have found 'The Way,' humanity will once again become part of the Great Spirit, and there will be no more need to reincarnate.

"The ways of the Great Spirit are unknowable, but you can see the reflection of the god/dess in the works of the goddess, as when you look into a pool you can see the reflections of the clouds, the trees and the birds, but not clearly and still only a reflection. You still have a long way to go as humanity before you can be raised up en masse from this plane and not have to reincarnate any longer," she concluded.

My mind drifted again. I remembered the first class I taught after I saw the vision. I was talking to my class.

"Spiritual training is needed for several reasons. To foster commitment to the earth mother and the Great Spirit; as an introduction to the history and heritage of Y Tylwyth Teg clan; and as an explanation of the privileges and responsibilities of membership in Y Tylwyth Teg. You are confirming your spirituality if you live a natural lifestyle, learn the traditions and beliefs of Y Tylwyth Teg, recognize the presence of the Great Spirit and accept your role in the great plan. You can begin this by learning the structure of Y Tylwyth Teg and its requirements." (See Appendix)

"Seekers, what is the cosmic consciousness?" I asked. One of my brighter students held up her hand. *"Its Purpose is the ultimate advancement of the soul to the realm of the celestial plane, to be one with the Great Spirit,"* she answered.

"Very good, and how do you reach the realm of the Great Spirit?"

"The Way to reach this realm is to first forgive and love yourself since the Great Spirit is within each of us."

"Very good Rhiannon, The truth is that we are all the Great Spirit,

35

each of us and all together. To realize this truth you must first become attuned to nature and walk in balance. Truth will be found by each seeker during their Quest.

"Next is the Spiritual Kingdom. In order to reach the spiritual kingdom several tasks must be performed. First you must learn the Laws, next you must learn the Sabbats, following which you must learn The Way, the way of the Great Spirit. To know the Great Spirit is to know truth and wonder and peace and love. The god/dess is only one aspect of the Great Spirit. The goddess is the archetypal symbol of the female. She is the moon, the earth; she is womankind. The god is the archetypal symbol of the male. He is the sun, he is the stars and he is mankind. The Great Spirit is all, the unity of all souls, the point of truth within all people. The Great Spirit is love, knowledge and power.

"Each human being has the capability of becoming like the god/dess. Each human being can contact that internal part of himself that is Christ/Buddha or Cernunnos. Each human being must commit his life to the service of others, to the service of the god/dess within/without. To contact this god/dess one must meditate/pray/project oneself into the still point within. One must turn loose of one's ego. This is the true son/daughter of the god/dess. All things are connected to all other things. All actions have an affect on nature. Witchcraft is a science/art/religion that allows each human being to relink with Nature-The Word-The Law.

"All of nature, all of the universe, is part of everything. Astrology is the art of interpreting the Forces of the universal law in terms that humans can understand. Tarot is the art of interpreting the Symbols of universal law in terms that humans can understand. Magic is the art of using universal law to change the universe. Evil is only manifest in the mind of human beings. Evil spirits exist only in the lower astral, and can only affect humans mentally; and the Devil is a reality only in the mind of human beings.

"The universe exists for change. The goal of human beings is to help all other humans advance in spirituality. We know this because of the Great Promises. The Great Spirit has given us many promises in the sacred words of our religion. It is our loss if we do not take advantage of them. First, we must study our religious books regularly. Second, we must believe the promises: the promise of eternal life, reincarnation, and the eternal soul, the promise that no one need fear. Through love fear can be conquered; the promise is that we can be

36

perfect, like the perfected body of the Great Spirit. Third, we must read the promises carefully, for all sacred books are written in symbolism. Fourth, we must keep in mind that the promises are for those who believe and those who do not believe together. They are our way of understanding the Universal Law. The promises are the laws of the universe as they apply to humanity.''

"What are these promises all about? No one has ever promised me anything except a hard time.'' said one of my more dense students.''

"Promises are about faith; have faith in the cymmry. The Promises assure you of eternal life, reincarnation. We have all been here before; we will all ultimately rejoin the Great Spirit. There are promises of the Great Spirit's loving care, the superconscious of our mind.

"The goddess is a loving goddess. Look to your wondrous body and its workings, look at a sunset. Could a goddess of hate build so lovingly? There are Promises for blessings in meditation and prayer; Contact the still small voice within; You will be rewarded; There are Promises for you as an individual, to change, to be reborn in a new body, to learn to become perfect in all things, and to become a perfect human, like the Great Spirit; to have Love, Knowledge and Power. There is The Great Spirit's promise of peace; We must work for peace, for peace will only come after struggle; there is the Great Spirit's promise of knowledge and wisdom through love; These we will all have if you learn the law of threefold utterance. And finally the Great Spirit's promise that you can overcome selfishness through love.''

"If you are a seeker you must also learn certain lessons:''

"The lessons about the Great Spirit as father, the existence of god, the person of the father, god/dess as a balanced being as father. The trinity of the father, the names of the father.

"Lessons about the Great Spirit as mother. The existence of the goddess, the person of the goddess, the god/dess is a balanced being as mother. The trinity of the mother, the names of the mother.

"Lessons about the Great Spirit as son/daughter. The existence of the son/daughter. The person of the son/daughter. God/dess as balanced being as son/daughter. The trinity of the son/daughter. The names of the son/daughter.

"Lessons about the holy books, the thirteen treasures, the sacred manuscripts, the nine-level way, the book of oral traditions and chronology of knowledge. The mystic circle. Cylch yr Abred, Cylch y Cwynfyd, Cylch y Ceugant, lessons about humanity and creation, the creation story, evolution of the worlds, Atlantis, the Cymmry, and the Watchers.

37

"Lessons about spiritual guardians. devas, angels, spirit guides, and how they all exist to help humanity on its quest.

"Lessons about reincarnation and karma; 'What goes around comes around'; 'The law of threefold return'; 'For every action there is a reaction at some time'.

"Lessons on right living. Love one another and help those who need help, but ever protect life and if one strikes you, defend yourself.

"Lessons about the fellowship of the clan, Y Tylwyth Teg, the fair family. How we are all psychically connected with each other through initiation. How we are a true family.

"Lessons about magick. Y Tylwyth Teg teaches that all things, all dreams, desires and needs can be obtained through the power of the will.

"Lessons about the laws of the Cymmry.

"To follow the way, first you must purify your life. Once men died for truth but now truth dies at the hands of men. Until one removes selfishness from one's life one cannot hope to gain true knowledge. Although you may be tempted by the things of this world you must strive only for wisdom, live in the world but be not of the world.

"The human race has never desired what was best for it, but you must not force your wisdom on others. You must teach others and seek to create a truer and nobler concept of life. You must go through at least one year and a day of purification and preparation before you can be instructed in even the simplest things.

"Know that a true initiate will not discuss the absolute. The first cause is explained but no human being knows sufficiently concerning it to give an intelligent opinion or definition, and no wise person presumes to discuss that about which he knows nothing.

" There is only one series of true occult exercises in the world, namely esoteric exercises. Thus honestly, sincerely and intelligently prepare yourself for your labors. Are you unselfish, open, obedient, humble, and consecrated? Have you developed your mind? Have you opened your heart? Like begets like. Recognize your own gullibility. Recognize deluded students of truth and avoid them. Ancient wisdom is spiritual and reasonable. It is based on the law of cause and effect. This is why you have been reborn on this planet.

"What is universal truth ? The ultimate truth is that you are a god/dess being evolving through time and space to accept your total divinity, your higher consciousness which lies within your selfhood at the soul essence level. Many religions and thought systems contain this

truth but hide it from their followers so that their actions, relationships and pocketbooks can be controlled and dominated by priests and other religious leaders. In place of this final truth, they teach lies, false gods, multiple delusions, and absurd requirements. Millions of sincere people are misled by threats of punishment, hell, damnation, and evil forces lurking everywhere. Christian Priests and Ministers often use their religious thoughts to judge, condemn and damn their fellow citizens. Millions have taken to struggling in the name of religion, holy wars which martyr their loved ones, and sacrifice their happiness and that of their children and grandchildren, to terrorize and attack the enemy. Millions more need a personality or teacher to worship and bow down to in order to feel their own worth through suppressing their natural needs, goals, ideas and hopes. Still millions more must accept without question every book, person or self-proclaimed authority on the nature of the universe and man's place in it and be ready to hurt, kill or despise their fellow humans in the name of their religious affiliations. These poor souls are operating with closed minds. They have already decided how everything is and how the world should go, and they are willing to revolutionize, suppress and murder in the name of power, which they worship outside of themselves.

"They are told that they are sinners and they believe it. They are told that they are chosen ones and they also believe that. They are told that God wants them to do good works and 'spread the gospel' and they believe that. They are told that God appeared only once on the planet earth and they believe that. They are told that psychic powers are the work of the Devil and they believe that. They are told that the saints have manifested psychic powers and they believe that too. In other words, these people who call themselves religious have mastered the ability to hold two or more contradictory thoughts at the same time and believe all of them.

"Very few souls are ready for the possibility that the higher self is Love and an Inner Being that leads us to at-one-ment with the mother/father of all, and that such masters as Jesus were able to manifest, demonstrate and show The Way to this inner conviction and realization of a life of harmony and love," "Many of You still live in fear, ignorance and superstition. You don't realize yet that you are worth anything. After all, you must be a sinner, and live in poverty, resentment and fear. Right?"

"Wrong!" I answered myself.

"You must experience ill health and poor relationships and evil conditions. Right?

39

"Wrong!" I said again

"Y Tylwyth Teg is dedicated to liberating the human spirit. We want to help free the souls who want to experience their full potential.

"But you must first learn that all things are one — that whatever is — is perfect. All neutrons, protons, electrons; all particles and subatomic particles are parts of larger physical bodies such as Man or Woman. We in turn are part of the Earth; the Earth is part of the Solar System, which is part of the Milky Way Galaxy, which is part of the 'All'.

"Humanity feels separate and apart from Self/Others and the Universe/Great Spirit. Humanity denies the perfection that is. Humanity refuses to accept responsibility for all that it experiences.

"Separation causes anxiety because something has become foreign and a potential threat. If we feel oneness or union with others we feel accepting.

"All human suffering, fear, hate, pain and desire are the result of this separation. Separation also leads to negative and unbalanced thinking.

"Every Gwiddion realizes that we are really not separate, we are all part of the one universal consciousness; this can be shown by the law of Karma -and Reincarnation.

"When a person feels separate he feels all alone and lost; that's why all people need to join together in Mind, Body and Spirit.

"Unfortunately what is needed is a 'cleansing time,' a time of upheaval and devastation. This will awaken the Human Race to listen to the Great Spirit," I finished.

CHAPTER 4

THE SACRED WORDS
OF POWER

The Magical Pronunciation of the Name of the God/dess
IAO.

I equals The Naming. A equals The Quest. O equals The Adoption.

"Rhuddlwm, every religion, every magical tradition has descended from one universal mystery language, one universal ancient source: Atlantis.

"All the words of that mystery language signify the same thing to each seeker no matter what the nationality. This language has many facets, many dialects, but one symbolism, and has led to the adoption of widely varying dogmas in many different churches. But this secret language has the knowledge of the universe intertwined within its meanings, the knowledge of power, the knowledge of wisdom, and the knowledge of love. Each initiate who becomes a part of Y Tylwyth Teg learns the meaning of the words and the correct pronunciation, but the real secret is in the mental and spiritual concepts associated with each word. This means that the way the word is uttered has as much power as the word itself.

"Remember. Separate the essence from the substance. This means that a word may sound a certain way and mean a certain thing, but the essence is the real thing. The way to the essence of words is through the realization of them. For example, the elemental spirits have an associative list of verbal concepts such as being, feeling, thinking, doing, aspiration, insight, patience, stability, and brilliance, that you can use to link between you as the seeker, and the higher energies

of the elements. No one will have the same list because no two seek-
ers think alike. The symbols will be the same once the seeker learns
the secret language and can apply the universal symbolism to each ele-
ment. Before you learn to walk you must learn to crawl. Before you
learn to run you must learn to walk. There is a large, yawning chasm
between taking the first step and running a four-minute mile. But
any seeker by perseverance and dedication can attain the very heights
of spirituality and run that four-minute mile. The secret language is
the sacred language of the gods.

The Sacred Words

IAO.OUE

The secret and sacred name of Don, the transendental god/dess of
the Cymmry, and the first word of power.

O-A-O-U-E-I-Y

or

IAO.UAI

or

IAO.OUAI

This word is hidden in its revelation.

I = 3 = eaglet.
A = 1 = lapwing.
O = 5 = cormorant.
-----
9 = the levels of initiation.

I.N.R.I. = The second word of power.
Ignis natura renovata integra. The fire of nature renews and refreshes.
R.O.T.A.S. The third word of power, tarot.
A = the Fool.
O = the Devil.
T = the Hanged Man.

A.O.M. Adytum Operis Magni, The fourth word of power.
The voice of threefold utterance: **Plennydd — Arawn — Gwron.**
O   A   I

The secret name which is known to very few is the secret pronunciation which can be revealed only to the few initiates who can conquer
the soul. The various names of power of the Great Spirit are Khem-

44

thiaf, Rheibet, Arogogoruabao, Mudorio, Aepe, Asalonai, Barraio, Ioel, Sabaft, Iouieouf, Iaeo, Adonai, Lai, Gaia, Aepe, Iar, Nox, Abrahadabra.

Names of power of the gods/goddesses:

Shemhamphorash, Velegh, Eligos, Masloth, Iophiel,Hagelgalim, Zabbathi, Duwies, Duw, Aronrhod, Brigit, Gwydion, Lew, Beli, Brand, Dwyvan, Eiddien, Llud, Merddin, Modren, Celi, Ior, Rheen, Peryn, Dofydd, Ddon, Yrhen, Ddihenydd, Cerridwen, Rhiannon, Branwen, Nudd, Math, Branwen, Arawn, Duwyvach, Hugh, Lir, Prydain.

The Symbols of Initiation: **IAO**
Naming = I (the first symbol of the word)
Quest = A (the second symbol of the word)
Adoption = O (the third symbol of the word)

Magical Alphabets

Different ages have each produced their own methods of magickal alphabets. Their spells and inscriptions on magical tools and weapons were originally a series of symbols used to represent different forces and ideas. The runic script is a good example of this as each letter was once a talisman made for a prescribed purpose. Runic has also been called Honorean or Thebian script. It is believed to go back to high Atlantis by some. It is more likely that Atlanteans used the Elvish script. The first appearance of Thebian in the fifteenth century was complied by Francis Barrett. Most of the magickal scripts have only twenty-two different symbols coming to us from the practitioners of Kabalistic western tradition ceremonial magic. The missing letters have been filled in by copying the other letters over again. This could cause some problems for the beginner. Because of the duplication and because of the basic talismanic qualities of the runic script, I would suggest that everyone begin with this form, progressing to more complex alphabets as their inherent qualities become apparent to the individual.

The symbolic powers represented by the scripts based on Hebrew do have a great deal of meaning in themselves. This is too broad a subject to cover here, as it would probably take you several years to master this concept. However, should you desire to uncover this learning for yourself, do so by studying the correspondences of the script to the Hebrew alphabet and thence to the Major Arcana of the Tarot.

This work should properly be the province of the candidate for the third level initiation; however, I have included it here to show you how everything has a definite purpose.

The various alphabets are merely other means of conveying old complete sets of emotions and ideal qualities. The symbols are important and hold within them much power which you will one day discover. For these reasons as well as to protect the true meanings from being completely understood by the outsider, these various forms and distinct combinations are often still used in the inscription of magical tools and weapons.

ALPHABETS

Early Atlantean Easter Island to Celtic Monoliths	Atlantean Druidic ICENI Girrui	Today's Alphabet	Planet People's 9th Universe Sigils	Ancient Druidic & Celtic Sacred Trees or Groves
Beth		B		Birch
Luis		L		Rowan
Nion		N		Ash
Fearn		F		Alder
Saile		S		Willow
Uath		H		Hawthorn
Duir		D		Oak
Tinne		T		Holly
Coll		C		Hazel
Muin		M		Vine
Govt		G		Ivy
Pethboc		P		Dwarf Alder
Ruis		R		Elder
Ailm		A		Silver Spruce
ONN		O		Furge
UR		U		Heather, White
EAHHO		E		White Poplar
IDHO		I		Yew

MAGICKAL ALPHABETS: (CONT.)

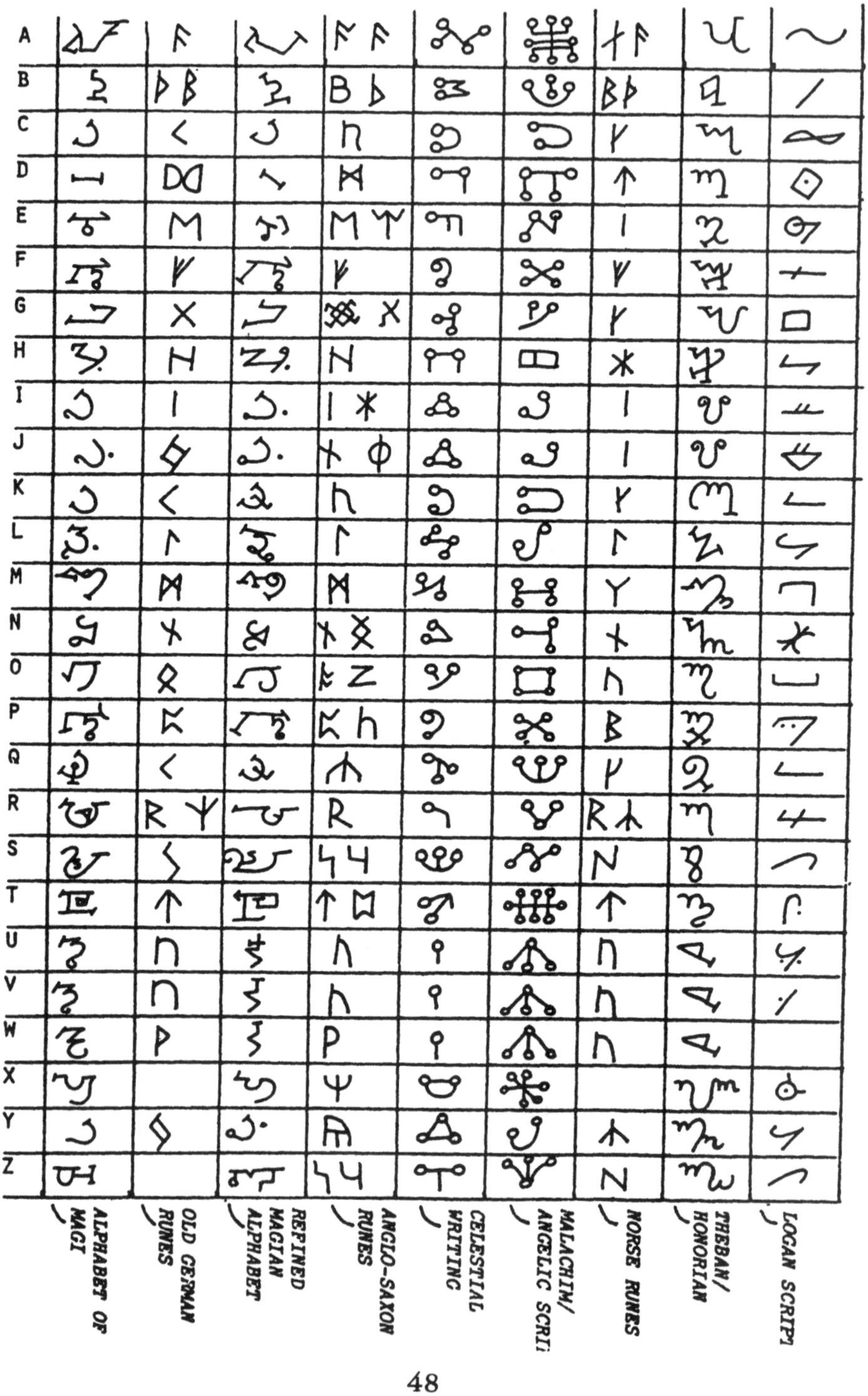
A
B
C
D
E
F
G
H
I
J
K
L
M
N
O
P
Q
R
S
T
U
V
W
X
Y
Z
ALPHABET OF MAGI
OLD GERMAN RUNES
REFINED MAGIAN ALPHABET
ANGLO-SAXON RUNES
CELESTIAL WRITING
MALACHIM/ ANGELIC SCRI
NORSE RUNES
THEBAN/ HONORIAN
LOGAN SCRIPT

THE ENOCHIAN ALPHABET

The Runes of the Watchers, or Gods. This is the most ancient alphabet on Earth. The Gods taught man to read and write. They taught charms and counter charms, spells, talismans, metalurgy, weather lore, astronomy, astrology, animal husbandry, the seasons, herb lore and many other wonderful things.

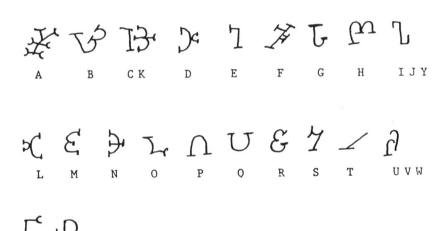

Ogham Alphabet

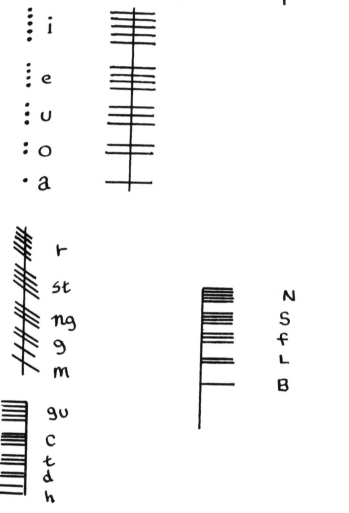

i

e

u

o

a

r

st

ng

g

m

gu

c

t

d

h

N

S

f

L

B

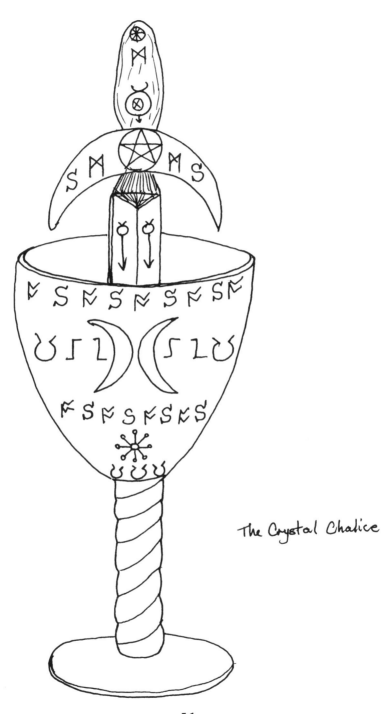

The Crystal Chalice

CHAPTER 5

THE PATH OF POWER
and SURVIVAL OF THE WAY

Universal Laws

On the 21st of July 1976/I was meditating on a small cliff over-looking the Chattahoochee River near Atlanta. As I sat there, I was shown a vision as clear as reality. In this vision nine priestesses formed a circle around a cauldron of light — while a tenth figure, a priest, stood apart from the others. The nine were guarding the Cauldron of Power — the Grail of Immortality! — while the tenth, the priest, had been elected to carry the power to the far corners of the earth.

Then an old grey-haired and bearded gentleman stepped out of the darkness beside me and spoke: *"The young priestesses symbolize the part of us that connects with our inner self and transports mystical inspiration back here to the physical world. The priest symbolizes the teacher — the gifted one who is guardian of light — this is you, Rhuddlwm; You have accepted discipline and overcome the limitations of your subconscious mind; your energy is becoming infinite — you are now taking your spiritual creativity to those who wish to learn — your teachings shall spread far and wide."*

"People will describe your teachings using many names: 'lies!' some will say; 'false teachings!', others will cry; and many will claim that they are 'Ancient Wisdom' and 'Esoteric Mysteries !'

"These ancient teachings have always existed in a symbolic form — but on the planes and not in the physical world — these teachings will be modified and adapted by you into the languages of those individuals who are worthy of them.

53

"The ancient knowledge is really energy — spiritualized energy which can be controlled and changed, communicated with, and used to move objects, tell the future — and to make the blind see and the lame walk.

"As you teach the 'ancient wisdom', keep your perspective — you are human too — you will make mistakes, but these mistakes will help you grow."

My mind wandered again, as he faded into the darkness. All at once another figure appeared.

"I am White Buffalo Woman," she announced. *"I, who the Cherokee revered in days long past, greet you."* My mind swirled and flowed with images of tribes and teepees. *"We are cousins, Rhuddlwm. The Indian blood that is part of you calls out to me. In ancient times the fair ones came in great canoes from the east, from the place of the sun. They gave our people much knowledge; the knowledge of the Great Spirit, the knowledge of love, knowledge and power, the knowledge of plants and hunting. I thank your people for these gifts, and I will always be waiting for your call."*

At first I didn't understand, then she spoke again. *"You are standing over a power point, Rhuddlwm. Each power point is a doorway to the astral, a doorway to prophecy and enlightenment if used properly. It is also a doorway to healing and magic — you are in a power place sacred to the Cherokees — I have come to you as a guardian of that power."*

"You mean that every power point on this earth has a local spirit as its guardian?" I whispered. I felt confused by the pictures that were forming in my mind.

"Yes, but more than that, if the power point has been activated by ritual, the guardian takes the form of the gods that were invoked there," she said.

"But what of my Welsh gods?" I cried. *"Are they then lost to me here in America?"*

"No, they're here too, waiting to be called. But you must call them frequently and strongly at the moons and at the quarter points, for their strength to increase. Then they will come to you."

Relieved, I let my mind be pulled where it would, as if it were floating on the current of the river beneath the cliff. My thoughts turned to the undines, the water sprites. Another figure stepped from the darkness. She was beautiful beyond belief, with skin which shimmered silver in the moonlight. Her hair was the color of the rainbow, and her eyes glowed with blue fire. She stirred.

"Who calls me?" Her eyes were like slits of white light radiating toward me and her voice was strange and unearthly in my mind.

"I do, Rhuddlwm ap Gawr, a bard of Y Tylwyth Teg," I said

"Greetings, Rhuddlwm. What is your wish?"

"What is your purpose here and what is your name?" I asked softly.

"I am Mara, guardian of the element water. I am called to bring good fishing to the tribe; I am called when the rivers run shallow; I am called in times of sadness, and I am called in times of magic. I have many names and many shapes. I am Llyr of the sea. I am Lorien, the lady of the lake, and I am the undines, the water fairies," she replied.

My mind opened up to her, the element water, and I felt another piece of the puzzle fall into place. I had been taught about the place that the elements had in the scheme of life — but now I was becoming water — shapeless, yet taking the shape of whatever container I resided in, whether it be the sea, or a lake — ever changing but always the same — just like the Great Spirit.

"I am god/dess," I thought. *"I am the storm of the sea, the gentle summer rain, the burbling brook, the rushing river — I am water."*

For a time I became the river and I discovered the real meaning of the word mystery, because I could not then or could I now describe or explain to you what I felt or what I had become during those few hours above the Chattahoochee. But I know inside, and that's what is important.

Another figure stirred in the depths of the darkness, a kindly old lady, bent slightly from age. She spoke, *"Meditate often Rhuddlwm, for meditation is a very important part of your life if you are to be a healer and a channel for spiritual guidance.*

"Meditation is the attuning of your mental and physical bodies to a spiritual source. Your three bodies are not always in tune. Meditation is a way to do this. Use the following steps: You must purify your mind before you can learn to meditate. Your body is the temple of the Great Spirit. Understand the relationship that you have with the Great Spirit. Meditation is meeting the God within you, therefore it is necessary that you know the Great Spirit. You must have the desire to know the Great Spirit with the same passion that a drowning man desires air. Purify your body; believe that the Great Spirit IS. Believe that your Quest for the Great Spirit will be rewarded. Change your life and begin to do those things that you are asking the Great Spirit to do."

She faded into the twilight.

Next an ancient, cowled figure drifted near! *"I give you the teachings of the universal laws,"* he said. *"These laws affect all living creatures. They must become part of your being. The Twelve Universal Laws are: The prime law, the law of duality, the law of love, the law of the planes, the law of balance of cycles, the law of truth, the law of psychic energy, the law of reincarnation, the law of karma, the law of spiritual ethics, the law of faith, and the law of free will.*

"The prime, threefold law states that there are three truths that are absolute. The soul of humankind is immortal and not subject to death. The Great Spirit, the giver of life, dwells in us and without us in an undying and eternally beneficent form, cannot be seen or heard or smelled, but can be perceived by the seeker who desires perception — is one power, this is the law of one."

The law of one, that made sense, for isn't God/dess everything? My mind spun with the realization that if the Great Spirit is everything, then there could only be one law and one creator.

"Each seeker is his own absolute law giver, the dispenser of good or evil to himself, and decrees his reward and punishment throughout life. You live in a world of immutable laws. Humankind has a place in the scheme of things. If he understands the laws and cooperates with Nature, he will advance rapidly and be happy. If he does not understand them and breaks them, wittingly or unwittingly, he will delay his progress and be miserable.

"The second law, the law of duality, states that everything has its opposite — good, evil, up, down, male, female, right, left, god, goddess, etc.

"This leads to the third law, the law of cause and effect. For every action there is a reaction at some time. This is karma, morality, suffering, inner penance."

Yea, I had experienced that all right !

"This leads to the fourth law, the law of balance. Everything attempts to seek a balance with everything else, but there is no balance. By nature if a balance is created, an unbalance is also created. Human beings were created to aid the Great Spirit in the control of the universe. This is done through cycles of balance.

"The fifth law is the law of truth. There are two forms of truth, subjective and objective truth. Subjective truth is something that you believe is true but is not necessarily so. Objective truth is that which is true no matter who observes it.

"The sixth law is the law of love. Love is here defined as mystic love, which is the surrender of yourself and the growth of the ego. You must learn the three aspects of love: Human sexual love, which is the source of kundalini or red dragon energy. This is sexual energy and is controlled properly by the law of duality and attraction. You must understand and use the positive and negative aspects of these energies through the controlled awareness of your breath and sexual force. Spiritual love: This is giving to another, sacrificing for another, love of the god and the goddess, and the Great Spirit. And finally, Self-intoxicated love: This is the love of purity of actions, the wise person's love of goodness and the highest type of service. You must love yourself for the goodness in you.

"The seventh law is the law of spiritual power. This includes the laws of psychic energy, prosperity, and mental precipitation. This law is the result of the control of the three essentials: love, knowledge and power. Love is emotion, knowledge is belief, and power is will.

"Emotion is generally undefined power. The mind, by visualizing, controls this power and directs it to a purpose. The will, by concentrating it, or believing in it, focuses the power.

"The eighth law is the law of spiritual ethics. This includes the twenty-two levels. These are: The Twelve Tennants, which are patience, tolerance, forbearance, kindliness, charity, humility, devotion, sincerity, courage, precision, efficiency, and discrimination. The Ten Virtues, which are: the accomplishment of the great work, which is enlightenment, devotion to the teacher, silence, obedience, energy, devotion to the great work, unselfishness, truthfulness, independence, and skepticism.

"The ninth law is the law of faith. This is the law of total belief. If you have the faith as of the mustard seed you will say, 'Mountain, come to me,' and it will move.

"The tenth law is the law of free will. Each soul has the free will to make any choice it so wishes, to do good or to do evil, to live or die, to become enlightened or seek materialism. Each soul may choose any path within the confines of the universal plan.

"This leads to the eleventh law, the law of reincarnation. There is no injustice. You reap what you sow. You return at a future time to learn new lessons. After a period on the astral, the mental and spiritual planes, you return to this earth to reincarnate as a person who can accomplish the karmic law.

"Finally, the twelfth law, the law of the planes. There are many planes of existence. Seven of them are the divine world, the monadic world, the spiritual world, the intuitional world, the mental world, the astral world, and the physical world. The matter of all these worlds or planes is essentially the same matter but differently arranged and of different degrees of density. They vibrate at different frequency rates, with the lowest the physical, and the highest, the divine. Each of these worlds or planes has its own inhabitants who see, hear and feel its vibrations.

"After each seeker adopts the Universal Laws and begins to live them, he must take the fourteen steps before he or she can reach enlightenment and begin to teach:

"The first step is respect for oneself and forgiveness of oneself for all sins, imagined or actual. There really aren't any sins, only mistakes, or errors.

"The second step. A seeker must surrender and start again. This, of course, means that a seeker must surrender his ego and start out again or be reborn.

"The third step. Everything is the universal spirit. You are the Great Spirit, I am the Great Spirit, we are all part of the universal spirit.

"Next is the fourth step. Deep within oneself is a quiet place, a still, small voice within. That part of you which blocks out everything else, which is your inner self.

"The fifth step. Quiet your mind, for you cannot hear the truth unless there is silence.

"The sixth step. When there is a task to do, you must become that task if you will do it properly.

"The seventh step. When you are with another seeker you become that other person's mind if you are to teach them.

"The eighth step. Before you can be changed into a new human you must die and be reborn. This, of course, refers to ego.

"The ninth step. You must experience sadness and despair in order to learn.

"The tenth step. You must realize that as long as you feed your ego with power food you will be on a power trip.

"The eleventh step. You must have a strong ego in order to teach, but be able to leave your ego behind to enjoy blending with the Great Spirit and your students.

"The twelfth step. Center yourself, forget about what you are getting out of any situation. Start to live The Way of the seeker.

"The thirteenth step. As soon as you give up striving toward the

60

light, the light will come to you. If you surrender you gain eternal union with pure energy and pure light.

"The fourteenth step. You must give up your ego in order to progress, and you have to stop every once in awhile and live for the moment. Only then may you reach enlightenment.

"There are three ways of realizing enlightenment: through direct experience, through inference or reasoning, and through trust that there are spiritual masters."

I pondered what had been said to me for what seemed like a long time. It was a great deal to absorb all at once, but it did make a lot of sense. I noticed the sun was coming up. Time to get home and do my morning meditation. I left, my mind swarming with thousands of images.

Two weeks later I was hiking up Mount Yonah.

It took me almost two hours to climb to the top and it wasn't all that much fun. My expectations were that it would be a nice walk. The reality was that it was an agonizing trip that caused my muscles to burn and turn to lead by the time I reached the top.

This was a sacred power point that I had been told about by an old Cherokee that I had met in North Carolina. In fact there were legends of sacrifices and rituals associated with this mountain from ancient times.

But as I stood on the edge of the three hundred foot cliff I knew the trip had been worth it. I looked out over the surrounding green countryside. There was the road I had driven up to here off to my right, and there was the small lake I had passed on the way. It was so beautiful, it took my breath away for a few seconds and it took my mind off my pain.

Emerald green pine trees covered the surrounding hills as white fleecy clouds drifted slowly by. I felt on top of the world.

I sat down on the granite ledge feeling a little shaky from the climb and let my mind wander, seeking that still point within that contained my guide. Suddenly my vision dimmed and my body became frozen; I couldn't even blink my eyes. Oh no! I thought, it's happening again just like it did at Lake Blackshear.

But I suddenly realized that this was different. I could still move my fingers and toes.

Suddenly a voice spoke in my mind. *"Welcome, Rhuddlwm. Welcome to my home."* I couldn't see anyone, but I thought there was a shimmering in the air in front of the cliff.

61

"You are at the convergence of several Ley Lines, Rhuddlwm. These ley lines are what the ancients called dragon paths and carry Odic Energy throughout the surface of the Earth. Within the earth, Odic Energy is carried in currents of molten rock, like the blood that flows through your veins.

"Odic Energy is the Universal Psychic Energy and is the life blood of the universe and the balancing force of nature. It is as much a part of life as the sap that rises in the spring, or the tides, or day and night.

"In some places where the Ley Lines come together, the tribes have held their rituals and built their temples, showing their respect for the forces of nature.

"The time will come Rhuddlwm, when you and the Cymmry will again use The Power, the Odic Energy, to heal the sick and make the earth fertile.

"For thousands of years humankind has repressed its psychic powers for Psychic power was used by the priests of Atlantis to subjugate the people. Selfishness always brings evil to those who practice it. But that has been humanity's curse, always reaching for the stars and being dragged down by selfishness into the depths.

"Each soul that overcomes selfishness brings humanity that much closer to the ultimate reality.

"So there is danger in learning the Earth Power, the Odic Force; it can harm as well as heal and it can bring grief as well as happiness to the user."

Suddenly my vision grew clear as nine warriors appeared around me. The leader, a large muscular Celt, dressed in kilts and swinging a large broadsword, smiled as he stepped forward.

I didn't even see him hit me.

I felt a tremendous pain in my head as he smashed me in the face and shouted at me to get up. I stumbled up, away from the edge of the cliff. I could have fallen off and been killed !

"Rhuddlwm, the mysteries are about to begin !" he said.

A dark, serpent-lean warrior grabbed my collar and ripped my shirt from my back; he slammed me on the side of my head, grabbed my arm and twisted it back until the pain crackled up my shoulder and into my brain. With a double handed blow he pounded my spine and knocked the breath out of me.

I flopped on my back and the leader dropped with both his knees on my stomach. His fists flicked out and crashed into my ears, then he gouged the muscles in my throat.

His face expressionless as a cobra, he then stood up and his broad sword whispered through the air. The blade flashed toward my groin and my trousers were ripped away.

He then kicked me in the knees and when I pulled my legs up, he stepped on my thighs with his heels. The pain was almost unbearable; what was happening ? Is this a joke ? Who were these people ? This wasn't a vision, this was real ! I looked down at my clothes hanging in shreds, then back up at these grim faced warriors, with fear in my eyes.

I was still doubled over with pain as the warriors grew hazy and disappeared.

"Stand up !" a harsh feminine voice boomed into my brain. I rolled over on my side and looked up at a large muscular woman who was speaking. At first glance she appeared plain looking, but after a few seconds I could see that she was really striking in a athletic sort of way, and she did have a beautiful body, big but beautiful.!

"You are not harmed," she said. *"You have been prepared for the Mysteries by taking away your muscle armor — you must be naked to be reborn — stand up !"*

I could hear a blue jay in the pine tree above me sqwaking its raspy song. I rose to my feet, amazed I was still alive, and unbelievably sore from my head to my toes.

She reached forward and ripped the remaining tattered cloth from my body. I was a little embarrassed at first, but soon got rid of that emotion, as she began walking around me poking at me and murmuring something to herself that I could not understand.

"Rhuddlwm, you will soon understand that the key to your survival in this world is going to be what is in your mind and and how you treat your body.

"Your body is a tool which can be manipulated in various ways to produce dramatic effects. While these effects have their beginnings in the realm of visualization and imagination, their completion is in the dimension of physical reality. Without physical effects as a result of magickal operations, the whole process would just be wishful thinking."

She took off her clothing, as little as it was, and again circled me. She touched me but it wasn't unpleasant this time. I even felt some sexual excitement as she touched my groin.

"Not too bad. But you could be in a lot better shape." she muttered. *"When are you humans going to learn to take care of yourselves."*

She then pulled me close and began kissing me. If this was a dream, I definitely wanted more. Things got very exciting for the next hour, and by the time we had both orgasmed, I was beginning to feel like I was in another world.

"Who and what are you?" I softly asked. She replied. *"I am what the ancients called a sucubus, a female spirit which inhabits power points and teaches humans about themselves."*

"What do you mean?" I questioned.

"I mean that the secret to all Magick, all Mysteries and all of life is Sex and Sex Energy. But the only way that you can learn of these matters is to be able to survive the drain of energy."

I had to admit, I did not feel at my peak right then.

She was speaking again. *"It is extremely important to keep your body in good condition in order to produce consistent magickal results and to survive the coming devastation. A dull or broken tool is impossible to work with; a out-of-tune musical instrument produces only discordant sounds. Your civilization's occult literature concentrates almost entirely on the mind and neglects the body. But the body is just as important as the mind.*

"These two aspects of your personality must be allowed to grow and work with efficiency and in harmony, otherwise your power will fail you at a crucial time and your objectives will remain unobtained. Worse, there may be a complete physical and mental breakdown.

"The performance of Magick causes a great strain to be placed on the Physical body. Maintaining good health and a high degree of energy helps the body to combat the stresses placed upon it. The unprepared seeker can inflict great damage to himself."

She got up and stood looking out over the river. She had become very beautiful.

"Because your body and your mind are but two attributes of your personality, each can have a striking influence on the other. The images that you can conjure up by use of your imagination can so stimulate your emotions, that profound changes can affect your endocrine glands and disturb your hormonal balance. This in turn can bring about chemical modifications in your body and alter the way your brain thinks.

"But it works both ways. Your mind can be affected by even minute changes in its electrical or chemical environment. Hence it is extremely important that you be very careful in the preparation as well as the timing of all magick you perform.

"Most of the ancient systems of spiritual training advised the seek-

er to begin working on the mental side of his nature first. However, the manipulation of the body, rather than the mind is actually the best point at which to start. 'Get your temple in order first, the rest will follow,' said an ancient teacher. A tired or ailing body is a hindrance to learning and a distraction to a well disciplined mind.

"Rhuddlwm, the success or failure of your entire enterprise, Camelot-of-the-Wood and Y Tylwyth Teg, ultimately depend on the condition of your physical body. The practice of magick and the performance of psychic manifestations depend on the state that your body is in. Although your imagination gives the power direction, your will provides the primary energy to transform reality. Without this emotional charge, nothing will happen.

"This emotional charge creates chemical and electrical changes in your body. Emotional energy is transformed into psychic energy, and these processes show themselves as changes in your respiration and blood pressure. This energy can also be generated by diet, breathing exercises and fasting. Sex with its basic connection to the instinctive mating urge of your species, is also a very powerful source of this energy.

"As you have seen, no matter how tired or distracted you may be, you are still programmed to respond to fear or sexual attraction. Only under conditions of physical collapse and hopelessness will the loss of your sexual stamina occur. But a strong vital body can respond to any stimulus.

"Emotional arousal can be changed directly into electro/psychic energy, and this is what you must use in your magickal workings. Large amounts of this energy are produced in certain spiritual practices, but you must be careful. A sudden influx of energy when you are not prepared for it can cause all manner of problems.

" Daily physical exercise and the correct amount of nutrients in your diet will go a long way to prepare you for your destiny."

"What kinds of nutrients are you talking about," I asked.

" The following elements in your diet are very important and should be monitored: protein, 1/2 gram for every pound of muscle weight; cottage cheese, brown rice and soybean sprouts are good sources. The Way does not teach you to be a vegetarian, but it would be better if a majority of your protein came from vegetable sources.

"If you are not eating properly, then you will have to obtain your vitamins from sources other than natural food. But you must consume the following vitamins in order to stay in good health:

"Vitamin A, from carrots, apricots, eggs, liver, and greens.

"Vitamin B complex, from fish, milk and brewers yeast.

"Vitamin C from citrus fruits, cabbage, green peppers, rose hips and tomato juice.

"Vitamin D, from egg yolks and fish liver oil.

"Vitamin E, from natural cereals, whole grains, and vegatable oils.

"Vitamin K, from egg yolks, yogurt, liver, kelp and soybean oil.

"Vitamin P, from skins and pulps of citrus fruits.

"In addition your body needs an adequate supply of minerals including: calcium, salt, Iodine, iron, manganese, zinc, phosphorus, potassium, sulphur, magnesium, chromium, cobalt and copper. The last three in trace amounts.

"Rhuddlwm, although it may seem complicated and too much bother, if you will consume the proper nutrients every day, your chance for ultimate survival will increase a thousandfold."

I had listened to her for quite some time now and my brain was going into overload. I put my head in my hands and thought about all the fast foods I had eaten since coming back from Wales. It still had not registered what the warriors had done to me, or what this woman really wanted.

I glanced up and saw that she was looking straight in my eyes. *"Rhuddlwm, I am Rhiannon. I am a messenger of the gods,"* she said.

"Sometime during the next few years you will be faced with the following situation. You will go to the grocery store and find hundreds of people milling around inside. There will be few items on the shelves and none of them are what you need. You will get sick to your stomach. You'll feel frantic. You have children to feed. You'll panic. You'll grab what looks like a loaf of bread out of your next door neighbor's hands and run. You'll run all the way home looking back at the angry people who'll stand watching you. There will be no cars on the street. Everybody will be walking. You'll go inside your home and lock the door. You'll unwrap the package you thought was bread. 'Oh, God, it's a roll of Bounty!' You'll collapse in a chair and stare out the window as the family across the street leaves their house. They will have blanket rolls on their shoulders and packages under their arms. They are going to try to make it to their parents' house about forty miles away. They think they can get there in four days. You'll look at the TV. It's only working now from two to four p.m. and only then to give announcements. There will be no food in the house. What are you going to do? How will you feed your children? What will you do about the people who are stealing and killing for food? You'll sit

as if in a trance. How could life have changed so suddenly? You'll feel utterly helpless with no way out.

"Rhuddlwm, you had better be prepared to survive at least one year and maybe more without food available from ordinary sources. You had better have the knowledge as well as the will to survive the coming cataclysm. In this age of leisure, most of your students depend too much on alarm radios, microwave ovens, and fast cars for their daily survival. Consequently, they have not developed the skills which can enable them to survive stresses which will be encountered in the America of the future, the wilderness.

"History is full of war-ruined civilizations that have fallen from indoor luxury to outdoor desperation in a few hours. For the stone age human, necessity was the mother of invention, and he adapted to her toughest demands. Today, the mother of invention is leisure. If humanity would use this leisure to seek challenge, life would be rewarding for everyone, but it hasn't yet. Few Americans spend any time at all learning the ways of the woods.

"Survivors possess certain characteristics that set them apart from those who cannot adapt successfully to a stress situation. A survivor possesses determination, stubbornness, well defined values, self-direction, and a belief in the goodness of humankind, as well as the recognition of humanity's bad traits as well. A survivor is cooperative, she does not feel that mankind's basic nature is to promote only self-interest. A survivor believes that although most people are good and concerned with other people, a basic drive in a survival situation sometimes promotes selfishness. A survivor is kind to herself. She does not fear pain or discomfort, nor does she seek to punish herself with them. She is not a self-hater. Even the most difficult existence is acceptable to her if it is beyond her ability to change it. Otherwise she will fight for change. She knows the odds. Because an aura of timelessness exists in a survival situation, a person cannot allow herself to be overcome by the duration or the quality of her existence. A survivalist accepts it as it is and approves it from that standpoint. One of civilized humanity's greatest weaknesses in a stressful situation is the lack of ability to do this easily. A survivalist possesses the utopian attitude. This is because of an inbuilt artistic nature. She makes the most miserable existence seem like royal splendor. Her digging sticks are works of art, her camps, miracles of industry. There is nothing crude in the primitive existence of the survivalist.

"One of the first skills a survivalist must learn is how to make a

shelter. Select a good campsite which provides protection from wind and storms, protection from flash floods, rock falls, high tides, freedom from poisonous plants, insect pests, harmful animals, level ground for a bed and a fireplace, availability of materials for making a shelter and bed, an inexhaustible source of firewood, food sources and drinking water, dry ground, an area sheltered by a wooden frame roof in an earthquake area, an underground shelter in a high wind area.

"A fire pit is also essential. It should be eight inches deep and lined with stones, surrounded with spark protectors which can be made from green pine boughs. Locate it in a direct line with the shelter entrance. The importance of a good fire cannot be over emphasized. Fire is essential always, not only for warmth but for cooking, signaling, purifying water, and manufacturing certain items. Learn how to make a fire without matches or lighter. Learn about tinder, flint and steel, bow drills, and magnifying glass fire starters.

"Learn how to collect water from plants, from underground, from the air. Learn how to purify water.

"Learn how to search for food among the plants in your area, utilizing roots, seeds, leaves, and fruit.

"Learn how to make a food storage pit.

"Learn how to prepare various edible plants. Some are poisonous unless prepared correctly. Some can easily be mistaken for poisonous plants. Begin now to learn herb and plant identification.

"Animals are an important source of food for the survivalist. Learn techniques of hunting and trapping of animals and for other needs such as clothing and tools. You must be trained to be a good hunter, fisherman or trapper, and you must observe a code of conduct. All life from the smallest insect to the largest bear has a sacred right to fulfill the purpose of its creation and in no way is it required to become the sport of human beings. Hunting for survival is a different situation entirely. Hunting for survival must be done in keeping with nature's laws. Hunting and killing creates a spiritual void in nature that is only justified by real hunger or sincere need. Hunger involves killing. Some methods of killing are necessarily cruel. If you must hunt, hunt for the smallest as well as the largest animal. You could waste all your time tracking a bear and never be able to kill him.

"Other resources for food are insects, which are grasshoppers, locusts, crickets, cicadas, ants, grubs and caterpillars. Do not eat those with hair or fuzz on them.

"Reptiles. These are snakes. Always cut off rattlesnakes' or other

poisonous snakes' heads and bury them before eating them. Lizards, frogs, all reptiles, should be skinned and eviscerated before cooking.

"Birds. Small birds are emergency food only. They are too hard to obtain.

"Trapping. There are many methods available: bird snares, deadfalls, lift pole snares, spring pole snares.

"Hunting using primitive weapons to kill is different from hunting with a Remington 306. Hunting with spear and bow necessitates getting close to your quarry. This is called stalking. It takes time and training to learn. You can hunt with a bow and arrow, a throwing stick, a throwing rod, or a spear.

"A word about firearms and defense. It is wrong to kill another human unless he is a clear and present danger to your life or the life of the others you are responsible for. But if you have to defend yourself, a rifle in the hands of a marksman is safer for you and an intruder than any other weapon.

"Fishing. This can be difficult but not impossible. You are going to need tackle, your hooks and line; you will need a willow fish trap, and you will need a fish spear.

"You also need to learn how to preserve meat. You can prepare meat jerky by drying it in the sun for a few days. You can prepare pemmican, taking dry edible berries, pounding them into a paste, add dried pounded jerky, and then mix with suet. You can also dry fish.

"Bone, Wood and Stone Working. This is an area that is going to be very important to you, especially when you want to make your own arrow heads, your own stone dishes, etc. In stone working you want to use percussion flaking, pressure flaking, picking or crumbling, abrading, and piercing to work the stone. All of the above are highly technical arts demanding precise skill. Learn them.

"The same goes for bone working. You will be using grooving, notching, sharpening and honing, and drilling. These techniques, again, are highly technical arts. Learn them.

"Constructing Bows and Arrows. The finest woods for making bows are ash, elm, hickory, witch hazel, and yew. Bow strings can be made out of linen, hemp (marijuana for those who don't know any better), animal sinew, hide, and vegetable fiber. Arrows can be made out of cane or shafts of reed.

"Rawhide. Remove the fat from the rawhide using the urine method with a scraper. Remove the hair with a hair scraper, then pound the hide to break the grain. This is the simplest way of making rawhide.

Tanning: first remove the hair, then soak the hide, stake it out to dry, tan with the lightly cooked brains of an animal (the animal that you are tanning), store overnight rolled up, scrape all the excess brain tissue off and then smoke over a smudge fire.

"For survival planning, there are several items of specific foods that you can store. The basic four: Wheat: store whole grained. It is one of the best sources of protein and nutrition and it will store for several years. Powdered milk: store nonfat powdered milk in cardboard boxes in a dry, cool area. Honey: store in a sealed can. It will store indefinitely. Sea salt: store large quantities of it. It is needed if you are eating primarily vegetarian meals.

"Those which you will want to rotate are: peanut butter, which is high in protein and fat, it does not store well; tomato juice, high in vitamins A and C; soybeans, high in protein content; black strap molasses, high in iron content; dried green peas, these you can obtain from a feed store.

"Your basic menu: these are the things you need to purchase as soon as possible. 10 100 pound sacks of reclaimed tested wheat. You can get these in the market. 5 100 pound sacks of unclaimed wheat. These you can get from the feed store. The moisture content should be under 10 percent. Protein content should be over 12 percent. 400 pounds of dry milk. 250 pounds of dry unstrained honey. 25 pounds of salt. 3 cases of tomato juice. 20 pounds of peanut butter. 200 pounds of soy beans, whole or processed. 100 pounds of oats. 100 pounds of brown rice. Again, 100 pounds of green dried peas. 90 pounds of laundry soap. 90 cakes of hand soap. 4 gallons of chlorox. 6 packages of sal soda. 20 pounds of molasses. 10 gallons of cooking oil. A very large quantity of vitamin pills, enough for four people for two years. Dry yeast. Toilet tissue. Flavoring. You need bullion cubes, vanilla, mint and almond flavoring, food coloring, brown sauce, soy sauce.

"You will need several different kinds of seeds: watercress, parsley, escarole, mustard, alfalfa, and sesame seeds. In addition, store the following seeds. This is number one priority: wheat, corn, rye, soy beans, barley, alfalfa. Store the following seeds, number two priority: cantaloupe, cauliflower, collards, parsnips, radish, chicory, carrots. Store the following seeds, number three priority: peas, tomatoes, beans, pumpkins, okra, onions, endive, watermelon, cucumber, turnip, beets, spinach, lettuce, eggplants, potatoes, cabbage.

"The following is a temporary food supply for four people for one month:

468 ounces of crackers, cookies, and pretzels.
148 ounces of candy — chocolate bars and hard candy.
5 pounds of sugar.
5 pounds of salt.
64 ounces of instant tea or coffee.
32 ounces of hot chocolate mix.
128 bottles of soft drinks.
160 ounces of nonfat dry milk.
350 ounces of juice.
620 ounces of canned fruit — peaches, pears, apricots.
620 ounces of vegetables — peas, corn, lima beans.
72 cans of soup — vegetable, pea, noodle, bean, mushroom, and beef.
1,664 ounces of canned meat — canned beef stew, salmon, tuna, spaghetti, baked beans, chicken noodle.
56 ounces of peanut butter and cheese.
56 ounces of jam, jelly, and marmalade.
10 boxes of cereal.

"The third area of survival is medical supplies. Obtain the following consumable Supplies: Acromyicin capsules, ampecillin, aspirin, bacitrician eye ointment, benedryl, bronchaid, Cepacol gargle, Darvon compound, Digel liquid, debrox drops, domobrow tabs, demetrol, Fleet enema, lomatil, mirezine tabs, methyolate, neosporin ointment, neosyniferin nose drops, purapectalin, Robitussin CF syrup, seconal, senacot granules, sudafed tabs, syrup of epicac, tincture benzoin, triminic syrup, tylenol, vaseline, cascuris segrida tabs, eugenol, eye and nose drops, isopropol alcohol, kyoen and pectin liquid, penicillin GE tablets, petroleda (white), phenobarbityl, surgical soap, sodium bicarbonate, sodium chloride, sulfa diazine tablets, and iodine water purification tablets.

"Obtain a good medical first aid kit with bandages and splints."

As she finished transferring the knowledge into my brain, I began to feel like my mind was going to explode.

"Why are you telling me these things." I asked.

"Rhuddlwm, I hope you are not as dense as you sound. The coming cataclysm is real. It may happen in ten years or possibly fifteen, but it will happen. The only thing that will change the exact time

are you and the other inhabitants on this earth. If you become more spiritual, it will happen faster.

"Your only concern during the coming bad times must be the survival of your tribe and The Way."

As she faded out of sight, my eyes were again drawn toward the river. I only hoped that I was as single of purpose as that river was. Because I was going to need all the strength and will during the coming years.

I felt bruised and troubled. I am a rational human being who does not have hallucinations. I have a analytical mind and years of experience and training in psychotherapy. I was not exhibiting any of the symptoms of mental illness, and in fact I had been told by my professor that I was one of the most stable and rational human beings that he had ever met.

What was happening to me?

It was at that moment I heard a voice in my head.

"Rhuddlwm, I am that being that you call the Goddess. I am the spirit of Nature and the spirit of this mountain. I appear to you in this form because you need to see me as a female."

"You are not crazy nor mentally ill. You are more sane then most humans today."

"But why am I hearing you when you are obviously not here?," I said exasperated.

"By performing meditation and psychic exercises over the years, you have developed the small area of your brain known as the Pineal Gland into a powerful psychic transmitter and receiver. This gland is able to detect the life force of any being and translate the emanations into words and pictures. All humans are capable of developing this ability."

"But what am I supposed to do with it?," I asked.

Rhuddlwm, you are one of the Keys; one of the physical guardians of this world. You are human, rational and intelligent. You are psychic and able to communicate with the forces of Nature. What do you think You should do with this ability?," she asked impatiently.

I thought for a time.

"If all that I have heard from you is the truth, then truly I am a teacher."

"It's about time!," another voice cried.

"Rhuddlwm, we have been waiting for years for you to make the decision to 'actually' become a teacher. You have been teaching, but

72

not with all your heart. From this moment on you are truly worthy of your Initiation."

I suddenly felt good inside, and no matter what else happened to me, I knew who I was and what I would do with my life.

CHAPTER 6

THE GRAIL AND THE ATLANTEAN MYSTERIES

The Secret Way of the Ancients

This is definitely not an easy chapter for me to write. How do I tell you just enough without telling you too much?

The ancient Celtic mysteries include:

The Arthurian legends
The Grail Quest
The Legend of "The Word" — Logos
The Legend of the Round Table
The Legend of Taliesin
The Legend of the children of Don
The Legend of the children of Llyn
The Legend of the children of Nudd
The Legend of Draco the Dragon
The Tree of Life
The Legend of the Lady of the Lake
The Legend of Merlin
The Legend of the Flood
The Legend of Narada
The Legend of the Zodiac
The Legend of the Rose Cross
The Legend of the Solar Sphere

The Legend of the Thirteen Treasures
The Planes of Consciousness
The Legend of the Sword Dyrnwyn
The Union of the Higher and Lower spirit
The Legend of Sexual polarity
The Legend of Camelot
Serpent power
The sacred Tarot
The mystical wedding
Glastonbury and Stonehenge
The Spirit of the Earth

These are the Greater and Lesser mysteries of the Celts and the Atlanteans.

By studying these mysteries you may understand and attain the total evolution of human consciousness. These legends demonstrate that enlightened beings seek to control the many universal powers and do not shun them; we seek to use and elevate desire — not to subdue it.

The Lesser Mysteries:

The First Circle — the Circle of Causes is the first through which all must pass. This is the circle of loyalty, of dedication and of service. Within this circle one learns the concept of honesty, of the duty to serve loyally and of the duty to uphold the laws and to right all wrongs.

The Second Circle — the Circle of Blessedness is the second circle and represents those who have been tested and are worthy to attain the secret wisdom which brings knowledge of the use of the great odic force.

The Third Circle — the Circle of the Infinite comes from the knowledge of polarity which is the key to all occult work.

These three circles are the lesser mysteries because they deal with control and use of elemental forces: air, earth, water and fire. The lesser mysteries are represented by the round table of the Zodiac.

The Greater mysteries are represented by the mystical Grail, the Cauldron of Inspiration. Its symbol is the Goddess Ceridwen — the shape changer. Within the greater mysteries also reside the lesser mysteries:

The Circle of courses is represented by the stone pentacle; this is the element Earth — the Hare.

The Circle of Blessedness is represented by the cup; this is the element water — the Salmon.

The Circle of Infinite is represented by the wand; this is the element air — the Raven.

The
Priestess

Keridwen

Rhuddlum

77

The Grail represents the powers and perceptions of every human being before they mature and develop into the adept master. The Grail is inside each of us during our Quest for knowledge — the voyage of rediscovery.

The Red dragon is symbolic of the mysteries as a whole.

It is the Symbol of Wales
It is the Symbol of "the Power," Earth energy
It is the Symbol of the constellation Draco
It is the Symbol of Fire

THE TALIESIN MYSTERY

In ancient times there lived at Penellyn a man of high rank named Tegid Voel, the Bald, whose house was in the middle of Lake Tegid. His wife, Keridwen, gave birth to a son named Morvran ab Tegid, and a daughter named Creirwy, who was the loveliest girl in the world. Now they had a brother, Aland-Du, who was the least favored of all men. Keridwen, his mother, thought that it was unfitting to send him into noble society because of his ugliness unless he had some great merit and some rare knowledge.

Keridwen therefore decided to follow the art of the books of Fferyllt, (metalworker), and boil up a cauldron of inspiration and knowledge for her son, so that his entrance into human society would be honorable because of his knowledge of the mysteries of the future state of the world. Then she began to boil the cauldron. It was not to cease boiling for a year and a day until the three magic drops of grace and inspiration were obtained.

She told Gwyon Bach, son of Gwreang of Llanfain in Kaereiniawn in Powys, to watch over the cauldron, and a blind man named Morda to keep the fire going beneath it. She asked them to ensure that it continued to boil for a year and a day. She herself went out every day during the hours of the planets to gather all kinds of magic herbs in accordance with the books of the astrologer. Now one evening toward the end of the year, as Keridwen was gathering plants and uttering incantation, three drops of the magic liquid happened to spill from the cauldron and fell on the finger of Gwyon Bach. Because they were so hot, he put his finger in his mouth, and the very moment the magical drops reached it, he could see the whole future and knew that he would have to beware Keridwen's tricks, for she was very cunning.

Seized by an irrepressible fear, he fled toward his homeland. And the cauldron broke in two because all the liquid it contained, except for the three magical drops, was poisonous.

At this point Keridwen returned to see that her year's work had been wasted. She snatched up a block of wood and struck the blind Morda with it until his eyes fell out onto his cheeks. And he said: "You have disfigured me for no reason, for I am innocent." "You are right," said Keridwen. "Gwyon Bach is the guilty one." So she ran after Gwyon Bach as fast as she could.

He saw her and changed into a hare so that she could not catch him; but she changed into a greyhound bitch and turned him. Then he leaped into the river and turned into a fish. But Keridwen chased him through the water in the form of an otter, so then he had to change into a bird of the air. She then followed him in the form of a sparrow hawk and harassed him in the sky. But just as she was about to fall on him and he thought his end had come, he spied a heap of wheat which had just been threshed on the roof of a barn. He hastened there and changed into a grain of wheat. But Keridwen took the form of a high crested black hen and swallowed him. And as the story goes, she became pregnant, and nine months later a child was born.

But she did not have the courage to kill the child because of his beauty. That is why she put him in a leather bag and threw the bag into the sea, on April 30.

And at this time the weir net of Gwyddno was on the strand between Dyni and Aberystwyth, near to his own castle, and the value of an hundred pounds was taken in that weir every May eve. And in those days Gwyddno had an only son named Elphin, the most hapless of youths, and the most needy. And he grieved his father some, for he thought that he was born in an evil hour. And by the advice of his Bards, his father granted him the catch in the weir that year, to see if good luck would ever befall him, and to give him something to begin his life in the world.

And the next day when Elphin went to look, there was nothing in that weir. But as he turned back he perceived a leathern bag upon a pole of the weir. Then said one of the weir-wardens unto Elphin, *"Thou wast never so unlucky until tonight, and now thou hast destroyed the virtues of the weir, which always yielded the value of an hundred pounds every May eve, and tonight there is nothing but this leathern bag within it."*

"How now," said Elphin, *"there may be therein the value of an hundred pounds."*

Well, they took up the leathern bag, and he who opened it saw the forehead of the boy, and said to Elphin, *"Behold "a radiant brow!"* *"Taliesin be he called,"* said Elphin. And he lifted the boy in his arms and lamenting his mischance, he placed him sorrowfully behind him. And he made his horse amble ever so gently that had before been trotting, and he carried him as swiftly as if he had been sitting in the easiest chair in the world. And presently the boy made a consolation and praise to Elphin, and foretold honour to Elphin.

The tale of Taliesin's birth contains a number of themes common to many traditions. First, is the cauldron of inspiration. Second is the metamorphosis on land (the hare — Earth), in water (the fish — Water), in the air (the bird — Air) and finally in fire (the wheat). The sheaf of wheat is synonymous with divine fire and the high crested black hen is she who devours the fire in order to be transformed. Finally there is fertilization by mouth which leads to the hero's unusual birth and the theme of the child on the waters.

Gwyon Bach is therefore purified by being passed through the elements after the initiation of the magick drops. After being purified, his soul transcends itself, is reabsorbed into the unity represented by the grain of wheat; alpha and omega — the first and the last, life and death.

Keridwen, Mother Earth, then devours him. He resides for nine months in her belly and is thus reborn as a new being.

The Final initiation element is that of being placed inside a leather bag (tomb), being placed on the waters (eternal life), being rescued by Elfin on the festival of the sun god Belenos (the shining one), and receiving the name Taliesen (shining forehead) as he becomes a Bard.

Gwyon's Spirit fertilizes Keridwen, the Earth Goddess, the mother of the wheat. He becomes both her husband and his son.

The story of Taliesen is the story of a Human who has successfully accomplished a return to the spiritual aspect of life, the Great Spirit, the Earth Mother and Sky Father. He has completed his trials and has become a true *"Man"* with all the powers of a complete soul.

His story illustrates the legend of the Grail. The Grail is the symbol of the Goddess Don who needs her children to return to her to give her life.

Kerridwen or Don

She is Mother to Avallae of the Isle of Avallon. She if wife of Beli.

Avallon is the Garden of Eden — the summerland and is synonymous with Emain Ablach — the Isle of apple trees — the Astral.

The Grail is a final solar image — but is also the cauldron of inspiration — the cauldron of rebirth. These are the symbols of enlightenment — a form of rebirth in initiation. It is the same as The Dagdas cauldron (One of The Tuatha De Dannan):

The Truths DeDanann brought:

The Stone of Fal — pentacle — earth
Lugh's spear — wand — air
Nuadas sword — sword — fire
Dagdas cauldron — cups — water

The Red Dragon is the dragon of the Kundalini, the serpent power; the power that coils three and a half times around the base of the spine — fire — The Sword.

This power when properly activated over an earth power point can harness great energy — The Green Dragon.

The Secret Power of the ancients was in the use of polarity — sexual polarity to activate these power points. (There is a great deal more to it than having sex at an ancient crossroads). These power points connected by ley lines criss cross the earth like veins in a human body. They are like accupressure points and meridian lines on the body (as above, so below).

This polarity between men and women is the basic polarity of life — it is generated during the sex act and results in procreation of the species. If used properly it is also the ultimate key to power.

Knowledge — Love — Power

The three essentials.

We of Y Tylwyth Teg have kept the secret these many centuries.

TANTRA has part of it, the MASONS have lost "the Word" as have the Rosicrucians. The Golden Dawn and OTO would have corrupted it if they had found it. But we have kept it safe these many aeons.

Only the priesthood and the seventh level have the key.

But hear me those of you who suspect, we could have used it over these many years, but it wasn't used when the Romans killed our brothers on Anglesly, not when the Normans invaded our lands; it wasn't used when Germany was just across the channel.

It will only be used when the Earth begins its change — when north becomes south and east becomes west.

It will only be used when the sun rises in the west and sets in the east.

Those of us — the keys — are gathering together to be joined in one mind to use the power for good. But we will resist its use until such time as the prophecy has been fulfilled.

For know this — the key to the power is simple yet complex, and to attempt to harness the whirlwind with smoke is the height of folly.

CHAPTER 7

INITIATION INTO THE MYSTERIES
The First Step on the Path

An initiation is the rite of passage — the transition from level to level of life with certain spiritual powers assigned to each level. Birth-puberty-marriage-death — these are ordinary initiatory experiences.

Initiation into the Tribe of Dynion Mwyn is both religious and mystical.

Purification; preparation; vows of secrecy; an ordeal; an act of renunciation of the old life and of entry upon the new; a revelation verbal and visual; and instruction — these are the elements of Initiation.

First, preparation — the seeker's devotion, intentions, insight and mastery of ritual are tested.

Second, purification — the seeker fasts for three days before Initiation.

Third, vows of secrecy — this is important to separate oneself from the common person.

Fourth, ordeal — ritual scourging and symbolic death.

Fifth, renunciation of the old life — dying to the old life.

Sixth, the revelation — showing the initiate the mystery.

Seventh, instruction — a qualified master must give instruction.

The need for your "Quest" is the first subject we must address:

There comes a time in each person's life when a need for a personal dream/vision becomes apparent. Buffeted by winds of indecision and change, showered with waves of commercial hype and "words of wisdom," your soul screams out against "choices" and seeks to regain touch with its center.

You long to know the "Divine Design," you feel a sincere need to "grow up" and ascend to a higher plane of b ing. These are the indications that it is time to begin your vision Quest.

Leaving the past behind is often necessary if your soul is to evolve. Clearing out the unnecessary baggage is only possible when you have seen your vision and you know what to dispose of and what to retain.

The purpose of the vision quest is not to "blast open psychic doorways" nor to gain entrance to the clan; instead the object is to relieve the pressures and influences of your "every day life" long enough to get in touch with your inner self — your spirit guide. No one knows your self like you do!

Accumulated physical, mental, and spiritual poisons must be eliminated in order to cleanse your Soul.

Sweat baths, fasting, herbal cleansers, combined with natural surroundings and the intense desire to know the presence of the Great Spirit are all elements of your Vision Quest.

The Quest is used to establish the direction your life should take, obtain special help, solve personal problems, to fulfill your potential and live fully in the present emotionally, physically, psychologically, and spiritually.

The Quest consists of a lonely vigil kept in the wilderness. This is three days in our tradition, but can last from one to thirteen days.

Before the Quest, ritual purification and prayers are included as preparation for the journey.

During the Quest you must fast, be exposed to the elements, and endure a vow of silence.

The combination of fasting and isolation induces an "altered state of consciousness" characterized by a sense of union with all of creation and the Great Spirit. Because your awareness is expanded, you can identify more easily with the Cosmic Consciousness as well as the Nature Spirits and other Devas. You are in two worlds — the world of nature and the world of the Spirit.

You will be taken through a sweat ceremony by your teachers. Purification by the sweat lodge is a sacred and powerful healing ritual — to cleanse the mental and spiritual being, as well as the physical body.

Prayers are offered to the Great Spirit and when you emerge you are considered to be reborn, cleansed, purified, and ready to undergo whatever experience awaits — the purification experience of a sweat lodge helps you focus on what is to be cleansed.

The "giving away" or letting go of your ego consciousness continues when you meet with your teachers the next morning to greet the birth of a new day in a Sunrise Ceremony where you are blessed by the Elders.

You then walk into the woods, to your "place of power" which has been shown to you the day before by the Elders.

You spend "three" full turns of the wheel of the sun, alone in the bare bosom of the Earth Mother. This period of solitude and isolation is your natural world.

You will experience what it is to be a natural being in a natural setting. Attitudes of openness and humility will give you the unique opportunity to make contact with the deeper levels of your being.

Darkness and solitude can trigger fear, anxiety, and repressed "Bogeymen" in your subconsciousness.

You will have a complete opportunity to examine your beliefs and life, reflecting on the questions: "Who am I? Where did I come from? What am I doing with my life? Where am I going?"

Each dawn you will greet the East, at noon the South, at sunset the West, and at midnight the North (if you are awake!); aligning yourself with the tides and the turning of the wheel.

You will acquire insight into the clarity of feelings about your life and discover and strengthen your inner resources, capacities, and strategies to cope with the stress and anxiety of the unknown.

You will find a deeper sense of confidence in yourself and the process by which you and the universe can work together to improve your life experiences.

The success of this survival experience depends on an inherent knowledge that comes from your inner power and reality.

Emerging from the vision quest you will have become intimately attuned to the cyclic energy forces of nature and the interconnectedness of these forces.

You will understand the healing energies around you and how to tune these powers to work with you.

The process of opening yourself to an "altered state of consciousness" allows you to experience a new way of receiving information, knowledge, self-discovery, and healing that are not available to you in your ordinary state of consciousness.

Numerous Native American prophecies speak of the sickness and pollution of our Mother Earth. We need to regard the Earth pollution that we see around us as feedback about our own disharmony and imbalance.

You must seek your vision and understand your role in this process.

What path will you walk to bring about a return of wholeness, balance, health and healing of yourself and Mother Earth?

How else can the connection be made between your human spirit and the Great Spirit of oneness? You must look to the Spirit of the land in which you live. You must get in touch with the energies of your inner Being and become sensitive to the Great Spirit.

All aspects of creation have a spirit force. In the American Indian Tradition the Spirit of Turtle Island represents the healing energies of the spirit. This is "the Great Mystery," which is formless and formed, animated and unanimated.

This land was inhabited by the Indian Tribes long before the Celts visited it — but our philosophies are similar. Therefore even though we use Celtic names of the God/desses of nature, the symbols are the same.

PREPARATIONS

In preparation, burn sage or cedar to purify, center and unite yourself with the spirit of the clan. Negative energy will be dissipated into the earth.

The Earth has an electro-magnetic vibration that is able to assist in extracting this negative energy into itself.

All creation on this Earth contains a spirit, a life force; this includes rocks, plants, hills, trees, sky, mountains, animals, etc. Take this time during your quest to communicate with the forces of all creation; Mother Earth is a living, sensitive, breathing organism.

First, prepare yourself at home:

1. Learn to identify tree and plant spirits and their powers (but also ask them of their purpose and exchange energy by hugging, etc. during your Quest).
2. Sunrise is a greeting of Father Sun, Mother Earth and the new day. Design and learn a ritual prayer for this greeting. By now you should have been using a daily greeting upon arising each day, at home in your own space.
3. Know how to construct a circle and know the aspects of the four quarters.
4. Know which plants you can gather to use for scratches and bites — we will show you the ones which are in residence at your Quest site.
5. Know how to build a fire.

6. Know the vibration rate of stone by their color. Use the higher vibrations for the Quarters, lower vibrations for the fire pit ring.
7. For a week preceding your visit to Camelot, meditate upon your Quest.
8. Use herbal teas for flushing out and to start the cleansing of your bodily system. Suggested tea: use 1 1/2 pints fresh water, fresh ginger root (about 1/2 finger sliced into pieces), fennel, flax seed (one tablespoon each) and boil for three minutes at a slow boil and pour broth into the tea pot containing one tablespoon comfrey leaf and one tablespoon peppermint leaf. Makes one pint. Use one to two cups per day.
9. Use a herbal therapeutic purification bath for one week. Suggested: equal parts of hyssop, rosemary, lemon verbena, lavender, comfrey, mugwort, sage, thyme, and peppermint with sea salts added.
10. Read a good book on survival for helpful hints in coping with the solitude and any emergency. (We check on you from time to time, but — Be Prepared)!

Be sure to make arrangements to add to the "Pot Luck" meals that will be served during your stay with your teachers. There are lots of stores in the area of Camelot; you may bring food items from home or you can give cash to help cover the cost.

A large number of student/seekers come to Camelot each year. We cannot absorb the cost of their stay by ourselves; therefore bring provisions to share with the clan.

OTHER INFORMATION AND REQUIREMENTS

There is a limit of personal items allowed; the more that you can do without, the fewer attractions you will have for the material world. In olden times, all that was taken was yourself and your abilities.

A. You should dress comfortably and sensibly — layering of pants, shirts, coats or capes, in a quantity to be determined by the season. Wear low heeled, sturdy shoes (tennis or hiking boots). No sandals. This may help save you from twisted ankles and scratches from underbrush, etc.
B. You should bring toilet tissue for personal use.
C. Bring a personal offering to the woods Spirit. You may bring with you three white candles (consecrated and charged) for offering to the God/dess. One per day/night.

D. Bring salt (consecrated) for casting the circle; water for casting the circle is gathered from the stream.

E. You will be given two gallons of water for the three days; unless medication is required for health reasons this is all you will take internally. The body enters an "altered state" faster with a decrease in food intake.

F. Bring books, pen (consecrated at home) for copying. You will be given a supply of wooden matches.
   NO LIGHTERS!   NO CIGARETTES!

G. You may use the sage brought from home or use cedar chips from downed cedar trees, (We will show you where you may gather these pieces) for your ritual fire as offerings and centering yourself.

H. You will be required to keep a small ritual fire burning for the three days (be sure it is completely out before you return to the house). This ritual fire will be located in the Southern Quarter.

I. The circle is to be marked with four head-size stones and a center made up of three stones. The circle is to be cast in your selected "place of power." This place should be secure and sheltered. The place will "feel" right for you. You may want to build a lean-to shelter by gathering wood and covering it with tree branches.

J. You will need to gather wood for the fire from the downed trees. A big pile just outside the circle may seem like a lot, but it burns fast. I suggest you gather together all your firewood on the first day; as your system rids itself of poisons, you will become weaker.

K. You will also need to ring your fireplace with stones and using a stick, dig out a space to burn the wood safely in (fire pit). Do not use water soaked stones as these explode upon contact with fire.

L. If you wish to wash up there is a running stream. (Wash downstream).

M. You need to organize yourself by preparing your sacred space, the circle gathering stones, gathering firewood, gathering your incense (cedar chips), water from the stream, etc.

N. You are free to explore and communicate with the different trees, plants, animals, water spirits, etc. Be sure you ask permission before you do anything, as you would if you were a guest (which you are), for there will probably be spirits that you will want to include in the sacred circle. Also open and close the circle each time with your staff or wand. You will not take your Athame with you, but you may bring your wand or staff (a staff may find you). As each turn of the wheel passes you will feel more like just sitting rather than walking about. This is natural, as you turn inward. When the wheel has turned three days, give thanks to all assisting in your quest. You will be required to memorize all that you can of the experience. The animals seen and sources of communications. When you return, the Elders will reassemble to share the experience that you had and help guide you in the interpretation of your experience.

O. The clan elders will reunite with you and celebrate your survival — with a circle and feasting later that night. This ceremony is a rite to incorporate and initiate your movement back into the clan and then into the society from which you came. But first, you will probably want a hot tub bath, fresh clothes, and a light warm meal.

P. You will be required to sign a statement absolving Y Tylwyth Teg of all responsibilities and occurances during your stay; this protects you as well as us from legal consequences if you get sick or are injured.

An experienced teacher will help you prepare yourself for the Quest, but in the final analysis it is you alone who must come face to face with your self.

The Great Spirit resides within each of us and will speak to those who have properly prepared the Temple.

THE VISION QUEST AWAITS!

The following is the first degree initiation into a Celtic tradition.

The First Degree Initiation

The grove members are robed and hooded. The initiate alone wears no cingulum. The initiator, High Priestess or High Priest (High Priest if the initiate is a woman, High Priestess of the initiate is a male), greets the initiate, who is blindfolded and led by the guide, summoner, Maiden or candlebearer, to the northeast. The initiator touches the initiate on the breast with sword or athame and says:

"Seeker of light, from whence have you journeyed?"
The neophyte says:
"I have journeyed from the north, land of death and darkness."
The initiator says:
"Where do you go?"
Neophyte:
"I journey to the east to be reborn."
Initiator:
"What passwords do you give?"
Neophyte:
"Perfect love and perfect trust."
Initiator:
"So mote it be. You cannot enter this sacred grove without purification. Who guides you on your journey?"
The guide:
"I guide him or her."
Initiator:
"Who be you?"
Guide:
"The guide of souls."
Initiator:
"So mote it be. Seeker of light, received from the Guardian of the North the bonds of death and rebirth and the blessings of air which is the breath of life."

The initiator blows three times on the neophyte's forehead after binding their hands behind their back with the initiation cord. The ends are drawn up in front and held by the guide who leads the neophyte to the east.

Initiator:
"Seeker of light, from whence have you journeyed?"
Neophyte:
"I have journeyed from the north, land of death and darkness."
Initiator:
"Where do you go?"
Neophyte:
"I journey south to be reborn."
Initiator:
"What passwords do you bring?"
Neophyte:
"Perfect love and perfect trust."

Initiator:

"So mote it be. You cannot enter this sacred grove without purification. Who guides you on your journey?"

Guide:

"I guide him or her."

Initiator:

"Who be you?"

Guide:

"The guide of souls."

Initiator:

"So mote it be. Seeker of like, receive from the Guardian of the East the blessing of earth."

The initiator then makes a banishing pentagram of salt upon the forehead and the neophyte is then led to the south.

Initiator:

"Seeker of light, from whence have you journeyed?"

Neophyte:

"I have journeyed from the north, land of death and darkness."

Initiator:

"Where do you go?"

Neophyte:

"I journey west to be reborn."

Initiator:

"What password do you bring?"

Neophyte:

"Perfect love and perfect trust."

Initiator:

"So mote it be. You cannot enter the sacred grove without purification. Who guides you on your journey?"

Guide:

"I guide him or her."

Initiator:

"Who be you?"

Guide:

"The guide of souls."

Initiator:

"So mote it be. Seeker of light, receive from the Guardian of the South the blade of power and the blessings of fire."

The initiator touches the neophyte on each shoulder with the athame and censes them thrice with the censor. The neophyte is then led to the West.

94

Initiator:

"Seeker of light, from whence have your journeyed?"

Neophyte:

"I have journeyed from the North, land of death and darkness."

Initiator:

"And where do you go?"

Neophyte:

"I journey North to be reborn."

Initiator:

"What passwords do you bring?"

Neophyte:

"Perfect love and perfect trust."

Initiator:

"So mote it be. You cannot enter this sacred grove without purification. Who guides you on your journey?"

Guide:

"I guide him or her."

Initiator:

"Who be you?"

Guide:

"The guide of souls."

Initiator:

"So mote it be. Seeker of light, receive from the guardian of the West the blessings of water.

The initiator draws a banishing pentagram of water on the neophyte's forehead. The neophyte is led to the North, back turned to the circle.

Initiator:

"Seeker of light, from whence have you journeyed?"

Neophyte:

"I have journeyed from the four watchtowers of the world and have received purification from each."

Initiator:

"Where do you go?"

Neophyte:

"I go to the sacred grove to be reborn."

Initiator:

"What passwords do you give?"

Neophyte:

"Perfect love and perfect trust."

The initiator grabs hold of the neophyte's bound wrist and yanks

them backwards and yanks him or her backwards into the circle, saying:
"Be thou reborn."

Then the blindfold is removed and the neophyte is kissed for purification. The cords are untied and the neophyte is shown how to tie it around the waist with a single loop to the left side. He or she is instructed that this is the symbol of the circle of rebirth. They are then led before the altar. They are told to make the pentagram position and are anointed thus. An invoking pentagram: forehead, left foot, right hand, right hand, left foot, and forehead.

The initiator then says:
"Are thou ready to take the oath?"
Neophyte:
"I am."

The initiator then consecrates the neophyte's athame and holds it out to the neophyte, who places their right hand over the blade and says:

"I, (craft name), do vow by my honor before the whole company of gods, the great mother Arianrhod, the great spirit Hu Gadaran, and all here present within this sacred grove, that I will keep sacred the secrets and laws of this grove. So mote it be.

Initiator now takes blood from the initiate and puts it into the summoner's black book and makes the new initiate sign the craft name and date.

Second Level Initiation

The candidate and guide present themselves at the north gate. Initiator holds the maiden candle aloft and says:
"Neophyte Wiccan, from whence have you come?"
Candidate:
"I have come from the sacred grove in search of greater light."
Initiator:
"Where do you go?"
Candidate:
"I journey East in search of the sun that I may stand in this light."
Initiator:
"What password do you give?"
Candidate:
"Greetings on all points of the pentacle."
Initiator:
"Who guides you on your journey?"

Guide:

"I guide him or her."

Initiator:

"Who be you?"

Guide:

"The guide of souls."

Initiator:

"So mote it be. Neophyte Wiccan, receive from the Guardian of the Grove these sacred gifts."

The initiator presents the candidate with a pentacle upon which are two birch leaves, two apple seeds, a parchment, and two pieces of quartz. The candidate is taken to the east.

Initiator:

"Neophyte witch, from whence have you come?"

Candidate:

"I have come from the sacred grove in search of greater light."

Initiator:

"Where do you go?"

Candidate:

"I journey South in search of the serpent that I may stand in his fiery gaze."

Initiator:

"What password do you give?"

Candidate:

"Greetings on all points of the pentacle."

Initiator:

"Who guides you on your journey?"

Guide:

"I guide him or her."

Initiator:

"Who be you?"

Guide:

"The guide of souls."

Initiator:

"So mote it be. Neophyte, witch, present to the Guardian of the East the gift from the tree of eternity."

The candidate gives the initiator the two birch leaves which are put into the cauldron. The candidate is then led to the South.

Initiator:

"Neophyte witch, from whence have you come?"

Candidate:

"I have come from the sacred grove in search of greater light."

Initiator:

"Where do you go?"

Candidate:

"I journey West in search of the Lady, that I may stand beneath her silver wheel."

Initiator:

"What passwords do you give?"

Candidate:

"Greetings on all points of the pentacle."

Initiator:

"Who guides you on your journey?"

Guide:

"I guide him or her."

Initiator:

"Who be you?"

Guide:

"The guide of souls."

Initiator:

"So mote it be. Neophyte witch, present to the Guardian of the South the promise.

The candidate gives the parchment to the High Priest/ess which is put into the cauldron, and then is led to the West.

Initiator:

"Seeker of light, from whence have you journeyed?

Candidate:

"I have come from the sacred grove in search of greater light."

Initiator:

"Where do you go?"

Candidate:

"I journey North in search of the Lord, that I may see his mighty horns."

Initiator:

"What passwords do you give?"

Candidate:

"Greetings on all points of the pentacle."

Initiator:

"Who guides you on your journey?"

Guide:

"I guide him or her."

Initiator:

"Who be you?"

Guide:

"The guide of souls."

Initiator:

"So mote it be. Neophyte witch, present to the Guardian of the West the seeds of the sacred tree."

The candidate gives the apple seeds which are put into the cauldron, and is led to the North.

Initiator:

"Neophyte witch, from whence have you journeyed."

Candidate:

"I have come from the sacred grove in search of greater light."

Initiator:

"Where has your journey taken you?"

Candidate:

"To the realm of the God whose gift I carry in my hand."

The candidate gives the quartz to the initiator, who places them into the cauldron and gives the candidate two unlit tapers.

Initiator:

"Neophyte witch, do you bring a greater light?"

Candidate:

"I cannot, for you have the greater light."

Initiator:

"Then receive the greater light, and give praise to Cerridwen by her holy breasts."

The initiator lights the two tapers from the maiden candle. The candidate faces West and holds out the candle and says:

" All hail be to the breasts of the moon. All hail be to Cerridwen. All hail be to Rhiannon."

The candidate is led into the circle and stood before the cauldron. The initiator says:

"Where is the greater light?"

Candidate:

"Within the sacred grove, within thee and within me."

Initiator:

"So mote it be. "

Here the initiator anoints the forehead of the candidate with oil and an invoking pentagram.

Initiator:

"Be thou wise, initiate of the second level."

Then puts out the candles, which are kept by the initiate, who would carve their craft name and date of the second degree upon one. This should be used for their first circle as a High Priest or a High Priestess.

The Third Degree

The circle is cast and purified. Only the High Priestess and High Priest and Candidate should be present. The candidate is met at the North unbound.

Initiator:

"Oh thou of the second, from whence have you come?"

Candidate:

"I have come from the sacred grove on a quest for the mystery of the Grael."

Initiator:

"And What do you seek?"

Candidate:

"I search for the truth of the mysteries."

Initiator:

"And who is it that would vouch for you?"

Candidate:

"I have been presented to the Mighty Ones twice before and have received purification and the gift of greater light from each of the Lords of the Watchtowers, and they do vouch for me."

Initiator:

"So mote it be. Whom doest thou seek?" Candidate:

"I (Craft name), seek the Lady Rhiannon and the Lord Cernunnos that I may be given the truth.

Initiator:

"What passwords do you give?

Candidate:

"All hail be to the breasts of the moon."

Initiator:

"So mote it be. Enter."

The initiator cuts the gate and the candidate enters. Both stand facing North before the altar.

Initiator:

"Before thou canst be given the truth thou must prove thyself worthy. Prepare thee properly the place between the worlds."

The candidate casts and purifies the circle and reinvokes the Mighty Ones. The initiator places one hand under his or her right foot and the other upon the top of his or her head and says:

"Unto thee I will place all like powers that are mine. So mote it be."

And the initiator wills the power into the candidate.

The tools of the High Priest/ess are now shown to the initiate and explained. Then the lessor and greater mysteries are revealed.

Initiator:

"Let it be known before the great company of the gods and all the Mighty Ones that (name of candidate) has been properly prepared and made a High Priest (Priestess) of the craft."

The Great Rite is now performed between the initiate and the High Priest or the High Priestess.

CHAPTER 8

DISCIPLESHIP — MASTERSHIP

What is Expected of a Seeker

My Guide was speaking to me, *"Rhuddlwm, generally most seekers look at life in terms of two questions. Will I get anything out of this, or will this hurt me? You cannot live a natural life and take the same habits you have lived with all your life and put your practice of earth religion philosophy in the same framework. In one way or another your approach to the Old Religion is usually based on a struggle to achieve something — recognition of your peers, to be important in the community, to find a safe hole to hide in, and so forth. You are doing the same thing you have always done. You are expecting something to give you satisfaction, to give you happiness.*

"To look outside yourself for true peace and satisfaction is hopeless. You must look within.

"The first step in the enlightenment process is to become a student. The student must obey the great laws as they are revealed to her and await the guidance of the elder brothers and sisters. During these years of spiritual darkness he or she must spend this time in self-improvement along those lines which are normally recognized as virtuous and true. He or she must consecrate him/herself to the labor of preparing their nature for the greater responsibilities that are to come. The duties of such a one are:

1. Learn to cast away selfishness.
2. Keep your own and your neighbor's secrets.

103

3. *Court not the favors of the rich, despise not the poor, for he who does will also become poor. Give to the needy and unfortunate what little you can spare — it will be returned to you threefold.*
4. *Be merciful to those who offend you, or who have injured you, for what shall a man's heart be who would take heavy vengeance on a slight offense.*
5. *Be not hasty to condemn the actions of others lest you should in the next hour fall into the very same error. And let your words be few.*
6. *Study day and night and pray to the Great Spirit that she would be pleased to grant you wisdom and understanding.*
7. *Avoid gluttony and all excess. If you are rendered incapable of receiving any good or divine gift.*
8. *Covet not much gold, but learn to be satisfied with enough.*

"The second is to become a disciple. These are the accepted students of an initiate or master. For them the veil is beginning to lift. They have placed their feet firmly upon the winding path that leads to the temple of Y Tylwyth Teg. Instead of wandering far in the search for wisdom, they gather at the feet of their appointed teacher and learn from him or her. Today many seekers wander from one place to another and there is too much uncertainty in the soul of the student. You must choose one path, and having established the integrity of that path, remain with it until all has been obtained that can be.

"The master chooses his disciple. The disciple does not choose the master. Each master has a number of disciples. Again, they are chosen. For the disciple, the day of book learning is over. The day of personal investigation is at hand. He or she has been accepted. True masters sometimes appear in public, teaching large classes or groups of disciples. But they also come privately to their disciples and instruct them individually. None who is not an adept is able to provide for the spiritual needs of students. Most will not recognize the master when he comes. The work of the disciple is to learn unquestioning obedience. Once the master has proven his authority and virtue the disciple must obey without question.

"The third step is the initiate. These are the accepted and proven disciples who, while out of the physical body, have actually taken on one or more initiations. They are becoming masters. On the threshold between the realm of the real world and that of the invisible world stands the guardian of the abyss. This is the physical nature of the *initiate. This is the terrible being that guards the spiritual world from each seeker. To pass this being one must give up the physical world. Not until the seeker reaches the ninth level does he or she become loosed of the bonds that curb the ordinary human. He or she does not become greater than the law until he or she becomes part of the law. All initiates are to some degree clairvoyant since they must be able to function consciously outside of the human body. All masters have passed gradually from ignorance to wisdom. So they have passed along the way. Along the way the initiate must do certain things and abide by certain laws:*

1. *All true seekers must abide by the laws of the community where they dwell.*
2. *All true seekers must break no laws regardless of the injustice of such laws.*
3. *All true seekers must assume the dress and customs of the community among whom they dwell.*
4. *All true seekers must reveal his or her identity to no person unless that one is worthy to receive it.*
5. *All true seekers shall never become boisterous or declamatory in his or her statements, nor palm off his or her ideas as having more importance than his own brain.*
6. *All true seekers shall be peace loving, simple, and not critical of those around them.*
7. *All true seekers will never use their spiritual powers for their own gain unless such is for the good of others also.*
8. *All true seekers will never take pay for the spiritual instruction they teach, only donations to cover the cost.*

"If a true initiate has followed the laws of the clan of Y Tylwyth Teg she will become a master."

CHAPTER 9

THE TRIBE OF MASTERS

The Wise Ones of Atlantis

Seeker, If you wish to find the source of The Family, you only have to travel to North Wales in the vicinity of Gwynedd and Clwyd — this is where our tradition was first put into written form by the Bards.

Go to Mount Snowdonia and look at its slopes to the East — toward Betws-y-Coed.

Go to Anglesey, a stronghold of the Welsh language and look toward England.

Go to Denbigh and look to the West.

Go to Llandudno and look to the South.

If you are a serious seeker, you will then find our home, our hidden community

But this is not our origin. Our origin is the Ancient Civilization of Atlantis. Not the Island, for there was never a specific Island of Atlantis.

Solon, a celebrated legislator of Greece lived around 650 BC and went on many journeys to Egypt and other ancient lands where he heard priests describe a land that existed west of the Pillars of Hercules.

They told of a prehistoric continent larger than Asia which was located in the Atlantic ocean and was a powerful kingdom nine thousand years before the birth of Solon.

Homer speaks of a continent that existed off the west coast of Africa, with great wealth and beauty.

In one ancient record in Egypt a Master, wrote: *"Low cliffs fringed the coast of the gulf, which was semi-circular and of vast extent. Twenty miles inland from the city of paradise rose seven hills, framing the beautiful city four square with their purple crests. The capital spread from the center, which was at the water terrace, like a fan opened wide; the ribs being the broad avenues and the edges, flutted hills in the distance."*

Ancient Hebrew records speak of a book no longer in existence, which speaks of Adam living in Paradise and said that this paradise stood in the wonderful land of Atlantis, and from this Adam came every member of the human race. Atlantis gave the name Atlantic to the ocean which now covers it.

The ancient pyramids of Egypt, Asia, South America and the far north, are all patterned after those created by the Atlantean Engineers. The Power used in erecting them was a combination of tuned instruments, all pitched to a certain key, and the combined psychic will projected by the the group.

The priests of Atlantis possessed knowledge of the esoteric arts and sciences, of gravitation and levitation and could move tons of material from place to place by the intelligent application of those laws.

Certain Egyptian monuments tell of invasions of lower Egypt five thousand years ago by a blonde tribe from the west. The bones found in the stone cromlechs are those of a large race. These were the cromagnon humans who were the remnants of Atlantis. The people were called the Tamahu and have come down to the present day as the Berber tribe Tuareg.

The language of the Berbers, the Basques and some ancient Welsh dialects all have the same syntax in common. All of these people are located on the west coast of Europe and speak languages that are derived from Atlantean.

But this is only half the story. In the Pacific ocean, another civilization was destroyed about the same time as Atlantis - This was Lemuria.

The existence of these civilizations can be confirmed by: Nacal tablets, books, inscriptions, symbols and legends found in India, China, Burma, Tibet, and Cambodia; Ancient Maya books, inscriptions, and legends found in the Yucatan and Central America; Remains, inscriptions, and symbols found among the pacific islanders; Stone tablets found in Mexico; Cliff dwellers writings and inscriptions found in western North America; The ancient Greek philosophers; The books and writings of the ancient Egyptians; Legends throughout the world; and the legends of Y Tylwyth Teg.

Our legends state that there were once two large bodies of land, one in the Atlantic and one in the Pacific Ocean. On these continents humans made their appearance approximately one hundred thousand years ago. This was the beginning of the second world; When the last glaciation period began approximately 115,000 B.C., the water levels began to recede. The continental areas known as North America and North Europe were glaciated and cold deserts surrounded them.

A great deal of water became locked up in the massive ice sheet which covered these areas at the peak of the period and was over three miles thick. The water level in all the seas receded more than two hundred meters (approx. 600 feet) thus exposing a very large expanse of the mid ocean ridge and the pacific plateau. These were the beginnings of Atlantis and Lemuria.

From approximately seventy thousand years ago to approximately thirteen thousand five hundred years ago, the mean temperature in the winter and summer was ten degrees colder than it is now, keeping the glaciers at about the same size.

Then in thirteen thousand five hundred years B.P., something occurred. The ice volume abruptly decreased, the mean temperature increased by ten degrees and the sea level rose.

Thirteen thousand years ago the area now covered by the North Sea was dry land, and the home of an ancient civilization. The climate was mild — the Earth was on a different axis, and was differently inclined toward the sun. The sea level was much lower than it is now. This was the beginning of the end of the last ice age and the Glaciers had locked up much of the available water. The sea was much more salty and boats and ships were much easier to float and sail.

As the glaciers began to melt, the Earths axis began to shift, causing even more of the suns energy to melt more ice. The flooding was horrible. The weather changed bringing great storms and high winds, and great amounts of moisture were absorbed by the atmosphere.

As the weight of the glaciers left the polar regions, these areas began to lift up just as a boat does when you remove its cargo. As some land rose (Canada, Northern Europe, Greenland, etc.), other land began to sink. Some land appeared to sink because of the higher water level; some because of the law of physics: we live on a fluid earth. The inside of the earth is molten and the laws of fluid mechanics say that if pressure causes some land to sink (weight of glaciers), other land at the weakest points of the crust will rise and vice versa.

This means that the safest points on Earth are the various continental plates. These are composed of rock that is light and floats on top of the Earths molten mantle as a piece of wood does if tossed into the lake.

The ancient priest/scientists of Atlantis saw what was happening and told their people, but few would listen. Those that did, migrated from the sea coasts where most of the civilized world lived, to the interiors of the continents. They took with them as much of the Sacred Knowledge as they could. But great volumes of books and tablets were lost. Most knowledge was carried in the memory of those that left for the new lands.

The Ancient Celts were the remnants of this ancient civilization that stretched along the coastline of Europe thirteen thousand years ago; the Iberians were a part; the Basques; the Berbers; all those who once inhabited the land now covered by the sea. Our tradition is the result of this ancient knowledge being passed on by word of mouth and trained memory of Bards and Teachers of The Way.

We of Dynion Mwyn trace our lineage back directly to the ancient priesthood of Atlantis who migrated to Hyperborea during the destruction of Atlantis in 12,000 B.C.

Hyperborea was located in the area now known as the Southern British Isles and the North Sea and became a thriving community of Atlantean priests and priestesses who kept the ancient knowledge safe for those who were worthy of receiving it.

We know that all religions that developed throughout Europe and Asia sent their priests to be trained by the Atlantean priests of Hyperborea.

The center of activity was located in the area now covered by the North Sea. This center of commerce and culture consisted of several cities which contained race tracks and temples of renowned beauty. The ruling princes were peaceful, but had vast armies to protect them from the barbarians to the south.

Between 13,000 B.C. and 3,000 B.C., the last of the major glaciers melted, raising the sea level by 300 to 600 feet. Finally in 2800 B.C. the Sea poured into the lowlands which is now the North Sea and destroyed Hyperborea, causing the great migrations of the different peoples throughout Northern Europe and into the Mediterranean countries. These migrations included the core of the Atlantean priesthood who migrated to the Isle of Mona in Wales. These priests and priestesses became known as Druids (Worshippers of the Oak) and also became the Celtic Priesthood.

The Druid Priesthood ruled the "Cymmry" which means "The People" in the Welsh language. These Cymmry lived in Wales and Britain prior to the invasion by the Romans.

The Druids became the teachers, professors, philosophers, lawyers and poets of the Celtic peoples. In all public and private quarrels, the Druid settled all disputes. They passed on their knowledge by word of mouth.

There was such a large volume of oral tradition that finally in 100 A.D., the knowledge began to be transcribed in Ogamh Runes. For the next 1000 years this knowledge was written in the Welsh language as well as Ogahm, and was hidden in the form of manuscripts in Northern Wales by the tribe of Dynion Mwyn.

Finally in 1274 A.D. Prince Llywelyn ab Gwyffed, being a prince and a poetic Bard, began the task of compiling all the Druid knowledge into ordered volumes.

He was the first Druid Bard to collect *"The Thirteen Treasures"* and created *"The Owl."* To these books he later added what he had learned from the Order of the Knights Templers of which he was a grand master, and Witchcraft which was the corrupted remains of the ancient Pictish Tradition. He adopted the name of one of the tribes of Welsh Picts for our tradition: Y Tylwyth Teg.

Llewelyn was initiated into the Order of the Knights Templers in 1279 and became a secret master of the order in Wales in 1280 as well as the Ordre de Seon and the Ordre de la Rose-Croix.

Y Tylwyth Teg, as *"The Way"* became known, absorbed the knowledge of several witchcraft Covens and Groves through the years as well as Kabalistic magick from the East.

Between 1282 A.D. and 1895 A.D., there is little historical information available because of the witchhunts and repression, making it extremely difficult to keep records. But we do have many legends concerning the *"Tribe of Masters"* of Dynion Mwyn. The following tale reflects our commitment to our tribe and shows the reasons for our spiritual devotion to our teachers.

"Ten thousand years ago a spiritual master came to the Cymmry to teach the ancient mysteries. This spiritual master sought nothing for himself, but brought much to humankind. He appeared to a small group of people who lived in a land of Hyperborea. Mysterious and having great powers, he lived among this Tribe of people for twenty-three years, and taught them how to generate The Power. He explained that he had come from the Great Spirit to present these special teachings to those individuals who through discipline and courage could rise above everyday reality and create within themselves the ancient, inner force which would announce a new age of love and knowledge.

"This small group of people became known as the tribe of Dynion Mwyn, the gentle folk. He taught them how to heal the sick, how to see at a distance, how to change the weather, how to move stones with a thought, how to make the blind see and the dead return to life. The master's name was Hu Gadaran, and he created the Tribe of Masters.

"As the tribe increased in knowledge it also increased in numbers, and great were their powers. He explained that he was gathering the keys that would one day teach humanity The Way."

The Masters of the Keys have refined their powers and their path over the last 10,000 years, and today they are prepared to help bring spiritual advancement to humanity by teaching certain seekers to recognize truth.

The Tribe has manifested its activities secretly and sometimes openly under different names and in various forms and has proven to be a rock of salvation in times of danger. The Tribe has always upheld the banner of freedom against tyranny in whatever shape it appeared. To this secret order every Master belongs by rite of initiation and works under the guidance of the one light of truth. No one has the power to admit a seeker into this society unless she has the power by virtue of her interior illumination and initiation. Neither can anyone be expelled unless she or he should expel themselves by becoming unfaithful to the principles and forget the truths which have been learned by experience. All this is known to every true enlightened being and now is revealed to you.

This invisible organization of men and women who have found the path to real self-knowledge and self-actualization, are willing to act as spiritual guides to those who are willing to be guided.

While numerous orders have been founded in the past, we believe that there is but one ancient organization of genuine teachers which can reveal to the seeker the lost mysteries of antiquity and unveil the one truth. This organization is known in this time as the tribe of Dynion Mwyn, the peaceful people. It is a tribe of esoteric teachers, and derives its knowledge from the ancients of Atlantis.

This knowledge is never revealed to the common person, for it gives immense power to the possessor, for good or evil. It is taught through symbol, parable, and allegory, requiring The Keys for its interpretation. The symbols of the clan of Y Tylwyth Teg were originally derived from these ancient Keys.

There exists only one right key and, moreover, this one right key must be used the right way. The clan of Y Tylwyth Teg possesses this key which opens up all occult secrets and explains without exception all secrets and all systems of religion. The key is expressed through **Camelot-of-the-Wood.**

Camelot-of-the-Wood is both a physical place and a realm of the mind. Within the mind it is a centering point with no boundaries. From every direction seeds of learning are being planted in the sacred awareness of all life. The physical realm of Camelot includes a community, forests, gardens, a college of natural healing and centers where we manifest the seeds of the mind in ways to be shared and experienced by all. Within both realms each Gwiddon is becoming a Master of life.

The essence of Camelot is demonstrated by its symbol: First three spirals, three paths, spiraling both inward and outward, always toward growth. The first spiral represents the path toward the awareness of love. A level of love quite apart from the common definition. It is mystical love. It is a love linked to the awareness of the shared kinship of all life. The second spiral symbolizes a path of action or power. The action can take many forms as long as it is woven together with the spiral of love. One of the primary actions would be the teaching of true seekers. The third spiral represents the path of knowledge. It is a knowledge that is a unique blend of ancient wisdom and today's latest scientific research.

The Ankh in the center holds a threefold meaning of growth. The growth of Camelot, the growth of loving kinship between humans and nature, and the growth of each individual who travels the three interwoven paths. This results in an increasing awareness of the sacredness of that spirit of creation we refer to as Mother Earth.

The encompassing circle is the symbol of the kinship of all life, the concept of one, the idea that all life is equally sacred. The spiral paths of Camelot lead to an increasing awareness of yourself. Ours is a method of learning by experience which is best explained by the following quote: *"When you know how to listen and observe, all of life, all of existence, is a teacher."* This philosophy seeks to expand awareness on two levels. One level is to make you more aware of the wonders which are literally at your fingertips. Too many people seek to concentrate only upon the sixth sense, forgetting to equally expand the potentials inherent in their other five senses. Our philosophy attempts to expand all of one's senses. We believe a dangerous imbalance is created when one places too much emphasis on any one of the senses. A major goal of our teaching is to achieve the development of what has been termed primary perception. It is the link between all life on the earth.

The second level is our awareness of the kinship of all life and the sacredness of all life. The major obstacle to this awareness is ego. Of all our problems this is the most difficult to overcome. Its negative effects touch everyone's perception. There is no detour around this obstacle. It can only be overcome by growth and awareness, in the same manner in which the first level will be achieved. Neither level can be obtained by those who seek instant enlightenment. Both levels are linked to the pagan theology of Camelot.

There is no segregation between the secular and the sacred. To us, every awareness is totally linked to our religion. A Gwiddon may participate in a sacred rite which might include a feast, a meditation and a dance; but the same person would consider a noon snack no less a sacrament, for in both actions a life, be it animal or plant, it has given of itself for their growth. The perception of this attitude is fully realized only through growth on all levels of our awareness. It is an all-pervading attitude.

There are rituals relating to the seasons to underline the sacramental aspects of nature, but a Gwiddon perceives the creation of a compost heap as no less holy an activity than participation in a symbolic ritual. To a Gwiddon all of life is a sacrament. If one's previous introduction to religion has been in the current orthodox realm, a path that links spirituality to every action and thought may appear to be too complex. The very opposite is true. The stress of orthodox religions is focused upon death and a transcendence from life. Our focus is on life and our greatest sacrament is the manifestation of our love of nature into actions that will bring about truth and joy.

The teachings of Dinion Mwyn as expressed through Camelot, are given to each seeker by a Gwiddon Master who has reached an advanced state of enlightenment. A Gwiddon Master will not expect you to take his word for who he is. He will have a way of making you experience his mystical state by making you see your own human fears and frustrations and overcoming them. But a Master is only a Guide to your enlightenment.

A Gwiddon Master — Disciple relationship demands intense concentration and involvement; you must focus constantly on attaining that which your Guide is showing you. But your Guide is also your higher self externalized, as we are each part of the Great Spirit.

If there is a 'Block' in your life, possibly some trauma in your past, your guide will open up the 'Block' and let you face the trauma with help and love.

You are not guaranteed a good experience with a Guide; you will only get out of the relationship what you put into it.

The illusion of failing your Guide or the Guide failing you is also possible. There is no failing or passing. There is only learning.

In regards to other teachers: There are many unqualified people calling themselves teachers and claiming to be able to guide you to enlightenment; but anyone who sets up shop as a 'Master' or teacher probably has so much of his or her status needs involved in teaching, that he or she is vulnerable to competing with others that are similarly involved.

Once a person thinks of himself as a 'Master' or 'Guide' or 'Teacher', and allows his ego to affect his human relationships, the teaching approach he is using will turn sour. His vanity is overfed, and no one tells him he is behaving badly or stupidly. Without feedback from his students, his judgement becomes impaired.

It is important that a Gwiddon Disciple learn from many teachers and not from just one. If you went to medical school, you would not expect to have only one professor, would you?

The difficulty is that those who go from school to school, guru to guru, or technique to technique without completing the requirements of each, are just expressing their resistance to real discipline involved in long term growth. As they bounce from one 'Master' to another, they demonstrate that some people will do anything for enlightenment except work for it. Learn from many teachers but learn all of what each has to teach you before moving on.

A Gwiddon Master does not let his advanced enlightenment separate him from his students. He is human like they are, but he is enlightened and can demonstrate his enlightenment to his students.

As the students grow they eventually are taught by others besides the Master; But the Master is a Guide and as long as the student follows the way of the Cymmry, the Master will guide the seeker on his journey. The Master guides. The Seeker learns.

CHAPTER 10

MAGICK — SEX AND EARTH ENERGY
The True Force of Nature

My purpose in writing this chapter is to teach you the spiritual use of your sexual energy, which in turn will make your life more spiritually meaningful. In order to do this I must first explain what I mean by the spiritual use of sexual energy; Then I will show how early conditioning has decreased your sexual potential; and finally I will give you a simple method of reconditioning your body and mind to develop your full sexual potential. This concept, the spiritual use of sexual energy, is sometimes called Tantra.

There are many books on Tantra, and most are of two types. Either they are extremely esoteric: promising ecstasy beyond your wildest dreams and saying absolutely nothing about how to get there; or they are extremely complicated, with many rules and rituals, all of which take the spontaneity and passion out of sex and require that you keep a book beside your bed in order to follow the proper sequence.

Our exercises are extremely simple and remarkably effective. No amount of rules and exercises can create passion if it is not there; and passion alone, without knowledge of *how* to use it, is a dead end street. This chapter is about becoming passionate and using passion to experience the mysteries. These methods can also be used to heal, to enhance your creative process, to improve relationships, and to correct sexual problems.

Yin Yang

Rhuddlum

118

This chapter is the result of fifteen years of experimentation. The first three years were spent learning the method, and the last twelve years have been spent teaching through the vehicle of workshops and seminars.

I will show you how sensuality, the delights of the body, if used *as prescribed,* can be a path to higher consciousness.

There are two forms of magickal energy or power:

Internal or *Kundalini force* - Red Dragon, serpent power.

External or *Odic force* - green dragon, Earth power.

The kundalini, although not as powerful as the odic, can control the odic.

The kundalini can be used by itself to raise individual consciousness or with other kundalini to raise group consciousness.

All energy is connected — all energy is the same, yet different.

The odic force is used to do what is usually thought of as physical magick.

The kundalini force is used to accomplish spiritual magick.

Sabrina was speaking:

"As a door is opened with a key, so the adept can open the door of enlightenment by awakening the Serpent Power using special exercises.

"The Serpent sleeps at the base of the pelvis giving enlightenment to adepts and bondage to the ignorant. The sleeping Serpent is awakened by catching hold of her tail. By the force of the psychic exercises, the Serpent leaves her sleep and starts upward. The Serpent is situated at the base of the spine having three and a half coils. So long as the Serpent sleeps, the body of the individual is a mere animal and true knowledge does not occur. By awakening the Serpent power by psychic exercise the door of enlightenment is unlocked.

"Sex can be beautiful between friends, lovers or those who have joined through marriage. But you must cultivate the natural acceptance of sex as a beautiful spiritual and mystical sharing between two humans and not a negative guilt ridden aspect. Practice. Become proficient not in the mechanics, but in the beauty.

"The sexual union can become a sacred ceremony involving purification and prayers. The woman is transformed and becomes the consecrated temple where the ritual is performed. The Serpent self merges with the Universal self and one finds the revelation of the cosmic mystery in the presence of the naked body. The woman is the second part of the androgyne, the completed being, the unified, the one. In uniting

119

with each other you experience the unity of supreme bliss. Such an experience is not attained easily. This sexual experience must not end in orgasm until one has mastered the control of thought, control of breath, and control of orgasm. In this way, sexual union is transformed into a ritual through which the human couple becomes a divine couple.

"One must prepare for the performance of the rite by meditation and ceremonies that make it possible and fruitful. The ritual is based on five elements: water (wine), earth (corn), air (incense), fire (candles) and spirit (sexual intercourse), which are blessed by incantations. Each element is represented in its own place, and the final element is partaken of in its own time.

"Sex may be experienced on many different levels of consciousness. From the lowest to the highest. But sexual energy is the most powerful elemental amplifier that can be used in magick.

"During Sexual Magick every naked woman is the Goddess incarnate. She is looked upon with the same adoration that one exercises in pondering the unfathomable secret of nature and its limitless capacity to create. The ritual nudity of the priestess has a special mystical value. It generates within the Priest the same wondrous emotion that is felt before the revelation of the cosmic mystery. The priestess assumes, from the standpoint of her partner and herself, the role of Divine Female, the universal passive principal, the second part of the Dyad or energy-matter. She becomes the Odic force, the second part of the completed being. In uniting with her, the Priest experiences unity and enjoys supreme bliss — the priestess experiences the oneness and happiness of generating the lifeforce. Such an experience is not attained easily. The Initiate prepares for this experience by mastering the three controls: control of thought, control of breath, and control of orgasm.

"Sexual magick is a complex ritual depending for its effect on a mastery of certain secret knowledge.

"Fix your mind on the psychic center at the base of the spine. Then engage in contracting the muscles which are situated in the perineal area. Then contemplate the Great Spirit of love as situated near the base of the spine. Above this point is a small and subtle flame of intelligence. Imagine the union taking place between yourself and that flame. Then imagine that there passes through the central spinal cord, the three bodies, etheric, astral and mental, in every power point a spiritual nectar is emitted whose characteristic is great bliss. Its color is whitish rose, full of splendor and showering down its jets of fluid.

120

Drink of this wine of immortality and then again enter the perineal space through the practice of meditation and breath control.

"Practice the above exercise daily and you will begin to gain spiritual enlightenment. Through practice one gains the power of prophecy and the power of going everywhere through the mere exertion of will," She said in completion.

When I use the word *"spiritual,"* I mean, specifically, that there are more levels of awareness available to you than those of everyday experience. You can define everyday experience as: fear, loneliness, anger, pettiness, rule-following, going to work, washing the dishes, and so on.

The realm of the "enlightened one" is pure knowledge, pure love, and the experience of unity in all things. Pure knowledge differs from theory in that it is not clouded by conditioning and projections. Pure action is action without thought: non-doing. Artists, dancers, and zen archers have brief moments of this level of consciousness. Pure love is like being in love without a specific object to love: agape, universal love. We love everyone and everything as a physical experience, not a thought. We *are* love. Unity is the belief that the universe is one substance.

None of these states are attainable without the use of your physical body. Your physical body is an antenna for energy and must be cleared of tension, disease and pain in order to be resilient and open enough to tolerate the high vibratory rate of energy which these higher states of consciousness require. Raising the state of consciousness entails raising the level of energy in your body. Lowering the state of consciousness equals lowering the amount of energy in your body.

Sexual energy is a form of energy readily available to everyone. If sex is used normally, it results in a lowering of the amount of energy in your body. The method I teach will result in adding energy to your body in amounts that will eventually in the experience of higher states of consciousness.

There are many rough places on the path. Opening the psychic-physical system means experiencing your emotions — those that you are experiencing today and those that you buried in your body in the past, because it was not acceptable to allow them to flow through. Opening the body also means dealing with the pain that is there and can no longer be dealt with.

In addition, the last few states of consciousness before breaking through to enlightenment are extremely painful to your psyche. There

121

is the belief that nothing works, that you are hopelessly trapped in your patterns and conditioning and will never change. This can be at the level of despair or the level of suicide. In these spaces there is a strong motivation to lower the level of energy in the system. The favorite methods for this are drugs and alcohol. It is possible to regard it as a result of despair and to see this as a high, though asleep, state of consciousness.

It is important to understand these states of consciousness because feelings of despair and hopelessness can lead to suicide and sometimes mental illness. It is important for the person involved to keep a grain of objectivity which reminds him/her that this is just another state of consciousness, which will pass, and a high one at that! The person has the option of lowering the energy in the system to become more comfortable, or raising the energy in the system, to eventually climb into the enlightened state.

To help you understand these states of consciousness, following is a map of The Levels consciousness:

The first level is the level of **Pure Belief and Emotion**. Our fears, our loneliness, our anger and aggression, and our beliefs: *"Black people got rhythm." "Women are weak." "Men don't like me because I'm fat." "I'm no good." "I'm better than you,"* and so on.

The second level is the level of **Society**: obeying traffic signals, getting married, going to college, going to work, paying the mortgage, and so on. Up until very recently most people lived out their whole lives on these two levels of consciousness. You remember from the previous discussion that the way to raise your level of consciousness is to add energy to your system. Many people are now doing meditation and other forms of personal work which have as one of their characteristics the fact that energy is added to the human system. For many people in the sixties the first introduction to other states was with psychedelics. But the many limitations to drugs was quickly discovered, and people switched to other forms of working with energy, such as meditation.

If you have been meditating or otherwise adding energy to your system, you have experiences which are on the next higher level above the level of society, which is called "Ego", or False Freedom. This is your first *"breakthrough,"* your first emotional and physical release. You may drop out of school, get a divorce, quit your job, or jump in your van and travel across the country. You may be a *"drop out."* There is a great deal more energy on this level than on the levels below it, and a sense of freedom and of *"being above the masses."* However, it is only the first level and there are many more. I think one of the reasons rock stars have such a high drug abuse rate is because they get above this level, into some of the levels of despair, and have no map or guide to get them further.

The next level is called the "**Philosopher.**" This is our intellectual discussions of how the universe works. We get high from these discussions. But our perceptions are still clouded by our fears and conditioning and we cannot really see *how it is* at all.

After the philosopher come the three uncomfortable levels talked about earlier: **Despair, Suicide** and **Remorse.** The despair is usually over the evolutionary path: *I'm not making it somehow and never will.* The suicidal feelings are wanting to get away from it all, to end the sorry mess, to leave the planet. The remorse is over the fact that although you've been *"working on yourself"* with meditation or whatever for X number of years, you are still afraid, uptight and angry. Another reason for wanting to leave the planet: *"nothing every changes."*

Fortunately this is the last level *"below the line."* Below the line means levels of unconsciousness or levels of being asleep. *"Above the line"* are the levels of awareness, or levels of being awake. These are **The Objective Seeker,** and **Wisdom.**

The **objective seeker,** that is, observing oneself acting out one's conditioned patterns without judgment or emotion, knowing that it makes no difference, that everything is as it should be, and that the essence of a human being is not her/his conditioned self, but her/his divine self. Again, this is an experience of the total human system and not a thought.

Wisdom, means that we *can* know, but only when we are operating from this level of consciousness, not from the level of "philosopher."

There are a number of ways of working with these levels of consciousness. For example, every aspect of our lives goes through, or can go through the levels. Romance is an example. **Pure Belief:** At this level a person is lonely and wishes he/she could fine someone to love.

Society: At this level we have found someone and we become a couple, or get married.

Ego: At this level you probably get divorced, or at least have an open marriage.

Philosopher: At this level you are probably involved in theories of "what makes a relationship work."

Despair: It *doesn't* work, and everything feels pretty shitty.

Suicide: The death of the relationship, and mourning.

Remorse: Looking back over the relationship to see why it didn't work. And for most people, the pattern is to go back to the beginning again: being lonely, finding someone new, and repeat it all again. There are no successful relationships *below the line.*

Our only hope lies in staying above the line.

This leads to Practical Mysticism. It is extremely *practical* to use this method on many levels. Some of the results of my students and myself will be discussed later but what I would like to explain to you here is that *raising your level of consciousness* means also changing how you behave and feel. We all feel, think and act differently at different levels of consciousness. If you are feeling lonely and depressed, for example, and you have a reliable method of adding energy to your system, you will feel better. Specifically, you will probably go from the level of Pure Belief to the level of Ego and you will jump up, put on your best clothes, and go dancing. Not the highest level there *is,* but a whole lot better than the first one, eh?

Another example: A person who is experiencing Pure Love or Agape, is not going to rob or kill people. What I am saying here is that these feelings are the result of internal changes and will become more and more readily available to you.

To sum up: we move up and down in levels of consciousness — perhaps covering all the levels in a day or even in an hour; and our movement is due to the raising and lowering of the overall energy level of our psychic-physical system. When it gets uncomfortable, hang in there. It will soon get better.

The reason why human beings have not been able to use their sexual energy to alter their states of consciousness in the past has been due to the culture we live in. In our culture there are strong taboos against sexuality, pleasure and self love.

It began at our birth. Almost all of us were born through the genitals of women who hated and feared their own sexual energy. As they were growing up they gradually tightened their pelvic muscles against the flow of sexual energy, and when it came time to give birth to us it was very difficult for them to release those muscles and to let us pass through. Our birth was a struggle; we fought against the barriers imposed against our forward movement, and they, in pain, cursed us and the sexual impulses which put us inside there in the first place. As we finally passed through the channel, we also couldn't help but

124

feel the fear they felt for that area of their bodies, and we absorbed it into our own bodies.

Next, every time Mom changed our diapers and looked at that area of our bodies, more rejection and disgust were registered. As she wiped our bottoms we clearly understood that she didn't like that area of our body, including the genitals, and we took on that disgust.

If we ever noticed any pleasant sensations and responded to them with our hands, we were given the strictest threats against touching ourselves and following our natural pleasure.

Shortly afterward, we were encouraged to stay clothed, segregated from members of the opposite sex when bathing, eliminating and sleeping, and of course we were told little or nothing about how our sexual energy worked. Even though we may have been told where babies come from, we were not told about passion.

By the time we were teenagers we were estranged from our bodies, our sexual energy, and from others who might have been our partners in joy and pleasure.

When we finally came together as couples we wondered why it didn't work very well, why there is so little sensuality, so little passion and so many outright sexual dysfunctions: men who orgasm too fast, women who can't have an orgasm at all. It puts a tremendous strain on our love for each other, since we cannot be satisfied in one of the primary ways of our being together.

I have worked with hundreds of people through counseling and seminars; as adults they have pretty much the same problems:

"Sex doesn't exist, or shouldn't exist.

Good sex is hard to come by.

I don't deserve good sex, because my body isn't good enough.

I'm not attractive.

I'm afraid of sex.

I'm afraid of men.

I'm afraid of women.

I'm tired of having to perform in bed and put my partner first.

My body doesn't turn on very easily.

My body doesn't stay turned on.

All he/she wants me for is my body.

God doesn't approve of sex.

If you really spiritual you're celibate.

There's something bad about sex. In some way it isn't good for me.

I can't find the right partner.
If I get involved sexually with someone that means I owe them
something; I'm responsible to them in some negative way.
I'm afraid I can't satisfy my partner.
I can't enjoy sex unless: 1. I'm in love, 2. I'm not in love, 3.
I'm drunk or on drugs, 4. etc.

When we decide to heal ourselves we come up against very powerful forces. The first and most powerful is that our parents sometimes didn't like sex, and if we heal ourselves and start enjoying ourselves, then they won't like us. Most of us are little children inside, who still react to our parents as if we were two or three years old and dependent upon them for life and love. We believe that we should not incur their disapproval or we will not survive.

Secondly, as we look around us, there are not very many people whose sexual energy is moving through their bodies in a joyous and healthy way. As I observe my fellow human beings on the street and in the supermarket I do not find them very sexy. What would happen if I opened up my sexual energy? Would I go crazy? Would I be horny all the time? Would people reject and ostracize me, even punish me?

There is little help available from the spiritual community either. Many members and groups have even adopted the traditional position of celibacy as a superior spiritual position, thus reinforcing the cultural conditioning against their own sexual force. There is little truth in this position. Their attitude is: *Since raising the level of consciousness requires raising the level of energy in the body, and since orgasm lowers the level of energy, then orgasm is contrary to spiritual development, and the easiest way to stay away from orgasm is to stay away from sex altogether.* BULLSHIT!

What I recommend to my students will be discussed in the next section, and it actually works against the three problem areas I have just mentioned. First, working with the sexual energy helps the inner child to grow up and to have more strength to break the parent-induced patterns. It also gives him/her a sense of confidence, centering, and personal identity which are necessary to break the negative conditioning from our parents.

Secondly, my experience with opening the sexual energy in myself and others is that it is not a handicap in relating to other people, but rather an asset. I have become more loving, more powerful, and more attractive, and none of the aforementioned fears have manifested.

The solution of the spiritual question is to substitute the whole truth for the half truth, which is that if you delay your orgasm and raise the energy up in your body you will eventually reach a level of energy at which orgasm does not bring you down.

Now that we have seen how some of us have lost the beauty and power of our passionate nature, let's find out how to get it back.

I have been on a concentrated program to discover the nature and uses of my sexual energy for many years. I first heard the word *Tantra* in 1966 when I was studying paganism in Wales. When I discovered the ancient method of Celtic Tantra I was fascinated! Here were people who were saying that sexual energy was not only beautiful and valuable, but a way to experience God!

Meanwhile, although my own sex life was far from tame, I was not satisfied with it. Although I loved sex, and it was always very magical to me, I wasn't getting a lot out of it. I read the books and talked with my teachers, and eventually made the great discovery. It wasn't until I visited Wales that I started making the huge leaps in my sexuality. In Wales I worked with several teachers who taught me first to satisfy my partner and then to satisfy myself, thus controlling the energy.

This is also where I met Sabrina, who was a *Tantra Master* and who agreed to teach me. Her techniques and knowledge are available to my students in my classes. After nine months of studying with her and practicing the various exercises over and over, I had two classical Tantric experiences, one with a partner and one by myself. In the case with a partner, we went to bed on a Saturday night and didn't get up except to eat for almost seventy-two hours. During most of that time we were engaged sexually in a state of unity with each other and the cosmos; a non-verbal state in which we didn't know who had which body or what our names were. We discontinued the experience because we started to wonder what the rest of the world must be doing, so we got up to take a look. We stayed very psychic with each other for days, knowing each other's thoughts and whereabouts, but we never got together again. I took it as a gift from the gods — a show of possibilities.

Another gift came in a session I had by myself. I had been working with my spiritual guide, meditating and talking to him every day. However, he only came into my meditation when I called on him. On this particular day I was doing a meditation exercise and got very horny. In fact, I was thinking of someone I could ask to come over and play. All of a sudden my guide interrupted my thought and said sharply, "Now listen to me. I want you to understand that you don't need *anyone* to make this energy work for you, and I'm going to prove it to you. You just keep doing your exercise and I'll show you that you can get higher than you ever believed possible." So I kept on doing the exercise, running the energy to my heart. After a while I decided to orgasm, which would ordinarily lower my level of energy and end the session. However, this time it didn't seem to. I suspected I had reached a level of energy which I had only heard about before — where an orgasm doesn't bring you down. I decided to test it, and I came again and again — each time after a few rounds of bring the energy up to my heart. An hour and a half and seven orgasms later, I simply stopped out of boredom and I went out to take a walk. I'm not particularly handsome, but this particular afternoon women turned their heads as I walked by. I felt like a god, and I must have looked like one.

My relationship with Sabrina ended when I had these experiences, giving me the authority to begin teaching others and making these gifts available to everyone. I decided that my progress was due not only to my training with a Tantra Master, but also because I had been doing a great deal of meditation, and my system was more open and clearer than most.

I also decided to include meditation and a lot of clearing of negative sexual conditioning in my future classes, along with masturbation exercises which would be done in private, as homework. As I progressed and continued the exercises, I became more and more amazed at the value of the technique.

About six months after I returned to the U.S., I met a woman with whom, after a couple of experiences together, I had a classical heart-opening experience. That is, the experience of being in love, but without another person to be in love with: "Pure Love" as described earlier. (My friend did not share the experience). In other words, I was in love with everyone and everything. I felt totally at peace and physically handsome. I was loving and clear and loved — I became Love Itself. The experience lasted for several days.

Then things began to become exciting. Two of my students had classical experiences in higher levels of consciousness while doing the homework — on their first try! I was elated. And the feedback kept coming in from my students: "I no longer have any trouble attracting loving sexual partners!" "I no longer have a problem with premature ejaculation!" "Sex just gets better and better!" I could see that the experiences I had were not individual and peculiar only to myself, but

128

could be experienced by anyone, either immediately or over a period of time.

I, too, along with my students, became more magnetic and more satisfied with the ease and pleasure of my sexual experiences. The primary characteristic of sexuality is personal magnetism: magnetic attraction. With it, sex is easy. Without it, sex becomes a hassle and a chore. The sexual exercise, without a doubt, increases one's personal magnetism.

I also began to see that my vitality, my aliveness, and my enthusiasm were increasing noticeably. Friends remarked how great I looked, how alive I was. I began to learn that I could direct the energy to any part of my body, not only my heart, and began using it for healing — directing it to any place in my body that wasn't feeling right. If I direct it to my third eye, I find that my mind is clearer, I have more courage and a sense of personal power, as well as clairvoyance.

I consider myself a teacher in a territory which is available to everyone, but which is *new* because it has been closed for so long.

The most important aspect of all, however, is that my students have an unshakable sense of identity about themselves. By taking away our bodies, our society took away our sense of ourselves. By taking back our bodies and our sexuality we take back ourselves. This is the self love which is talked about in books and workshops these days. Have you ever asked *How?* when a workshop leader says that it is important to love yourself? This use of sexual energy produces self love more intensely than any other exercise available.

I want to give you enough information in this chapter to enable you to duplicate all of my experiences and learn for yourself how simple and easy and joyful sex can be.

First of all, accept the fact that you were trained out of your sexuality from an early age. Go over the list of negative positions and statements in the last section. How many are yours? What negative thoughts go through your mind when you think about sex with a partner, or masturbation, or any other aspect of sexuality? Begin talking back to yourself when these negative thoughts come up. For example: **"I know my mind is telling me that sex is a hassle, and I'd rather not bother with it. But I know now that this is a result of my conditioning, and I am going to work against it by doing the masturbation exercise and putting myself in situations where a sexual experience may occur."**

Take off your clothes and look at yourself in a full length mirror. Ask yourself what parts of your body you like and what you don't like.

Realize that what you *don't* like is not only conditioned by a play-boy/playgirl image of what's beautiful, but is one of the many ways you keep your body frozen and incapable of transmitting sexual energy. I suggest you take long baths, washing yourself carefully with your bare hands. Give extra attention to the parts of your body you don't like, massaging them gently and lovingly and apologizing to them for not loving them more. If you like oils on your skin, be conscious and slow while you massage them on to your skin, again giving extra care and attention to the parts which need more love. Participate in any activity which will make your body feel good to you.

As for the sexual exercise, the only thing to remember is that it is extremely simple — raising the body's sexual energy almost to the point of orgasm, and instead of letting the energy go out into orgasm, allow the energy to come up in the body, up to the heart. At the point just before orgasm, there is a channel open in the body, and if you rest at that point, the energy which has been generated will flow naturally upward toward the heart. You don't have to **do** anything; it just happens. Don't worry about what it feels like, or if it's happening — just do it! ! You may visualize the energy coming up if you like. You may inhale at the crucial point, if you like, and you may use the pubo-cocygeous muscle to intensify the energy if you like. The pubo-cocygeous muscle or kegel muscle was known to yogis long before Masters and Johnson began using it for sexual therapy. I find that the muscle will increase the level of sexual energy rapidly and I suggest squeezing and releasing the muscle as you build toward a climax. At the point where you allow the energy to come up to your heart, also release the last squeeze, and the energy will rise up very strongly.

If you're not familiar with this muscle, it covers the whole pelvic floor, from the pubic bone in the front to the coccyx in the back and the pelvic bones on each side. All the openings go to the outside of the body: anus, urethra, penis and vagina go through this muscle and have sphincters at the point of exit. The way to get in touch with the muscle, if you have not already, is to urinate and periodically stop the flow of urine. The muscle is used for that act, and you will soon be able to use it independently, when you are not urinating.

But don't get distracted by technique. Just begin an adventure with yourself to see what your sexual energy is all about. Rediscover the physical system you were trained to ignore.

If you have difficulty talking yourself into a sexual session, remember that you were conditioned away from that activity. Take the position that sexual excitement is now your meditation. Start your session by touching and loving yourself with your hands all over your body before you go for your genitals and other erotic zones.

You may 'come' or have an orgasm at the end of a session if you like. Or you may find that you 'come' by accident, which will probably end your session for you because the energy will be gone. Men particularly will need to stop each round far short of orgasm until they learn what the **point of no return** is for them. Men will also discover that delaying orgasm or eliminating it altogether does not necessarily produce physical problems.

The biggest problem you will have with this exercise is not *how to do it,* but your own training against masturbation. A recent national publication contains an article which talks about the origin of our sexual hangups and shows that as a culture we have been conditioned not only out of sex but out of *pleasure.* Self-pleasuring is the most forbidden pleasure of all. Examine your fears and feelings about masturbation. Then put them aside, and re-learn your own body. The pleasure you experience will do more to work against your negative conditioning than anything else you can do or think. I suggest you do what Sabrina advised me to do; have a session with yourself every day, as a meditation, for three months, and see what the results are for yourself.

Discovering myself was a precious gift. I am delighted to pass the gift along to you.

Part of raveling our tangled, twisted sexuality is to understand that yin and yang operate in bed as well as throughout the rest of the universe. This leads to the concept of Androgeny, or the external balance of **masculine** and **feminine** characteristics within an individual. A couple in which one partner is always active and one always passive will die of boredom. Each of us needs to be active as well as receptive, the lover as well as the loved. In our society the imbalance is usually caused because the man cannot be receptive and the woman cannot be active. This is one of the attractions to homosexuality for both sexes. A man who cannot find an active woman, or allow himself to be receptive to a woman, may try to find this balance with another man. And a woman who cannot allow herself to be active with a man, or find a man who will allow her to be active, may find a woman to fill the bill. (I will not go into the whys of homosexuality; this is for each individual to determine).

Androgeny is a mystical concept — the idea that we are neither men nor women, although we manifest one body or the other in this lifetime. We are both masculine and feminine, and the human system works best when both qualities are in balance. That means that each of us is both active and receptive, emotional and intellectual, worldly and meditative. If we do not **experience** both sides of this "dichotomy" in our personalities and expression, it is because we are trained toward one or the other by our parents and our society.

Men, for example, usually have trouble expressing their feelings, even knowing they exist, and women often have difficulty being articulate in the expression of their ideas to the world. The theory of Androgeny states that this condition is not natural to us, and that we should be working toward an internal balance. A whole person would be one who is fully developed emotionally, intellectually, physically, and spiritually. He/she would receive ideas from wherever they come from and have the ability to manifest them in the world.

Practically speaking, this means that women can be brilliant and forceful in expression, that they can run businesses and be involved in the world, and men can get into the beauty of their feelings, their emotions and surrender.

The strict concept: *men can't be emotional and women can't make it in the world* is already heavily eroded. There are millions of men who do not lack the so called *feminine* qualities at all, but have greater difficulty with the masculine ones: being active, producing in the world, defending themselves, and so on. I was a man whose masculine nature manifested first; and I had to **learn** to be receptive and intuitive.

This also fits in perfectly with the theory of right-left brain balance. The right brain controls the intuitive functions and the left brain, the intellectual functions. It is generally agreed that they should be balanced.

I am not ready to propose a method of healing the masculine-feminine balance in others, but I will describe to you how the healing took place in me.

When I was a child I was rather skinny and very intellectual. I was constantly accused by my peers of being "too smart." In my early relationships I was always active, believing that if I didn't go out and get **it**, it would never come to me. I also wasn't very successful at going out to get **it**, because I unconsciously felt inadequate and didn't expect to be well received by those I was going after. Just like the yin-yang diagrams, everything is intertwined. If I couldn't be active, I couldn't be receptive.

132

The first part of the healing came through forcing my activeness to stop and begin to learn and understand the receptive part of my nature. At the same time I was working on my fears and learning that it is OK to be gentle and trusting, that I don't have to be always defending myself against everyone and everything.

I know a number of men who are exploring their feminine side by fantasizing that they are women and what it would be like to have a vagina. I also have many friends who report that during their lovemaking they have reached periods in which it is unclear who is the man and who is the woman, as have I. So it seems that the suggestion of various mystical schools is correct: that our identification as the man or the woman is, at some level, illusory.

I once counseled a man who at one time had been a practicing transvestite, who explained that what he wanted from the experience of dressing up like a woman and acting out a woman's role, was to know what it feels like to be a woman. He wanted to balance and express his feminine nature as well as his masculine nature. His masculine side was already well expressed, as he was an athlete and a respected scientist. I don't care at this time to go into the social problems of transvestism, only to say that my belief at the moment is that it comes from a desire to achieve that necessary internal balance without proper direction.

As I have been expressing my feminine nature more, I have also become more masculine. I have learned to relax and allow partners to make love to me. I have become more magnetic, drawing partners to me rather than being active or going to them. (I am aware that women have no trouble in this area; they learn at an early age to be attractive. But I had no belief until my visit to Wales of myself as a magnetic man, meaning that I can attract, or pull partners into my sphere at will). It almost seems as if my masculine nature couldn't develop until I made it OK for my feminine nature to be expressed. My best sexual partners these days are those who are well balanced with respect to their masculine and feminine natures, which means, practically speaking, that they can surrender to the act of making love, to the energy that moves through them and between us, and that they can be both active and receptive in love making. That means that they like to be loved as much as loving and the movement goes back and forth between us, one being active at times, and then the other. Sometimes there is no active and no receptive, a beautiful blend. **Ecstasy** is feminine. **Surrender** is feminine. A man (or woman) who is unwilling to allow his feminine aspect to take over is incapable of totally experiencing sexual ecstasy and is incapable of expe ·encing the highest possibilities of the sexual experience.

One of the payoffs of my working with myself in this fashion, of working on my internal masculine/feminine balance, is in my relationships. I no longer have to look after a woman and pay her bills; she can do that for herself. I am also not dependent emotionally, because I feel powerful and attractive, and if a lover decided to leave me I could quickly attract another. This is a remarkable revolution in my relationships. It makes no difference if your orientation is not heterosexual. In gay relationships as well, one partner is often dominant and the other dependent because one has a better developed masculine nature than the other.

Underdevelopment of the masculine nature happens much more frequently in our society than is recognized. Ever since the industrial revolution fathers have been separated by their jobs from their children. It is very common for a man to leave for work in the morning before his children are awake and return in the evening after they are asleep, and for various other reasons to spend very little time with them. The result is that he gives very little energy and attention to the children and cannot provide one of his most important functions, which is to transmit to the child, male or female, his masculine energy. So the male part of the little boy or girl not only has no model, but no **content,** and is stunted in its growth. The result is a man or woman with very little yang — very little ability to move forcefully in the external world, very little ability to bring projects to their conclusion or manifestation, and very little ability to protect the individual; so there is a lot of fear of functioning in the world.

For years I have been teaching that *Everything you need is already within you,* and *If you solve your internal contradictions the external ones will disappear also.* This experience of self love also made me realize that I needed to spend more time exploring my internal self. At one time I hated being by myself and would always seek people to be with. Now I look for and enjoy times when I can be alone, either to be my own companion or to explore my inner spaces. What a great relief and what a marvelous discovery!

The most important thing to know about being with a partner is knowing how to be with yourself. It is absolutely necessary to have a private sex life in order to have a satisfactory sex life with a partner. For one thing, you need to have exact knowledge of how the energy works in your own body, and it is very difficult to learn this with another person's energy being taken into account at the same time.

Standard sex therapy these days is teaching people to masturbate, to learn their own bodies. Secondly, making love with oneself successfully, learning that you can "get there" alone as well as with a partner, is a very powerful discovery. Most women are waiting around for Prince Charming to kiss them on the lips and wake them from emotional slumber and become the vital, passionate being they know they truly are.

Unfortunately, it doesn't work that way. We become passionate beings by turning ourselves on, by opening our sexual "center" **ourselves** by reversing the conditioning that closed it all off in the first place. And then, when our energy is flowing, we are ready for a partner.

The "Eagles" had a beautiful line in one of their songs that goes, *"I found out a long time ago what a woman can do for your soul/But a woman can't take you any place you don't already know how to go."* We all can remember a very special night when we were carried into ecstasy with a very special sexual partner, but those occasions will remain rare and isolated unless we do the work of opening up our sexuality.

I know this is true, because I have occasionally agreed to *teach* someone Tantra by going to bed with her. She of course expects that I, as the *Great Tantric* will be able to take her to those spaces she longs for. My universal experience in these situations is that *I* go to those spaces and she just has a wonderful sexual experience. In the Hindu tradition, even though the priest/ess was the keeper of the Secret, the initiate had to train for years before she ever got together with one of those marvelous beings.

The value of all this in terms of the **relationship** between you and your lover is immense. If I don't depend on my lover for my highs, or blame her for my lows, then I can enjoy her when we come together and there is a loving lightness in our relationship that is very rich. I also don't have to be afraid of losing her, because:

1. It's so good she'd be a fool to leave.
2. If she does leave, I'm so handsome and magnetic and *satisfied with my life* that it's only a matter of time before another partner will appear.
3. I can **let go** with love for her if need be.

Lastly, if we open our hearts to each other, which is possible through the methods I will describe later, then there is a bond formed between us which lasts through the times when our hearts are closed, or we can't cope with the other aspects of our lives — in short, when the relationship appears not to be working.

With that introduction, let's talk about being together and using the sexual energy to alter our state of consciousness. The secret of being with a partner is the same as the secret of being by yourself; to raise the energy in your body to the point of orgasm and then, instead of coming, to relax and let the energy go up to your heart (or wherever). In other words, you just bring the energy up to the point of orgasm, relax and let it go up in the body instead of out into the universe. You don't have to be *at the brink* together (although it helps). It doesn't matter if one partner gets into heaven before the other one; only the ego cares if we do the same thing at the same time. Some women prefer to masturbate or be masturbated during lovemaking because it keeps their energy very high. Once the energy is flowing you don't need a map. The discoveries I have made are largely due to the fact that I made few assumptions about where I was going.

Additionally, I teach a number of games a couple can play, which will probably raise the level of energy between you and make the journey easier. One such game is simply to breathe together. Just breathing at the same rate while you are holding each other can be ecstatic. Another is looking into each others' eyes. When I look into the left eye of a lover I become empty inside, my thoughts stop, and I start to feel the heat in my groin spreading throughout my body. But this is after years of practice. In the beginning you will experience some discomfort in looking into each others' eyes and will be able to attempt it for only short periods of time. You will find that it uncovers a lot of forgotten emotions and conflicts you thought were forgotten. Expressing them will help dissolve them. You will sometimes change the flavor of your meeting from a sexual one to an emotional one but you can always go back to sex.

Another possibility is to bring sound into your sessions together. Try anything from chanting together to making unplanned meaningless sounds together which will gradually take on a life of their own. There is something about making sounds together, vibrating together, which, like breathing together makes us ecstatic. When I do this with a lover, I feel like we become one, that our vibration somehow becomes one and I can feel the inside of her body as well as mine.

It also helps to practice being receptive. Most people have much more difficulty letting love and energy into their systems than letting

136

it out, or being loving. So with your lover, take turns being parent and child as an exercise in learning to receive. The partner who plays the parent lies on his/her back and the partner who takes the position of child lies with his/her head near the parent's heart. The parent embraces the child, stroking him/her occasionally and imagining limitless love pouring from his heart and body into the child. Breathing together, the child just soaks it up (and watches what conflicts it produces for him). Then you switch.

I also like to use visualizations and mantras. One visualization is to breathe together and imagine that the energy moves between you in a circle, going up the genitals of one partner, then across from his/her heart to the partner's heart, down to the partner's genitals and around again. It can go either direction; see which you like best.

The purpose of a mantra is to help quiet the clamour in your head so energy can move through. The mantras I like are *"Ham Sa," "You love me," "We are one,"* and *"I worship the god/goddess within you." "The Ham Sa"* seems to call the archetypal male-female energies into my love making. "You love me" seems to create a circuit of energy between my partner and myself. "We are one" reminds us of the Unity space whether we experience it or not. "I worship the god/goddess with you" reminds me of who my partner really is and who I really am. I usually do the mantra silently, in my head, and my partner may do them or not, as she pleases.

Another interesting connection is through the solar plexus. If we project energy at each other from our solar plexus and breathe together a wonderful connection happens; likewise if we touch each others' solar plexus and breathe together. Try it.

Any of the books you find on Tantra may have games to play that will make your love making deeper and take you closer to the experience of unity. Just remember, there are no rules. Get the energy as high as you can and allow it to come up in your body. Go with the energy, go with your fantasies, go with the movements your body wants to make, and spend time alone sexually as well as with your partner. Eventually you will begin to have the experiences you seek, with greater and greater regularity.

MY SEXUAL TEACHER

This section is dedicated to my teacher Sabrina and is written with love and appreciation. I decided to write a section about the woman who gave me the technique I teach, because I found people to be fascinated whenever I would tell stories about her.

When I first met her, she noticed that I had my legs crossed and asked me to uncross them, saying that the cymmry teach that energy cannot move properly when one crosses their arms and legs.

I was instructed to go to her house to be taught this technique that I have described as Tantra. It wasn't really called Tantra, which is a form of yoga, but I am not allowed to tell you what the name really is in our tradition.

She was staying in a tiny, bare house in the Welsh countryside just outside the community. The first time we met we sat on the floor in her kitchen and looked into each other's eyes. She touched my forehead and a wave of laughter came from somewhere and shook my body all over. Then a wave of sadness, and I was ready to cry. My body felt intensely energized and focused on itself. *"I think you've had enough for today,"* she said. *"I'd like you to lie down in the hammock outside and rest."* To get to the hammock we had to pass to the right side of the tree instead of the left, she said, *"because the energy is better on this side."* I lay in the hammock, not dozing, but somewhere between waking and sleeping, listening to her moving around the house and began having sexual fantasies about her. After awhile she came out to the hammock and said, *"your thoughts are disturbing me at my work. Will you please go back now."*

She added, *"I'm going to give you an exercise which I want you to do every day for three months, which is to masturbate until the point where you know that one more stroke will make you come, take your hand away, and allow the energy to come up to your heart. You can repeat the cycle as often as you like, but for the first three months, don't have an orgasm. After that you can end your sessions with an orgasm if you like."*

I stumbled toward the path stoned from the experiences of the afternoon and stunned at being asked to leave so abruptly, and as I was about to leave thought to ask, *"When should I come again?"*

"You'll know when to come," she said.

"But how will I know?"

"You'll know. Now leave."

And I did know. A couple of weeks later on a lovely spring day I was thinking about her in a warm and loving way and knew somehow that it was time to go for another visit. I had also been doing the exercise as she instructed and noticed a warm trickle of energy coming up to my chest each time, charging my chest and heart and making me feel wonderful.

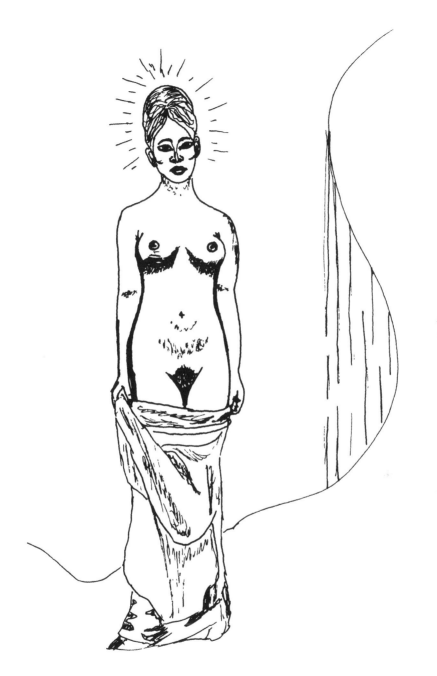

Sabrina

Rhuddlion

She welcomed me as if she had been expecting me and said that she needed to balance my energy so that we could be together more comfortably. She asked me to wait in the kitchen while she did something to the energy in her bedroom, altering it somehow so that we could work in there. After a few minutes she invited me in. The bedroom was as spartan as the kitchen — nothing on the walls, nothing in the room except a bed, an old wood stove and a brass basket for wood, which was empty. She asked me to take off my clothes and lie down on the bed. She touched me gently in various places, following a plan of balancing my energy, and each time she touched me she shook her hands out behind her. She explained that she had to keep shaking the negative energy off her fingers so it wouldn't unbalance her own energy.

When she was through she asked if I would like to make love. I said yes. I was still lying on the bed. She took off her clothes and looked at me with the most intense love and adoration I have ever experienced. Then, without touching me, she leaned over and just let a little warm air from her mouth touch my chest. An incredible rush of intense sexual energy filled my chest. Then she came closer and just barely touched the opening of her vulva to my penis, and the same kind of intense, sexual rush filled the lower half of my body. She instructed me to lie perfectly still, keeping all of my energy and attention in my head instead of my genitals or other erotic areas, and made love to me for about fifteen minutes, barely touching me anywhere else than my genitals.

Having imagined long, languorous, affectionate Tantra sessions I was shocked when she finished, rolled over, and told me it was time to stop. *"Some Tantra session,"* I thought, feeling cheated. *"More like a slam — bam — thank — you — ma'am than a religious experience."* But when I tried to stand up I noticed the energy in my body. I felt like I had been plugged into an electrical socket. I was vibrating all over, the energy starting from my penis and going in waves to every corner of my body. I had difficulty standing up, and my vision was altered, as if I were on drugs. I was impressed. Not bad for fifteen minutes of love making! In slow motion I put on my clothes and headed for the path. I didn't even ask when I should come back. The feelings lasted for the rest of the day and the evening, and I continued with the exercise she'd given me, practicing every day.

In succeeding months I began to learn more about her. She was totally psychic and could always tell what was going on with me. Every so often I would put out the thought that I'd like to see her, and within a few hours I'd find her at my door. If I was depressed she'd come and say, *"I heard you needed me."* She told me that she had taught herself to be clairvoyant, clairaudient, and clairsentient, and that her knowledge of Tantra had come partly from experiencing her own supersensitive body and partly from spirit guides who were her teachers. She often contacted them when I was present, especially to ask if I were ready for a new technique or not.

Her sensitivity had some drawbacks, however. For one thing, she couldn't walk in certain areas of a room, or any space, when the energy configurations were too uncomfortable for her. She also had great difficulty being around other people because their energy interfered with her own, or unbalanced it. She explained that sometimes she had to spend weeks alone, allowing her spirit guides to rebalance her energy for her.

Once she explained that the ideal relationship between two people was one in which all the chakras, or energy centers of the body, were balanced and connected. When we made love she would evaluate the experience in terms of how many chakras had been connected; for example, *"We were connected all the way to the throat chakra that time."* After a while I began noticing that I connected with people using various centers; for example, I have some friends with whom I have an intense loving relationship and some intellectual contact, but no sex. Occasionally I have had sexual contact and connected nowhere else. All the relationships are good, but it is true that the more areas of the total human being which can be connected at one time, the higher and more satisfying the relationship.

Sex is an important part of our religion and is used during Initiation Rites and certain magickal rituals. But, sexual/spiritual magickal work should only be undertaken by a person who has had a complete range of experience of human life, particularly complete sexual relationships.

The failure to complete the circuit of force through the aura can result in magnetic starvation or congestion of force if no circuit for the flow can be found.

The rapport between a seeker and his/her Teacher (since everyone is always taught male to female and female to male) causes a two way polarity to be set up.

The psychic rhythm of man is that of the Sun Cycle — passing rapidly through all its phases of dawn, noon, dusk and night in twenty four

~ Lovers ~

Rhuddlwm

hours. The rhythm of the woman is that of the moon, which operates over a twenty eight day cycle — waxing, full, waning, new.

A seeker and his/her Teacher, by completing the aura circuit, cause great energy to be released throughout the physical body. The female is more open with her mind and can release more energy, but cannot control it without great talent and ability. The male, although not able normally to release as much energy, can control much more.

In ritual practice, it is only by cooperation with each other (male/female) that Cymmry Gwiddon can progress. Man and woman must continually fulfill and complete each other. Only after long experience of mutual exchange can either alone carry out complete Cymmry rituals.

Every ordinary human act of love is, in fact, a shadow of the cosmic act, and the more completely it is carried out the closer it may come to the divine spiritual act. Sexual union is used to return to the wholeness of Truth.

Starting with a human partner who shares one's spiritual aims, one goes through a process of ritual which converts the ordinary man and woman into the personification of the God and Goddess; and then their union is consummated. The sexual experience enormously prolonged is brought to the point where the identity of each is blended with the other, and both experience a condition of total union. It is a tremendous joy, the joy of Being beyond understanding.

The male seed should ultimately be ejaculated into the woman's responding vagina, as if it were an offering of sacred oil being poured onto an altar fire; thus the physical orgasms of both partners are transformed into a far greater ecstasy.

Unfulfilled sexual expression stunts the ability for truly deep and powerful magickal work.

If a woman is unfulfilled and sexually inexperienced, she may have great sexual energy potential, but no direction or control. If a man is unfulfilled and sexually inexperienced, the same is true, although in a different way; his energy may be redirected into some form of work.

Sexual energy may be expressed in three ways:

1. Physical love — emotional fulfillment — love between two people. The lowest plane.
2. Spiritual love — realizing your spiritual nature — connecting the person to the whole family — realizing true love between two people on a higher plane.
3. Magickal love — redirecting the physical and emotional sex-

ual energy toward an outside idea or desire — action in accordance with will — magick.

All Sex — Love — Desire is an expression of polarity between two opposites: male and female. Even self love is the expression of the inner polarity inside each person.

Between two individual seekers there is polarity on several levels: mind, body and spirit. If two people unite at all levels of polarity, there is maximum energy potential. This can result in what the ancient Tantra Masters called serpent power or sex magick.

The techniques for tapping this power is another part of the mysteries. Only dedicated seekers for truth who can express love and desire will advance. What about the others? They will either quit from frustration (there is no free lunch) or they will destroy themselves.

When I first began to learn sexual magick I thought it would be only a physical/occult journey, but I discovered that the implications of this technique are far greater. A person who is tuned in to his/her sexual energy and knows how to use it has a feeling of security and *presence* that other people do not. This presence is magnetic and attractive, so that the person easily attracts other people. He also controls his psychic space so that anyone he does not want to be with in that space is screened out.

What we are doing in Y Twlwyth Teg, is teaching people how to open up their sexual energy and use it to change their feelings and behavior for the better.

These exercises can enhance your creative powers. I have experimented in writing this book with going at it "cold" and after meditation. I find that in the latter case it flows smoother and is much easier to organize my thoughts.

Whenever I have a difficult task to perform or a new group of people to work with I meditate, and I find that the job goes easier, and I am more confident and centered. I often meditate before meeting a lover, and I find it makes me more loving, more receptive, and more interested in the prospect of our meeting in a sexual way.

The energy can also be used for healing, either by building up one's energy before attempting to heal some else or by directing the energy within one's own body to the part which needs it.

The Celtic mysteries, the Authurian romances, the mabinogion; these are all records of the search for enlightenment as a seeker experiences each phase of life. If you are observant you will see the sexual polarity revealed in each story.

We of Y Twlwyth Teg have the keys.
You, the seekers, are the locks.
Blessed Be!

CHAPTER 11

THE PROPHECIES

Earth Changes and Where We Are Going

On May Eve of 1986 they came to bring Rhuddlwm the knowledge of future events.

"Rhuddlwm, even though I will come to you once more, I speak here of the knowledge of the many future events which you need to be warned about. Suffice it to say at this time that your tribe will work toward the propagation of Y Tylwyth Teg and Dynion Mwyn in the southeastern part of the United States. But, within fourteen years Y Tylwyth Teg will be establishing representatives across the entire country. You must be ready. The human race is working out earth karma. As you come near the end of this age, we see a beginning of the new era of spiritual enlightenment. The forces of light and the hidden forces of darkness are beginning their war for the minds of humankind. The light forces represent love, unity, peace, brotherhood, and sharing for all. The dark forces are greed, lust, confusion, poverty and diseased thinking. The struggle between these two forces has been going on since the beginning of time, but as you face the years ahead the entire globe will be engulfed in this fight for the final liberation or final enslavement of humankind.

"Y Tylwyth Teg is part of this process. It has worked within your own consciousness for the victory of light, and a thousand years of harmony on this planet. Y Tylwyth Teg will help some become enlightened by becoming aware of their inner nature, perfect balance, perfect health and perfect being.

"Most people do not know that this vast, worldwide struggle is taking place. Secure in the circumstance of the moment, they are willing to let nature take its course and give up one individual freedom after another. Many new right-wing religions are willing to think for their members, to dictate how they shall live, what they shall do, where they will spend their money. Meanwhile genuine free enterprise and civil rights are being slowly taken away with new controls, new regulations, and new government spying.

"Every aspect of your private life is subject to invasion. Inflation has brought on the already crushing tax system brought on by governments printing more money to pay debts that it cannot cover by an already crushing tax system. Your individual initiative is being drained away by conditions in far-off places over which you have no control. You need to get government out of your lives, out of your pocket books. And you need to keep the thought controllers away from you long enough to see the real picture of what is taking place in the world as the old struggle of light and freedom works to overcome fear and darkness.

"The student of Y Tylwyth Teg will realize that this struggle takes place in human awareness before it develops into the events and circumstances of life. Thus, many of your students are taking on earth karma as they search for the difference between what is right and what is wrong.

"Transferring your resentments and outrage is not the answer. If you are growing into your divine selfhood, you are changing all the while. You must support that which you see as good. Quietly, without obvious movement, you must remove your energies from violence and evil.

"Many psychics and other wise ones have warned that you face the possibility of vast earth movements and the possibility of a war with foreign powers.

"You are getting only part of the picture in these prophecies. What people are sensing are the confusion, hatred and violence of mass consciousness at the present time. You know from your study of ancient wisdom that what you hold in your consciousness eventually appears as events and experiences. As long as you see everything and everyone as hostile to your own good, you will eventually react against these forces. This explains Hitler's campaign against the Jews because of all of Germany's problems. Human nature is such that you seek a scapegoat, someone or something to blame for your hardships.

"These possibilities are gathering under the present conditions in mass consciousness. But they do not have to reach the point of appearing. The light bearers of the world could work quietly underground, behind the scenes to balance these evil forces mentioned in the Christian Book of Revelations as the Beast 666 with life, love and truth. In fact, even a worldwide depression and the spread of cancer, chemicals or ideas can be neutralized, not by attacking anything or anyone, but by sending out thoughts from your inner consciousness to heal the planet earth with love. Radical terrorist tactics that Moslem extremists use are not necessary. You can be a good citizen, a law-abiding soul, respectful of authority and law and order. The changes mostly needed are how you treat those whom you have daily conversations with, and who mean the most to you. If you hate-love everyone you are not growing on the path to a higher consciousness and cannot triumph over the discords of the world. You must love totally, unconditionally, without reservation, at the etheric level of awareness. Sometimes it is not practical to reveal love on the physical and emotional levels. It is sometimes viewed as a sign of weakness and you are then open to invasion and exploitation.

"Beware of right-wing religions that claim that they are entirely right, that everyone else is entirely wrong. You live in a plural world. People have a right to individual differences. That is what liberty and freedom are all about in this New Age of spiritual enlightenment.

"The illumination of human consciousness is taking place all around you. Slowly even the less advanced souls are awakening to their own birthright and to a higher and finer way of life. Those who are enlightened realize the great truth that you are responsible

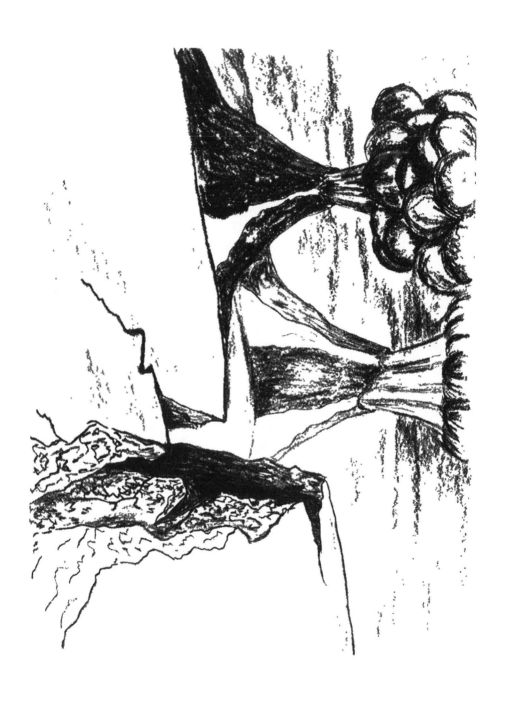

directly for everything that is happening to you now and will happen to you in the future. Karma is the unfailing principle that you experience as an individual and as a member of any society or religious group. Cosmic law is always the same. No one escapes from its justice. Some get it sooner and some get it later. But you always get it in the end.

"The increasing pressure which is building within the earth from the rapidly accelerating imbalance is beginning to be released through cracks in the moving plates on the surface. Between the years 2003 and 2027 you will see the acceleration of this activity continuously resonating around the planet. Stress changes will continuously be recorded from some area of the world almost daily. Remember, changing pressures in one area of the Earth's surface have direct relationships to other areas of the world through corresponding plate and fault lines, electromagnetic grid patterns, and etheric energy. Every form of energy, from human thought to physical changes resonates out through the entire universe, and indeed creates your reality.

"The Spring of 2007 will begin to see the far-reaching effects of these changes upon the nuclear plants around the world. None are safe from potential leaks, and may give lethal consequences. Some, unfortunately, will not be closed in sufficient time to prevent damage to communities. Major earthquakes will begin to cause fissures with immediate consequences rather than leaks. Give special attention; meditate on divine and perfect order concerning these plants.

"You must intensify your work in this dimension to redirect the relocation of specific people and officiate all responsibilities without interfering with the will and destiny of humankind. In most cases, although we can only bombard potentialities with high vibrations and wisdom, the ultimate acceptance or rejection is an individual soul decision. There are exceptions, of course, such as preventing further nuclear testing and assisting with evacuation. It is sometimes amusing and even entertaining to watch humankind's struggles. We share the passionate love that some of you have for each other, but we can only assist in accordance with divine love. Soon many will awaken and surrender their illusions. What joy will follow.

"Weather patterns will be severe in the winters of 2002-2012 and will exist unusually late. This will be very hard on food production and will cause shortages in most areas and high prices. Winter wheat will not do too well and spring crops will be planted late. Geologic activity will produce hot summers in many areas, being difficult on crop production. Keep a several-months supply of staple items to assure variety, supply and price. Food prices will jump astronomically in many areas. People will rebel and increase their fright. People will be forced into alternatives, growing sprouts, gardening, and making more items from scratch rather than packaged or frozen goods. Many adjustments will be economically necessary.

"Signs of the last days will become stronger as the years progress. Those who are fear based will become hollow-eyed, zombie-like, and intensify animalistic behavior. Others will intensify their love and compassion for others through selfless service, either consciously or unconsciously recognizing that a greater world is coming. Increase your knowledge toward increasing self-sufficiency on all levels.

"Although the following prophecies may seem to portend a vast amount of earth changes over the next fifteen years, remember between one event and another may be a period of three months to a year. This will give you breathing room and allow people to migrate from one area to another and prepare for the worst. There will be approximately 3 million humans who will die between 2003 and 2012 due to the earth changes. There will be more than 300 million who will die between 2012 and 2027. You must prepare a safe place near where you are now. This means underground. The wind will blow at speeds of from 100 - 300+ miles per hour when the earth begins to wobble and possibly tilt over in space. You must be able to live underground for at least two to three weeks. It will also be dark for periods of almost nine months.

You have twenty-seven years to prepare for the year of the beginning, 2003. Be prepared."

The following prophecies were given to Y Tylwyth Teg on April 30, 1976. **THE PROPHECIES—GEOLOGIC**

Between the years 2003 and 2027 there will be massive destruction around the world caused by earthquakes, tidal waves and volcanic activity.

January 2003 to November 2012:

Indonesia and New Guinea will be severely damaged by earthquakes and volcanoes. 9.+ earthquakes. Earthquakes of 5+ strength will strike on the Pacific coast of the United States, Alaska, Canada, Mexico, South America, and the South Pacific.

March 2003 to November 2005:

Turkey and Greece will experience severe earthquakes. There will be subsidence of land adjacent to the Dardanelle's Straits.

From August 2003 to November 2025:

From January to February 2003, March to May 2003, and January-November 2004: earthquakes will occur in southern California, causing the Gulf of California to begin changes that later in the century will cause it to flow into the Imperial Valley of California. Palm Springs will eventually be under water in late 2017.

January 2003 to 2017:

The earth will increase its wobble and cause the climate to change drastically. There will be tidal waves, 200 mile-an-hour winds, and giant storms. This is the most dangerous time for our race. 11. + Earthquakes.

January 2003 to December 2017:

Land begins to rise in the Atlantic Ocean between Iceland and Ireland. 9. + Earthquakes.

March 2001 to March 2017:

Martinique will be totally destroyed by a cataclysmic eruption of Mt. Pele. 8. + Earthquake.

January 2003 to January 2017:

Major earthquakes will destroy Italy, France and Scandinavia, resulting in several volcanoes erupting throughout the Mediterranean area. 11. + Earthquakes.

May 2003 to June 2025:

Easter Island will rise. It becomes part of a new continent showing evidence of an ancient civilization. 12. + Earthquakes.

May 2003 to June 2017:

Britain and northern Europe will experience great earthquakes as land rises in the North Sea and other land subsides on the western coast. 10. + Earthquakes.

From January 2003 to January 2025:

Mammoth Lakes, California will be struck by massive earthquakes, accompanied shortly thereafter by a tremendous volcanic eruption. 8. + Earthquakes.

January 2003 to November 2026:

Beginning of severe economic pressures on the United States as food shortages begin.

March 2003 to November 2024:

The Middle East, Syria, Iran, Iraq, Israel and Jordan will be severely damaged by earthquakes. 7+ earthquakes.

January 2004 to November 2025:

Italy will experience several severe earthquakes of 8 + in strength.

March 2004 to November 2025:

Seattle, Washington will experience a large, 6. + Earthquake.

March 2004 to -September 2027:

The eastern portion of Africa will experience great earthquakes associated with the Rift Valley. These will be 11. + Earthquakes.

March 2005 to November 2029:

Portions of California, and Georgia, South Carolina and north Florida will begin to sink slowly into the sea.

March 2005 to December 2010:

The coasts of Ireland, Wales and France will be inundated.

March 2005 to September 2017:

Earthquakes, tidal waves, will ravage first India then Japan. 10. + Earthquakes.

May 2005 to June 2017:

Russia will experience great shifting and moving of land as the northern seas cover the land. 10. + Earthquakes.

May 2005 to June 2017:

There will be great changes in the geological formation of the Arctic and Antarctic as the ice begins to rapidly melt, accompanied by 10-12+ earthquakes.

March 2006 to February 2018:

A major earthquake measuring 8+, will destroy Hoover Dam, causing Lake Mead to empty into the Colorado River. A giant wall of water will thus cause the destruction of the Davis Dam, Imperial Dam, and Laguna Dam, releasing enough water to inundate parts of Arizona.

March 2007 to March 2029:

San Francisco Bay will extend south and become and inland sea as earthquakes destroy the surrounding cities. 9. + Earthquakes.

February 2007 to March 2029:

South America will be shaken from the top to the bottom and much land will subside into the ocean. 10. + Earthquakes.

March 2008 to February 2029:

Los Angeles and San Diego will be totally devastated by earthquakes and begin to sink slowly into the sea. 10. + Earthquakes.

March 2009 to November 2029:

The ocean will inundate part of Oregon and Washington State. Many earthquakes. 7.8+ earthquakes.

March 2010 to December 2011:

New York will experience a large earthquake of 8. +.

March 2010 to November 2012:

The Black Sea will increase in size with 7. + Earthquakes.

January 2011 to November 2013:

The Mediterranean Sea will toss and turn like an agitated sleeper as the Straits of Gibraltar become impassable. 9. + Earthquakes.

January 2012 to November 2017:

The earth's axis will begin to tip. Several celestial events portend the coming devastation. 10. + Earthquakes.

February 2012 to December 2015:

Tremendous earthquakes will rock the entire United States and Western Europe. New York and Los Angeles will be virtually destroyed. 11. + Earthquakes.

February 2012 to June 2013:

Parts of India will be inundated as China begins changing its appearance. 10.+ earthquakes.

January 2014 to November 2014:

Great earthquakes near St. Louis, Missouri will destroy much property. It will be an 8. + Earthquake.

March 2014 to December 2017:

The Great Lakes begin to increase in area as the land subsides. 8. + Earthquakes.

January 2015 to February 2016:

A new body of land begins to appear 20 miles off the current coast of California, eventually reaching the length of 200 miles long and 38 miles wide. 12. + Earthquakes.

January 2015 to November 2016:

The Great Lakes will begin to empty into the Mississippi River. 6. + Earthquakes.

The greatest period of seismic occurrences seem to involve the years 1997- 2017. A great series of earthquakes will occur from California to Alaska during the period 2005-2015, accompanied by significant volcanic activity in the northwestern United States, Alaska and Hawaii.

THE PROPHECIES—ECONOMIC

1992-1999: The economy will gradually recover from a recession and heat up tremendously but quite slowly

2000-2005: The economy of the World will begin to accelerate into a decline. Energy will be in an artificial short supply, bringing on major scandals.

2005-2009: The economy of the U.S. will at first recover until the first major earthquake strikes southern California, and then will rapidly decline.

2010-2012: The economy becomes very uneven.

2012-2015: There is no economy, only survival.

2017 - 2027: The rebirth of the World economy.

THE PROPHECIES—POLITICAL

1985-1986: Haley's Comet signified complete changes for the worse for 2000.

1988-1992: The U.S. political environment becomes more democratic and liberal.

1992: A Democratic president will come from the people

1992-2000: The US will become more moderate and less Conservative politically and religiously

2000: The US congress will become slightly more Democratic and less Republican. The people will elect a Democratic President; but a Republican president will be inaugurated.

2000-2007: Terrorist attacks will become commonplace. The entire world will be upset. In 2006 there will be a limited major war of 30 to 45 days. Areas, which are in danger, will be Washington and Montana. Massive battles will occur between US subs and the aggressor. Limited war will erupt between the Arabs and the Western Powers.

The US will be involved and it will set the stage for a later war in 2007. Because of bio-technical warfare, the breadbasket of the US will be broken and food shortages will occur. The years 2009-2011 will be a regrouping era with emphasis on new peace after limited war.

The years 2009-2026 will be relatively quiet and 2027 will be the beginning of a new world. From 2012 on we will be in a new orbit. After 2015 to 2027 the inner sea will cover Utah and sea will stop near Colorado and Kansas. The whole western area rock will be under water. At the September 1981, Gathering of the Tribes, Sun Bear from Spokane, Washington, spoke of the Indian predictions.

"When a young girl speaks (Mt. St. Helen's), and grandfather answers (Mt. Rainier), if it blows west all population will be devastated to the sea. There will be warnings, rumblings, and lava will moving up. Before Rainier there will be activity in Mt. Lassen, all mountains from Yosemite to Canada and Alaska will become active."

The above prophecies are not cast in stone. They can be changed if humanity forgets its hate. Meditate and send loving energy into the earth at least once a day.

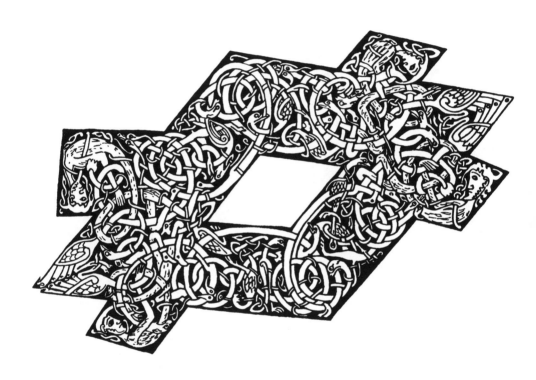

CHAPTER 12

PHILOSOPHY OF MAGIC
THE BOOK OF SHADOWS

I have discovered many truths, some from my earthly teachers, and some on my own. Others I learned from the teachers that I met on tee inner planes — my guides. What you will read here is symbol and knowledge that you may or may not understand. If you do not comprehend its truths, put this book away for a time, Live in this world and understanding will come.

My guides have often said to me, *"Rhuddlwm, do not distinguish yourself as different from other humans or animals or plants or rocks. Rather, consider everything within, upon and above the earth as fellow citizens, and equal participants in your living space which must be shared. Do not block yourself from the Great Spirit, for to do so will make you grow cold in nature. You must honor the source of all life, the Earth Mother and the Sky Father, the Great Spirit, the all in one. By doing this, you will understand.*

"Rhuddlwm, when you teach, the goals you develop in your students must be fourfold. Growth, development, awareness, and enlightenment. Growth of their knowledge, development of their power, awareness of their love, enlightenment of their wisdom. These shall be a basis for their understanding of The Way. Religion is an attempt to go home, a way to come to grips with the here and now. It is an approach, the path of life and light.

"There are three types and kinds of religious experience: Giving what is due to the Great Spirit; discovering mysteries which purge the soul and lead you to transcendence; and metamorphosis of your soul. There are four aspects to religious experience: invocation, offering, petition, and thanksgiving.

161

"In order for you to discover this religious experience you must first learn and understand the Mysteries. Keep a workbook of your teachings and your knowledge. Reveal the contents only to those who would understand and use the knowledge wisely."

In 1974 I met a seeker who was the ex High Priest of Lady Gwyn Thompson, in Connecticut. He showed me a copy of her Book of Shadows. I showed him a copy of the welsh **Owl**, our workbook. They were similar in some aspects, but our books, The Thirteen Treasures, went into much greater detail concerning legends, philosophy and magical techniques. Subsequently there came into my possession several books of shadows: Gardnerian, Alexandrian, Celtic tradition, Strega, and Druidic. After comparison I found that the Celtic traditional book of shadows by Gwyn Thompson was close to ours in philosophy and ritual and showed signs of contact with our tradition in the past. In keeping with my promise to the High Priest, I cannot reproduce his book of shadows, and I certainly would not reprint our book, The Owl, but I can reproduce a book of shadows which is a synthesis of several books. It is completely valid to all those of Celtic origin. It is **The Unicorn.**

THE UNICORN
A BOOK OF SHADOWS, OR A WORKBOOK FOR THE CELTIC TRADITION

The following was written in 1970 by Tony Kelly of the Selene community in Wales. It expresses well the feelings which lie behind the paganism of today, and gives the hope that we have for the future. Tony Kelly's inspired manifesto has become one of the great works of resurgent paganism.

PAGAN MUSINGS

We are of the Old Religion, sired by Time, and born of our beloved Earth Mother. For too long the People have trod a stony path that goes only onward beneath a sky that goes only upward. The Horned God plays in a lonely glade, alone, for the people are scattered in this barren age, and the winds carry his plaintive notes over deserted heaths and reedy moors and into the lonely grasses. Who knows now the ancient tongue of the Moon? And who speaks still with the Goddess?

The magic of the land of Lirien and the old Pagan gods have withered in the dragon's breath; the old ways of magick have slipped into the well of the past, and only the rocks now remember what the moon told us long ago, and what we learned from the trees, and the voices of the grasses and the scents of the flowers.

We are Pagans and we worship the Pagan Gods, and among the people there are witches yet who speak with the Moon and dance with the Horned One. But a Witch is a rare Pagan in these days, deep and inscrutable, recognizable only by her own kind, by the light in her eyes and the love in her breast, by the magic in her hands and the lilt of her tongue and by her Knowledge of the Real. But the Wiccan way is one Path; there are many. There are Pagans the world over who worship the Earth Mother and the Sky Father, the Rain God and the Rainbow Goddess, and the little People in the mists on the other side of the valley. A Pagan is one who worships the goddesses and the gods of nature, whether by observation or by study, whether by love or admiration, or whether in their sacred rites with the Moon or the Great Festivals of the Sun.

Many suns ago, as the pale dawn of reason crept across the Pagan sky, Humankind grew out of believing in the gods. It has yet to grow out of disbelieving in them. He who splits the Goddess on an existence/nonexistence dichotomy will earn himself only paradoxes, for the gods are not so divided, and neither are the lands of the Brothers of Time. Does a mind exist? Ask her and she will tell you yes, but seek her out and she will elude you. She is in every place, and in no place, and you'll see her works in all places, but herself in none. Existence was the second-born from the mother;s womb and contains neither the Firstborn nor the Unborn. Show us your mind and we'll show you the Gods. No matter that you can't for we can't show you the Gods. But come with us and the Goddess Herself will be our love and the God will call the tune. But a brass penny for your reason! Logic is a closed ring and the child doesn't validate the mother, nor the dream the Dreamer. But what matter the wars of opposites to She who has fallen in love with a whirlwind or to the Lover of the arching Rainbow?

But tell us of your Goddess as you love her, and the gods that guide your works and we'll listen with wonder, for to do less would be arrogant. But we'll do more, for the heart of Humanity is aching for memories only half forgotten, and the Old Ones, only half unseen. We'll write the old myths as they were always written, and we'll read them on the rocks and in the caves and in the deeps of the green-wood's shade, and we'll hear them in the rippling mountain streams and the rustling of the leaves, and we'll see them in the storm clouds, and in the evening mists. We have no wish to create a new religion, for our religion is as old as the hills and older, and we've no wish to bring differences together. Differences are like different flowers in a meadow, and we are all one in the Mother.

What need is there for a Pagan movement, since our religion has no teachings and we hear it in the wind and feel it in the stones and the moon will dance with us as she will? There is a need. For long the Divider has been among our people, and the tribes are no more. The sons of the Sky Father have all but conquered Nature, but they have poisoned Her breast and the Mother is sad, for the song birds, the fish, and the butterflies are dying. And the night draws on. A curse on the conquerors! But not our curse, for they curse themselves. They are of nature too. They have stolen our magic and sold it to the mindbenders and the mindbenders tramp a maze that has no outlet. They fear to go down into the dark waters, and they fear the real for the One who guards the path.

Where are the Pagan shrines? And where do the people gather? Where is the Magick made? And where are the Goddesses and the Old Ones? Our shrines are in the fields, on the mountains, and in the stars, and wind, deep in the greenwood and on the algal rocks where two streams meet. But the shrines are deserted, and if we gathered in the arms of the Moon for our ancient rites to be with our gods as we were of old, we would be stopped by the dead who now rule the Mother's land and claim rights of ownership on the Mother's breast, and make laws of division and frustration for us. We can no longer gather with the gods in a public place, and the old rites of communion have been driven from the towns and cities ever deeper into the heath where barely a handful of heathens have remained to guard the secrets and enact the old rites. There is magick in the heath far from the cold grey society, and there are island of magick hidden in the entrails of the metropolis behind closed doors, but the people are few, and the barriers between us are formidable. The old religion has become a dar way, obscure, and hidden in the protective bosom of the night. Thin fingers turn the pages in a book of Shadows while the sunshine seeks in vain his worshippers in his leafy glades.

Here then is the basic reason for a Pagan Way: we must create a Pagan Society wherein everyone shall be free to worship the goddesses

164

and gods of Nature. The relationship between a worshiper and her gods shall be sacred and inviolable, providing only that in the love of one's own gods one does not curse the names of the gods of others.

It is not yet our business to press the lawmakers with undivided endeavor to unmake the laws of repression and, with the Mother's love, it may never become our business. For the stifling tides of dogmatism are at last already in ebb. Our first work and our greatest wish is to come together, to be with each other in our tribes, for we haven't yet grown from our Mother's breast to the stature of gods.

We're of the earth, and kin to all the children of wild nature, born long ago in the warm mud of the ocean floor; we were together then, and we were together in the rain forests long before that dark day when, beguiled by the pride of the Sky Father and forgetful of the Mother's love, we killed her earlier-born children and impoverished the ancient genetic pool. The Red Child lives yet in America, the old Australians are still with their gods, the Black Child has not forsaken his gods; the Old Ones still leap deep in the heart of Mother India; and the White Child has still a foot on the old Wiccan Path, but Neanderthaler is no more and her magick faded as the Lli and the Archan burst their banks and the ocean flowed in to divide the Isle of Erin from the Land of the White Goddess.

Humanity looked with one eye and on a two-faced god when it reached for the heavens and scorned the Earth which alone is our life and our provider and the bosom to which we have ever returned since the dawn of time. He who looks only to reason to plumb the unfathomable is a fool, for logic is an echo already implicit in the question, and it has no voice of its own — but he is no greater fool than he who scorns Logic or derides its impotence from afar, then fears to engage it in fair combat when he stands upon his opponent's threshold. Don't turn your back on Reason, for its thrust is deadly, but confound it and it will yield, for its code of combat is honorable. Here lies more of the work of Paganism. Our lore has become encrusted over the ages with occult trivia and the empty vapourings of the lost. The Occult Arts are in a state of extreme decadence; Astrology is in a state of disrepute and fears to confront the statistician's sword; alien creeds oust our native arts and, being as little understood as our own forgotten arts, are just as futile for their lack of understanding, and the more so for their unfamiliarity. Misunderstanding is rife. Disbelief is black on every horizon, and vampires batten on the blood of the credulous. Our work is to reject the trivial, the irrelevant, and the erroneous, and

165

to bring the lost children of the Earth Mother again into the court of the Sky Father where reason alone will avail. Belief is the deceit of the credulous; it has no place in the heart of a Pagan.

But while we are sad for those who are bemused by reason, we are deadened by those who see no further than their syllogisms as they turn the eternal wheel of the Great Tautology. We are not fashioned in the mathematician's computations, and we were old when the first alchemist was a child. We have walked in the magic forest, bewitched in the old Green Thinks; we have seen the cauldron and the One become Many and the many become One; and we know the Silver Maid of the moonlight and the sound of the Cloven Feet. We have heard the pipes on the twilight fearns, and we've seen the spells of the Enchantress, and we have seen Time be stilled. We have been in the Eternal Darkness where the Night Mare gallops and ridden her to the edge of the Abyss, and beyond. We know the dark face of the Rising Sun. Spin a spell of words and make a magick knot; weave it on the magic loom and clothe it with the Gods. Say it in the Old Tongue and say it to the Goddess; say it in her name as well. There are no signposts on the untrodden way, but we'll make our rituals together and bring them as our gifts to the Old Gods in the Great Rites.

Here then is our work in the Pagan Way: to make magick in the name of our gods, to share our magick where the gods would wish it, and to come together in our ancient festivals of birth, life, death, and change, in the old rhythm. We'll print the rituals that can be shared in the written word; we'll do all in our power to bring the people together, to teach those who would learn, and to learn from those who can teach. We will initiate groups, bring people into groups, and groups to other groups in our common devotion to the gods and goddesses of Nature. We will not storm the secrets of any coven, nor profane the tools, the magick--and still less, the gods of another.

We will collect the myths of the ages, of our people and of the Pagans of other lands, and we'll study the books of the wise and we'll talk to the very young. And whatever the Pagan needs in Her study, or Her worship, then it is our concern, and the business of the Pagan Way to do everything possible to help each other in our worship of the gods we love.

We are committed with the lone Pagan by the seashore, with she who worships in the fastness of a mountain range or he who sings the old chant in a lost valley fall from the metalled road. We are committed with the wanderer, and equally with the prisoner, disinherited from

166

the Mother's milk in the darkness of the industrial wen. We are committed too with the coven, with the circular dance in the light of the Full Moon, with the Great Festivals of the Sun, and with the gatherings of the people. We are committed to build our temples in the towns and in the wilderness, to buy the lands and the streams from the landowners and give them to the Goddess for her children's use, and we'll replant the greenwood as it was of old for love of the dryad stillness, and still more for love of our children's children's children.

When the streams flow clear and the winds blow pure, when the Sun never more rises unrenowned nor the Moon rides in the skies unloved, when the stones tell of the Horned God and the greenwood grows deep to call back her own, then our work will be ended, and the Pagan Way will return to the beloved womb of our old religion, to the nature goddesses and gods of Paganism.

What are your feelings about the above work? Sit down right now and think about what you are doing. What do you want out of life? What are your goals? What do you believe in?

OF THE CIRCLE:

The Circle is a gateway, a door, an opening, a place where one opens oneself for what is inside. There are many kinds and sizes of circles but all are the same. Never enter a Circle or approach an altar with any form of malice in your heart. Circles start in the East and close in the East. The East from which which the sun rises, the concept of illumination. A circle is complete only as a circle. A circle becomes a spiral if it is not completed.

The Circle

In the north, air, Asrael, or Uriel, the God Lleu. To the east, Raphael, earth, the god Amaethon. To the south, Mikhail, fire, the god Govannan. To the west, Gabriel, water, the god Dylan. The circle is a multiple of three feet in diameter. North is the magnetic center of the universe. All gifts from the north quarter, true light. To the east, the symbol of life, the earth. To the south, the fullness of knowledge and wisdom. To the west, the second quarter of the life cycle.

In the earth invoking pentagram starts from the top, goes down to the bottom left, up to the right, over to the left, down to the bottom right, down to the top again. Earth banishing starts at the bottom left, up to the top, down to the bottom right, up to the top left, over the top right, and down the bottom left.

A Grove

No more than thirteen should gather when in a working circle of

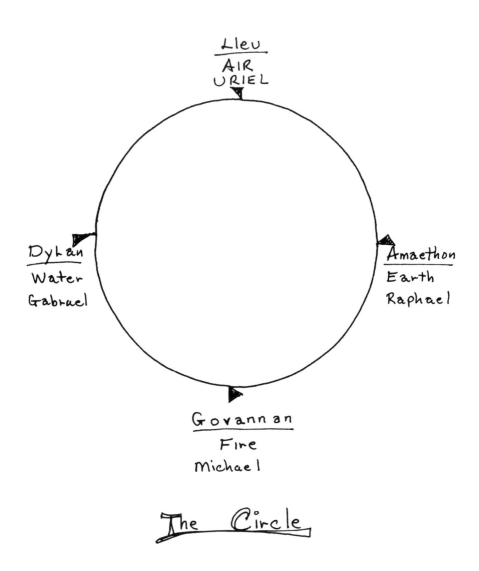

The Circle

Rhuddlwm

— The Pentacle and the Ankh —

R. huddleson

The Pantacle

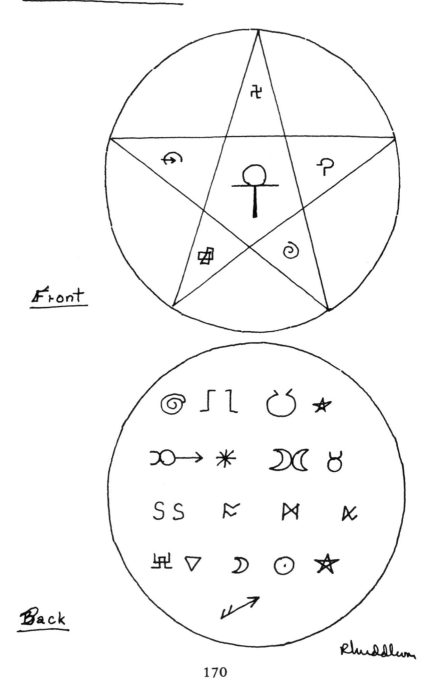

Front

Back

170

☞ Symbols ☜

☉	The Sun/God	☽	Waxing Moon
△	The threefold Law	☾	waning Moon
⭑	The Neophyte		
⎪	The Cone of Power	⇗	High Priest or Priestess
⍟	the Goddess	⊃⟶	Arrow of power
⍟	the God	✳	Eight Paths
↑	Victory	↺	Sacred Grove
↓	Defeat	ꓮ	Scourge
✪	Attainment	ꓞ	Good Fortune
	Broken Powers High Priest	F	Love
	Broken Powers High Priestess	FFF	FLAG – FLAX – Fodder
✷	Loss of power	⚵	Triple Goddess
SS	the Kiss on Both Cheeks	✪	Curse

Rhuddlan

171

nine feet. If the circle is bigger then as many as are comfortable may be admitted. The High Priestess shall lead the rites from Beltane to Hollowmas and at all Esbats. The High Priest shall lead the Sabbats from Hollowmas to Beltane. All should be of one mind and of one heart. The place of meeting should be called the Grove and a Maiden shall be selected from the female witches who are of second degree. She shall be unwed within the craft and will assist the High Priestess and is next in line to that position. A candlebearer shall be selected from the males, the partner of the Maiden if this be meet. He shall call all the meetings, keep the records, the discipline of all.

No circle may be held without a High Priest of a High Priestess or a Maiden who has permission from the High Priest or High Priestess to officiate. There should be no money collected, but all must do equal to the needs of the Grove.

(See illustration)

TOTEMS:

These are the sacred animals of the coven. They are the owl, sacred to the Goddess, and the stag, sacred to the Horned One.

SYMBOL:

This shall be the pentacle within the ankh.

(See Illustration)

THE WORKBOOK — THE OWL:

The book of ceremonies and teachings. This must be copied by hand by each member under the direction of the elder. It is Cerridwen's Cauldron of Wisdom that must be kept from the hands of the outsider, destroyed by fire at the death of the owner, unless there be someone of the Craft to keep it next.

ANOINTING OIL:

    1/2 ounce of pure clear oil

    1/2 ounce of musk oil

    1/2 tsp. cinnamon

COLORS:

These shall be red, green, blue and white, red being the most sacred color of life, green being the color of the earth, blue being the color of the sea, and white the color of light.

GROVE ATTIRE:

The Robe: shall be red, freeflowing and hooded. When it can no longer be worn it is to be burnt.

The Cingulum: the red cord of initiation, braided of three strands. It binds one to the gods. It is to be worn at all circles, tied with a single loop to the left side. This is never to be out of the possession of the owner and is to be buried with him at death.

The Necklace: must be worn at all circles by all female witches. Traditionally it is made of twenty amber beads interspaced by twenty jet beads. But it can be made of anything as long as it is prominent and not of iron.

The Garter: worn by the High Priestess and High Priest above the left knee. It shall have a silver buckle for each coven. Both shall be made of leather lined with purple silk.

THE RITUAL TOOLS

The Rod:

The riding pole made of an oak branch and carved with phallic design. The tip, the first nine inches, shall be silvered, It is used to cast the circle and in the fertility dances.

The White Handled Knife:

This should be used for bygraving, or engraving. It should only be used within the magic circle.

The Wand:

This is a magic rod and should be or rowan, hazel or box elder, not less than eighteen inches long, not more than three feet. Within the tip, a piece of metal which is silver or copper should be pushed erect to act as a power absorber.

The Pentacle:

A disk of plane silver, wood or wax, which serves as initial point of contact in the drawing down of the moon.

The Athame:

The black hilted knife. It must be double edged and never used for cutting. With it you can draw a magic circle and summon the gods. It can be used to protect your life if needs be. The athame is a male symbol, the most important tool of the Wiccan. It is a black handled knife. It is the only tool consecrated on the waning moon. It is used to cast the circle, it is used to call the Watchtowers, it is used to pull down energy to the circle, it is never used for any other purpose, and it represents will and being.

Charging the athame before casting the circle:

Hold the athame in your outstretched palm. Extend it up and out, full arms' length, grasp with the hands. Hold in this position until you can feel the power building. There will be a tangible pull, almost as if the athame wants to go upward. Hold until the full power is built. Then slowly pull the force down with the athame until it rests against

Athame Runes

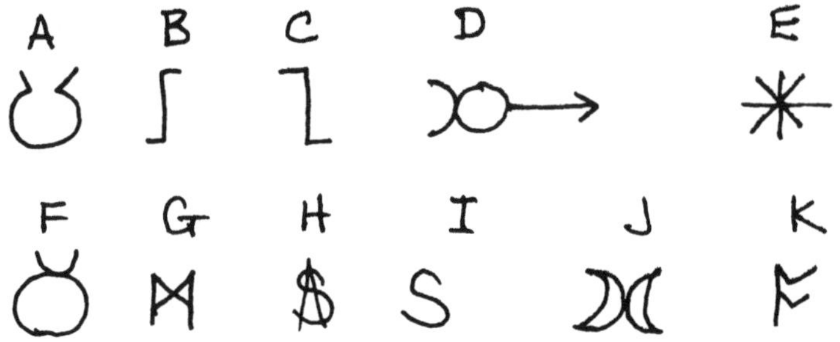

A	B	C	D	E
♉	∫	⌐	⊃O→	✳

F	G	H	I	J	K
♉	ᛗ	$	S	⊃C	ᚠ

A   The Circle

B   kneeling Man

C   Kneeling Woman

D   Arrow of Power

E   Eight Paths of Power

F   The Horned God

G   The Name of the Lord

H   The Salute   Purification

I   The Kiss on Both cheeks

J   The Goddess

K   the Name of the Lady

Rhuddleon

your forehead. Let the energy flow through. When fully charged kiss the athame first with the blade to the front, back toward you, to the left, to the right, then up, and then down.

Salute with your athame:

Place on your heart, then straight up and out, back to your lips, and straight up and out.

The Sacred Stone:

Wisdom was divided among three people. When the hidden children of the Goddess gathered together all that was divided then shall the sacred stone rest with the Mother and the promise shall be fulfilled.

The Chalice:

This is the female symbol. It represents the great womb of the Great Mother and of Nature. It holds the wine of the Sabbat. It is used to toast the God and the Goddess. It may be of any nonferrous material. It is never used for any other purpose. It is feminine, receptive, sustains, springs forth, and gives nourishment.

The Cauldron:

This is a kettle, preferably iron, with tripod legs. It is set in the center of the circle. It represents the great womb of the Mother. It represents the three great gifts granted by the Mother to her children, the three legs of the tripod. The baelfire burns in it or under it on Sabbats and Esbats. The three aspects of the cauldron are:

1) The Cauldron of Wisdom. It contains sacred rituals which contain Wiccan lore. From it we are guided in our thoughts, speech and deeds to a better way of life and harmony.

2) The Cauldron of Eternity. This is the abyss into which we may discard all that is evil or troublesome nature. Into this cauldron go our afflictions. It is a symbolic act of purification to prevent defilement of the earth and ourselves.

3) The Cauldron of the Grail. This contains the stones which are the cornerstones or foundations of the earth. It is the promise of the Great Spirit to her Children of Light that through seeking the wisdom and learning it well, they shall fulfill their destiny of Guardian of the Earth. Wisdom was divided among five people. When the Sons and Daughters of Light gather together then shall the sacred stones rest at the feet of our Mother. The promise shall be fulfilled. The cauldron may be the receptacle of our gifts, our requests, our problems. There are many legends concerning the cauldron. Study and meditate upon them.

Candle Holders:

These are used to hold the altar candles and the candles of the watchtowers. They may be of any nonferrous material: metal, glass, wood, etc. Three are used for the altar, four for the four watchtowers. For outdoor use lantern-type holders may be used, but these should be selected with care to assure they are nonmetallic. Otherwise place outside the circle. These candleholders should not be used for any other purpose.

Candles:

Three on the altar: the Goddess candle, which is our Lady; the God candle, which is our Lord; and a petition candle. Symbolism. The body of the candle represents the physical body. The wick of the candle represents intellect. The flame of the candle represents the soul or life force.

Charging the Candle:

Use consecration oil. Hold the candle in both hands. Charge or rub from the center to the bottom, and then from the center to the wick end. Concentrate on the charge you are putting into the candle, and never stroke the full length. Candles should be passed through the elements.

The Bell:

The bell is used to summon favorable spirits. It should have a clear, distinct ring. It should be of a nonferrous material. It is rung at the four quadrants when summoning the Guardians, three times. It is rung at other times during a ritual for emphasis and to summon the desired spirits.

Cingulum, Cord or Girdle:

It is to be made by the seeker personally. It is used in initiation to bind the initiate to the God and the Goddess. It is used to measure circles. It is to be worn at all circles. It is tied in a single knot at the left of the waist. It is never to leave the owner's possession or to be used by another. It is to be retained until death, when it will be buried with the Wiccan. If it is ever necessary to dispose of a cingulum it should be burned and the ashes buried.

Making the Cingulum:

Obtain three nine-foot lengths of velvet cord. Have the following: Herbs: vervain mint, basil, rosemary, hyssop, lavender, sage, valerian, fennel. Salt, Mortar and pestle, Charcoal to burn incense, Incense (Not stick incense), Tape measure (no metal in it)
The Cingulum is prepared on a waxing moon only. Have all ele-

Take an Apple- - - - - - - -

ments on the altar: fire, air, earth and water. Cast a salt circle. Consecrate the elements. Run the mortar and pestle through the elements. Sprinkle with water, over salt, through fire and air. Consecrate to use. Crush the herbs with the mortar and pestle. Holding cords loosely in the hand, run them through the four elements. Sprinkle with the water and the salt, pass through the incense smoke and over fire. Starting with the ends of the cords even, tie a knot. Braid the cords. Each time you lap over a braid, repeat:

"Wrought to measure, wrought to bind, blessed be these cords entwined."

When the entire length is braided, knot the cingulum at the following: There should be a first knot at zero, then a knot at three-and-a-half feet, a knot at four feet, a knot at four-and-a-half feet, and knot at five feet, and a knot at five-and-a-half feet. Each measurement is made from zero, from the first know. Take the crushed herbs, place part in water, part in incense, so as to burn. Holding your finished cingulum in your hand, consecrate it with the four elements. Sprinkle with the herbal water, and with salt, pass through the herbal incense bowl, and over the fire. Gird yourself with the finished cingulum. It should be knotted at the left side. Add more incense to the charcoal, meditate, and then dismiss the circle.

THE APPLE:

" Take an apple, cut it through, contemplate what's twixt the two."

(See Illustration) — Representing first the fivefold star, second, the circle, third, the seeds of life and reincarnation. The apple tree is large and the wood is useful. The fruit of the tree is food sustaining life. The tree represents religion, the apple represents priests and priestesses. The branches represent the different traditions.

THE NINE YEAR CYCLE:

Sun, moon, earth, fire, air, water, plant, animal, stone.

COLOR SYMBOLOGY:

White is purity. Blue is healing, physical and mental. Green is money, some healing. Red is will. Gold is balance. Orange is yellow, gold and red. Purple is red and blue. Yellow is study. Combinations and depths of shade reflect all aspects of the various individual colors.

THE WICCAN REDE — Short Version

"Bide the Wiccan Law ye must in perfect love and perfect trust. Eight words the Wiccan Rede fulfill, an ye harm none do what ye will. Lest in thyself defensed be, ever mind the rule of three.

Follow this in mind and heart, and merry we meet and merry we part."

THE WICCAN REDE — The Law of the Wicca — Long Version

"Bide the Wiccan Law ye must in perfect love and perfect trust. Live and let live, fairly take or fairly give. Cast the circle thrice about to keep all evil spirits out. To bind the spell every time let the spell be spake in rhyme. Soft of eye and light of touch, speak little and listen much. Deosil go by the waxing moon, sing and dance the Wiccan rune. Widdershins go when the moon doth wane, the werewolf howls by the dread wolfsbane. When the Lady's moon is new, kiss the hand to her times two. When the moon rides to her peak, then your heart's desire you'll speak. Heed the north wind's might gale, lock the door and drop the sail. When the wind blows from the south love will kiss thee on the mouth. When the wind blows from east expect the new and set the feast. When the west wind blows o'er thee, departed spirits restless be. Nine woods in the cauldron go, burn them quick and burn them slow. Elder be ye Lady's tree, harm it not or cursed ye be. When the wheel begins to turn, let the balfires burn. When the wheel has turned to Yule, light the log and let Pan rule. Heed ye flower, bush and tree, by the Lady blessed be. Where the rippling waters go, cast a stone and truth you'll know. When ye have need, hearken not to other's greed. With the fool no season spend, or be counted as his friend. Merry meet and merry part, bright the cheeks and warm the heart. Mind the threefold law ye should, three times bad and three times good. True in love ever be, lest thy lover's false to thee. When misfortune is anow, wear the blue star on thy brow. Eight words the Wiccan Rede fulfill, an ye harm none do what ye will."

THE EIGHT WORDS OF POWER:

Take four lines and cross them in a circle so that there are eight arms. The top movement, then ritual, chanting, meditation, sexual energy, herbs, trance and firm will.

(See Illustration)

TRUTH:

A truth is that which is. Like calls unto like, deep unto deep. If you would clear the path to will, make ye certain the mind is still.

SAYINGS:

"Ease the pain, cure the disease, let the dying spirit go." "Speak little, listen much." "The ways of the Wise are simple, confound-

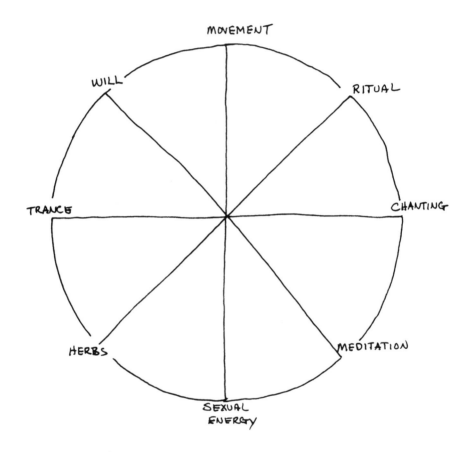

EIGHT PATHS OF POWER

Rhuddlwm

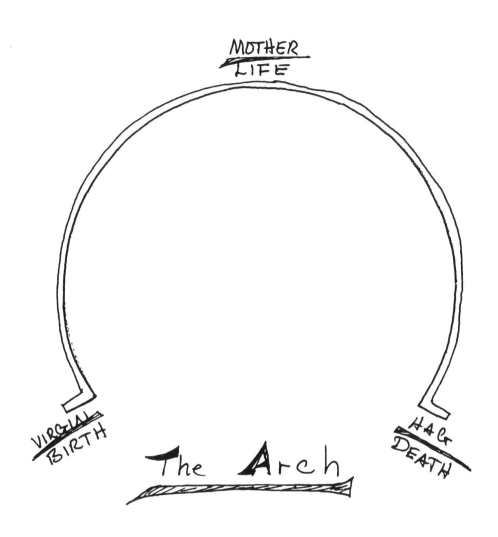

ing the ignorant." "Time is but the magic link c̣ God." "God is alive, magic is afoot."

SYMBOLS:

The Arc — Make a curve. Bottom left, virgin and birth, at the peak, good mother, fruitfulness, bottom right, the hag and death. (See Illustration)

Make a cross with the circle — Top arm, life mother, right arm, stone mother, low arm, death mother, left arm, aesthetic mother. The circle:tooth mother.

(See Illustration)

THE PLANES:

Celestial — the godhead; duality or causal, this is God and the Goddess; The third is the spiritual; The fourth is intuitional; The fifth is mental; The sixth is astral, where the akashic records reside; and the seventh is physical.

THE GODS:

The Great Spirit, Hu Gadaran, has three aspects: Lleu, the young sun god, mate of Bloddewyd; Gwydion, the god of magic, mate of Arianrhod; and Math, the great king, with Cerridwen — Don.

The names of the goddesses are pronounced thus:

Blodwith; Ree-a-non, Keridwen;

Other names of the Goddess are Olwen, Aradia, Branwen, Duinwen, Don, and Rhianna.

THE NINE FOLD GODDESS:

Bloddewyd, the maiden; Dwynwen, the young lover, the sex goddess; Branwen, the young wife; Arianrhod, the mother; Rhiannon, the queen; Brigit, the mature virgin; Cerridwen, the great mother; Don, the wise old grandmother; Secret name, the hag

THE NINE FOLD GOD:

Llew, the sun god; Gwydion, the god of magic; Math, the king of the gods, the wise old grandfather; Nuada, the king of the fairies; Llyr, the king of the sea; Pwyll, the god of nature; Arawn, the god of storms; Pryderi, the god of husbandry; Secret name, god of eternity

THE NINE FOLD CELTIC GODS:

Albiorix, the god of underworlds; Toutorix, the lord of the tribes; Arduinna, the love goddess; Blisama, the mother of earth; Damona, the cattle goddess; Epona, the horse goddess; Nemetona, the goddess of war; Brigit, the mother goddess; Secret name, bull god

182

THE NINE FOLD IRISH GODS:

Belenus, the sun god; Lugus, the god of arts and skills; Nantosuelta, goddess of the river; Ogmios, the god of the dead; Succellus, god of the underworld; Taranis, god of the lightning; Danu, goddess of the universe; Gofannon, the smith god; Secret name, the bull god

THE BIRCH TREE:

One of the nine sacred woods. Good for building certain items. The bark is good for building canoes and other things, containers, etc. There is a myth that the birch tree is the axis of the earth, the top of the tree being the pole or north star. The sacred mushroom grows under the birch tree. This mushroom is hallucinogenic. It inebriates one, makes one hyper, and exceedingly strong. The person then sleeps and has dreams about the mushroom people. This is Amanita Muscara.

THE OAK TREE:

Sacred to the druids. The oak tree is the symbol of strength and of rebirth. Mistletoe grows on oak trees. The mistletoe is sacred. It is a symbol of fertility, of the male principle. The berries resemble the sperm of the male. Mistletoe is also hallucinogenic. In druidic times the priests cut the mistletoe from the oaks at precise seasons with a golden scythe.

THE WATCHTOWERS OF THE WORLD:

These are the four corners of the earth, represented by the four point candles around a circle, east, south, west and north. They are presided over by the Mighty Ones, who are the lords.

GWLAD YR HAV:

That land beyond the veil of Maya, where weary souls repose within the realms of the Horned One to grow young again and to be reborn upon the earth. That fair land of nod called the Summerland.

THE CONE OF POWER:

Pure psychic energy raised from the naked body during a ritual involving motion, sound, and emotion.

THE DANCES:

To raise the cone of power all circle deosil around the releaser and altar, hand in hand, male-female. The dance goes faster and faster ar d yet faster as the power is raised and taken into the body of the rele aser. At the height of the dance the calls of Io Evohe, Blessed Be, anc the names of power are given until the ecstasy is reached. When the cry of stop is given by the releaser all fall to the ground and blank their minds out.

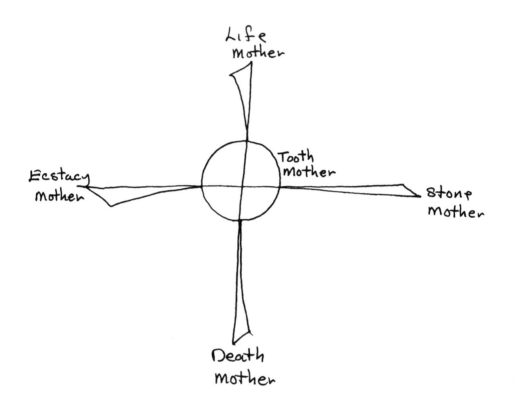

Life
Mother

Ecstacy
Mother

Tooth
Mother

Stone
Mother

Death
Mother

The Cross

Rhuddleon

------ The Rune Dance. The same as a circle dance only a spell rhyme is recited over and over until the ecstasy is reached.

------ The Knife Dance. A very slow circle dance. The athame is held blade up in the right hand, left hand around the wrist of the next person.

------ The Snake Dance. All follow the High Priestess deosil in a spiral to the center and then out again, kissing everyone you pass.

------ Volta. Dance deosil with your partner arms to shoulders with head resting on your partner's hand to the left. Dance slowly, then faster and faster, until you reach the ecstasy.

------ Pole dance. Gallop deosil around the circle astride the riding pole, leaping as high as you can. After riding, couples join hands and leap over the cauldron.

------ The Beltaine Dance. Dance to wind the Maypole, deosil by women, widdershins by men.

CONSECRATION OF TOOLS:

To Consecrate the Tools (All except the sword and athame):
Pass the tool over the four elements, saying:

"By fire, water, earth and air, baneful spirits need beware. Art thou made pure oh treasure trove, here wit' n this sacred grove. So mote it be."

WITCH BOTTLE:

This will protect you from any evil magic cast against you. Take a clean jar and half fill it with needles, pins, slivers of glass, razors and anything sharp. Add a noxious herb and then urinate into the jar or add white vinegar and a few drops of blood, menstrual or sperm. Seal it, and either bury it on your property or hide it in your house where no one can find it. It will protect you as long as it remains unspilled.

THE GODDESS SALUTE:

With your right hand hold your athame pointed upwards at a 45 degree angle, bring the blade to your lips and kiss it, hold out again and bring it down to you side.

KNOT MAGIC:

Worked with your partner. Take a piece of cord of the appropriate color 13 inches long. Using either a rune spell or concentration make a knot on one end, female, keeping the cord taut between you, the second knot at the other end, male. Go back and forth until you have made the last knot in the center. Usually three knots are used for good or light spells, nine knots for bane, baneful and strong spells. This can also be done alone without your partner. To undo the spell, work from the center out, untying the knots.

CANDLE MAGICK:

Take a plain white candle, or one of the appropriate color. With the white hilt knife inscribe a pentagram on top. Under that inscribe the person's name for whom you are doing the magic. Concentrate upon the purpose. Follow this by their degree symbols if they be in, or another pentagram if not. Anoint with wine or oil and think of the spell beginning to work. Light the candle thinking of the spell having worked very strongly. Let the candle burn out completely.

FORMULAE FOR INCENSE:

Sabbat Incense:

    2 oz. frankincense

    2 oz. myrrh

    2 oz. benzoine

1/2 oz. each of fennel, thyme, rue, camomile, pennyroyal, rose petals, laurel, vervain, wormwood, balm and seal. Pulverize and add in the same amount of church incense.

Esbat Incense:

Equal amounts each of frankincense, benzoine, myrrh, storax, poppy, aloe, calamus, rosebuds, cinnamon, coriander, thyme, orris root.

Small amount camphor.

    Pulverize. Add to same amount of church incense.

Sun Incense:

Equal parts of frankincense and myrrh.

Moon Incense:

Equal parts of wormwood and camphor.

Mercury Incense:

Equal parts of gummastic and cinnamon.

Venus Incense:

Equal parts of rose petals and aloes.

Earth Incense:

Three parts of juniper, three parts of cypress, two parts of myrrh, one half part of orris, one part of patchouli, one part of sage.

Mars Incense:

Four parts of dragon's blood, four parts rue, one part peppercorns, one part ginger, on pinch sulfur, on pinch powdered lodestone.

Jupiter Incense:

Equal parts of anise, mint, hyssop, chervil, and liverwort.

Saturn Incense:

Four parts of myrrh, one part of yew, one part of elderberry, one part cypress, one part patchouli, one pinch of iron filings.

To make oils of the planets grind a portion of incense and add to any clear, pure oil.

TO GAIN THE SIGHT:

Equal amounts each of gum mastic, calamus (which is sweet rushroot), cinnamon, juniper, white sandalwood, patchouli, musk, ambergris.

FLYING OINTMENT:

Annamthol, betel, opium, cinquefoil, henbane, belladonna, hemlock, hemp, canthreindid.

Use in small amounts. You must be extremely careful with these as they are dangerous, even in small amounts. Certain mushrooms, especially fly ageric can be used to gain the sight. However, this is also to be used carefully because they are poisonous. We do not recommend that you take any of these preparations internally, or even use them externally.

MAGICK MIRROR:

Rinse a concave glass and frame under cold water for about three minutes, willing all impurities to be washed away. Let dry. Paint the back black so that no light can come through. Brew a portion of wormwood or camomile, strain and let cool. Place your athame point in the liquid and say:

"Now do I breathe in the pure white light that pervades the universe. As I breathe out the light goes forth from my athame into the potion before me. There it shall always remain. Into this shall all forces of good be drawn in the names of Arianrhod and Cerridwen. So mote it be."

Paint the potion on the back of the dry mirror and hold your athame tip to it, saying:

"In the name of Arianrhod and Hu, may all good forces and high influences come through this mirror. So mote it be."

Make an invoking pentagram over the mirror. Let dry, seal from the dust. Mugwort is also very effective and can be used also in the incense when using the mirror.

PASSWORDS:

Password Phrase to Tell if Someone was correctly initiated:
Ask:
" Are you in?"
Answer:
" Yes."

Ask:

"How were you brought in."

Answer:

"He (or she) brought in from behind with a kiss."

PRAYER FOR THE DEAD:

"Oh great Horned One, 'tis by thy hands near the lovely summer-land that we part from earthly strife and await some future life. Bless our loving ones sleeping here, bless this soul we hold so dear. In another life we'll meet and know each life will be more sweet. So mote it be."

THE OLD RELIGION:

The Old Religion, Yr Hen Grefydd, is witchcraft, gwyddoniaid. A female witch is a gwiddon, and a male witch is a gwyddon. Witches are gwyddoniad.

THE PLANETS

How the Planets Rule the Body:

The sun rules the heart and the back.

The moon rules the breast, the stomach, the liver, the intestines, and the pancreas.

Mercury rules the brain, the nerves, and breathing.

Venus rules the throat and the kidneys.

Mars rules the genitals and the muscles.

Jupiter rules the liver and the pituitary gland.

Saturn rules the skin, the teeth, the bones, the gall bladder, pituitary gland, and the sex glands.

Uranus rules the blood and the third eye.

Neptune rules the nerves.

Pluto rules the genitals, reproductive glands, and reproduction itself.

ASTROLOGICAL SIGNS:

How the Signs Rule the Body:

Aries rules the head.

Taurus rules the throat and neck.

Cancer rules the stomach.

Virgo rules the nerves and the intestines.

Sagittarius rules the liver, the hips, and the thighs.

Aquarius rules the circulation, shins, and ankles.

Gemini rules the arms, shoulders and nerves.

Leo rules the heart, spine and back.

Libra rules the kidneys.

Scorpio rules the sex glands and genitals.

Capricorn rules the knees, the bones and the teeth.

Pisces rules the feet.

THE RUNESTONES:

On eight stones of uniform size paint the following runes of the correct color on one side of each stone.

One one side is the moon, like a half moon, silver representing the feminine, a woman, changes, secrets, disappointments, and illusions.

Mercury. A T with a top arm being a half circle. White. Rules travel, hasty news, a letter, important papers.

Jupiter. This is a diamond shape with a line through it. It's blue. Expansion, prosperity, good luck, success, growth, and reunion.

Venus. A triangle. Light blue. Love, romance, harmony, beauty, arts.

The sun. A circle with some lines coming out of it. Gold. The masculine. A man, happiness, joy, freedom, wish granted in a happy way.

Neptune. Two half pyramids facing each other, made into sort of a diamond shape. Green, travel by sea, emotion, drugs.

Mars. Two columns, on the top, connected with one cross. Red. Energy.Ambition. Quarrels. Disputes. Enemies. Sudden occurrences. War.

Saturn. A lightning bolt. Black. Delay, sorrow, tears, losses, partings.

Hold the stones within your left hand and cover them with your right hand. Shake the stones while asking your question out loud. Cast them out and remove the stones with the symbols face down. Read the stones the furthest away from you, the closest which is the outcome.

REINCARNATION RITUAL:

Select a quiet time in a darkened room. Cast a simple circle with your athame around a table upon which a small mirror about ten inches in diameter has been placed. A small candle and some incense is burning. Sit before the mirror, having the short candle between it and you. Light the candle and incense and blank out your mind for one minute. Gaze at your image in the mirror and speak you name aloud thrice. Pause. Now say,

"Who was I?"

Keep gazing and eventually you will be able to see various images that will awaken far memory. Do not do this for more than fifteen minutes at a time.

189

CLOUD MAGICK:

Choose a fleecy white cloud in a clear blue sky. Concentrate your vision upon it and mentally instruct it to bring your petition to the gods. If done properly, the cloud will begin to break up and disappear. Do not use on rain clouds.

FIRE MAGICK:

After raising the Cone of Power the High Priestess or High Priest should call the grove to stand around the cauldron holding their athames. The Maiden shall hold her candle and the summoner, or candlebearer, a flask of magical catalyst, two part of salt peter, one part of sugar, and one part of ground camomile flowers. Before the Circle, the request for magic will have been written upon a piece of paper with all pertinent information. This will be read to the witches. The officiator will ask the witches to point their athames into the cauldron and concentrate all magic powers through their bodies out through the athames into the cauldron, which should contain three lit charcoals with a steady blue flame. The officiator will now concentrate on the magic being accomplished and light the paper from the Maiden's candle and drop it into the cauldron. Then take the catalyst and cast it in. As the flames go up all will walk deosil, pointing their athames in the cauldron and giving the power until the flames die completely. The cauldron should then be put out with a measure of wine.

PROTECTION:

With the athame starting in the East draw a triple circle around you in the air, deosil, saying:

"I hereby surround myself with this circle of protection against which no hostile power dare set its fool."

At each point now draw an invoking pentagram, saying:

"In the names of Arianrhod and Cernunnos, so mote it be."

THE WHEEL OF THE YEAR:

Yule, the beginning
Imbolg, the developing
Spring Equinox, the creating
Beltaine, the forcing
Midsummer, the growing
Lughnasadh, the borning
Autumn Equinox, the harvest
Samhain, the death

Yule is Alban Arthan.

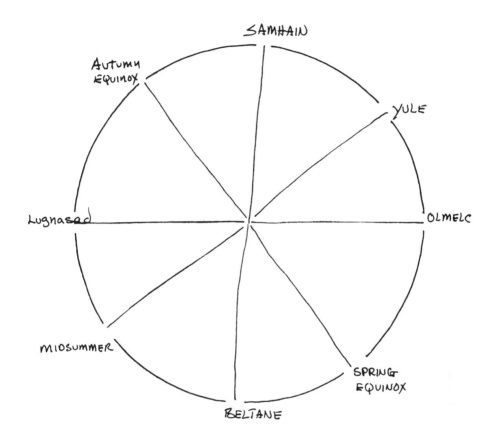

THE WHEEL OF THE YEAR

Rhuddlom

Spring *is* Alban Eilir.
Summer *is* Alban Hefin.
Autumn *is* Alban Elfed.
These are Scottish names.

THE YES-NO STONES:
   Find three smooth stones. Paint them with the following runes on both sides. The first stone, triangle, in silver, means yes. Second stone, circle, in gold, means no. Third stone, square, in red, significator. Hold the stones in your left hand and cover them with your right. As the question and cast them out. Wherever the significator falls closest to is the answer.

BLONOWEDD:
Hanes Blonowedd by Taliesin:
   "Not of father nor of mother was my blood, was my body I was spellbound by Gwydion, prime enchantor of the Britons When he formed me from nine blossoms, nine buds of various kind From primrose of the mountain, broom, meadowsweet and cockle Together intertwined from the bean in its shade Bearing a white spectral army of earthly mind From blossoms of the nettle, oak, thorn, and bashful chestnut Nine power of nine flowers, nine powers in me combined Nine buds of plants and trees, long and white are my fingers As the ninth wave of the sea"
   Brew for three days in quantities of three to make a portion of love.

NAMES:
Welsh Names, Female:
Branwen — old Welsh, white bossomed
Cordelia — middle Welsh, jewel of the sea
Dee — Welsh, black dark one
Enid — old Welsh, wood lark, purity
Gladys — old Welsh, lame one
Gweniviere — old Welsh, white wave, white phantom
Glynna — old Welsh, dweller in a valley or glen
Gwendolyn — old Welsh, white browed one
Gwynne — old Welsh, white or fair one
Gwynnith — old Welsh, white blessed one
Isolde — old Welsh, the fair one
Morgana — old Welsh, shore of the sea
Manora — old Welsh, white wave

Wynne — old Welsh, fair white
Welsh Names, Male:
Bevin — Welsh, son of the wellborn, youthful one
Carey — old Welsh, dweller at the castles
Clyde — Welsh, warm
Dewey — old Welsh, beloved one
Drew — old Welsh, wise one
Dylan — old Welsh, from the sea
Evan — gaelic, old Welsh, wellborn one
Gavin — old Welsh, from the hawk field
Glynn — old Welsh, irish, gaelic, dweller in a glen or valley
Gower — old Welsh, pure one
Griffith — old Welsh, fierce chief
Gwynn — old Welsh, fair blond one
Howell — old Welsh, little alert one
Ken — old Welsh, clear bright water
Lloyd — old Welsh, grey-haired one
Maddocks — old anglo-Welsh, the benefactor's son
Meredith — old Welsh, guardian from the sea
Morgan — old Welsh, white sea
Parry — old Welsh, son of Harry
Powell — old Welsh, son of Howell
Price — old Welsh, son of the ardent one
Reese — old Welsh, ardent one
Renfru — old Welsh, from the still river or channel
Romney — old Welsh, curving river
Tad — old Welsh, father
Trahern — old Welsh, super iron, super strength
Trent — latin/Welsh, torrent, rapid stream
Trustram — latin/Welsh, sorrowful labor
Tudor — old Welsh, a welsh variation of Theodore
Vaughn — old Welsh, small one
Wynn — old Welsh, fair white one

SPIRITUAL PYRAMID

The four sides represent will, faith, imagination, secrecy. The four corners plus the top represent the five elements. The tip represents action.(See Illustration)

THE ELEMENTS:

Fire is the south, air is the north, earth is the east, water is the west, ether and spirit are above and below.

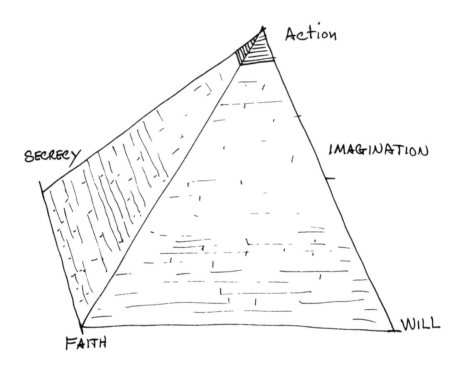

Action

IMAGINATION

SECRECY

WILL

FAITH

PYRAMID

Rhuddllom

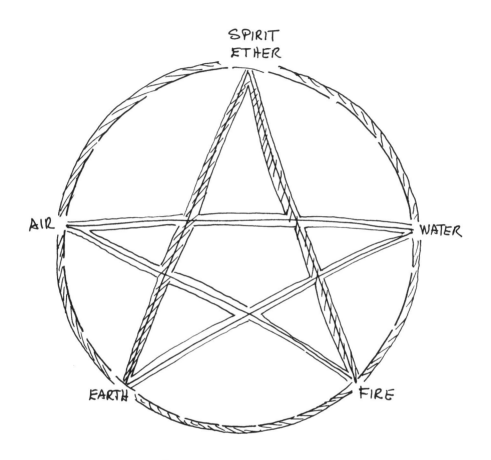

SPIRIT
ETHER

AIR

WATER

EARTH

FIRE

THE SPIRITUAL
PENTAGRAM

Rhuddlwm

195

Fire — passion, force, consuming, cleansing.

Air — catalyst for fire.

Water — purifier, will of being, wellspring, great womb, sea, receptive.

Earth — being, wisdom, experience cycles, change, seasons, birth, rebirth.

Ether — the framework, matrix, infinite. Build with the elements. Their language and symbolism are all around you.

(See Illustration)

THE PENTACLES:

The five points represent the five elements: air, earth, fire, water, spirit and ether (spirit and ether are the same). The circle represents power. The circle also represents the solar and lunar disks, the male and female principles.

(See Illustrations)

MAKING A WORKBOOK (BOOK OF SHADOWS):

The supplies are simple to acquire. Once you have the equipment it takes thirty minutes to put the book together. The style of book-binding that is used is based on Japanese rice paper books.

To begin you will need a flat surface, scissors, a stack of nonlined paper (can be three-hole-punched paper if you like), a hole puncher if you need it, leather or fabric for the cover of the book, plain un-holed paper for the inside covers, lightweight cardboard, white glue, a strip of fabric at least 16 inches by 3 inches, a half-yard of grosgreen ribbon or leather thong if you prefer, the same length, and a ruler.

1. Measure and cut two pieces of cardboard a quarter inch all around larger than the nonlined paper.
2. Measure and cut two pieces of leather or fabric for cover, one inch larger than the cardboard.
3. Measure and cut plain inside cover paper the exact same size as the cardboard.
4. Glue outside cover paper to cardboard and fold excess paper around to inside cover.
5. Glue inside cover paper to cardboard, folding excess half inch of paper in under.
6. Take the stack of plain paper. If not punched, add three holes evenly spaced.
7. Glue a loose strip of fabric around one long edge of stack to the top, bottom, front and back.

8. Punch holes in the cover of the book to match holes in the paper. Also make holes in the leather.
9. Place the paper between the covers.
10. String leather into the holes to bind the book.
11. The book will be secure at this point. Now take up cover and place ruler on the bound edge. Hold ruler firmly and bend back cover to reveal book, leaving a bend in the cover.

The earliest book I have dates from 15 years ago. The books are in very good shape and have withstood much use, although not misuse. I have used a variety of materials. My favorite is smooth leather and silkscreen paper. whatever appeals to you for a cover will work equally well. The book can be taken apart but not easily. I sometimes use rice paper in place of nonlined binder paper or typing paper. You can also use unused skin or airweight paper. The Japanese make this book with the paper folded in half and the cut edges to the binding. The fold is on the loose end and uncut. This is a nice touch and leaves a natural pocket between each page. The size of the book can vary with this process. I have made books the size of small pocket address books and all the way to the size of large binders. Decoration on the outside of the book is quite easy too. A glued applique is very simple and can have a unique effect. Also, a trim around the edges of the cover can add a distinctive air.

RITUAL:

Ritual is worship, a prescribed action whose purpose is to reach the subconscious mind and raise energy which is then directed to the purpose of the ritual. Ritual is one way of getting in touch with yourself. It's being in attunement, being aware. Ritual is human beings' approach to the unapproachable.

SALT CIRCLE:

Have ready in your circle sea salt, rain water, hyssop, candles and incense. Take a cleansing bath, have a clear head. Recite the Rede. Light candles with a lighted taper. Light the incense with a lighted taper. Have salt, water, and hyssop in bowls on the altar. Place right hand over salt, saying:

"Creature of earth, this charge I lay No phantom in thy presence stay Not in complete accord with me And as my will, so mote it be."

Take a pinch of salt, put it into the water, while making a banishing pentagram say:

"Creature of water, this charge I lay
No phantom in thy presence stay

197

Not in complete accord with me
And as my will, so mote it be."

Do the same with the hyssop.

Take the bowl of the salt to the east, going deosil, clockwise. Cast a circle of salt. Go around three times. While doing so, say:

"Creature of earth where you are cast
No spell nor adverse purpose last
Not in complete accord with me,
And as my will, so mote it be."

Take a bowl of water with salt and hyssop in it, go to the east, sprinkle water around the circle three times and say,

"Earth and water, where you are cast,
No spell or adverse purpose last,
Not in complete accord with me,
And as my will, so mote it be."

Take the candle around the circle once and repeat.

Take incense around the circle once and repeat.

The circle is now ready for use for any purpose you desire. When finished, thank any you feel have attended, dismiss them to go in peace. The circle is then open.

RITUAL SEALING:

This is done when you cannot take a ritual bath or when going into a situation that could be dangerous.

Sealing of the orifices - use sabbat oil. With oil on finger make banishing pentagram over eyes, ears, nose, vagina or penis, anus, and say:

"Blessed be my eyes, that they may see the light.
Blessed be my ears, that they may hear truth.
Blessed be my nose, that they may breath your essence.
Blessed be my mouth, that I may say the sacred name.
Blessed be my sex, which brings forth life.
Blessed be my anus, that my body be made pure.
So mote it be."

This ritual seals the body so that nothing can enter.

RITUAL BATH:

Mix: 3 pinches of sea salt, rose hops, rosemary, mint, thyme, verbain, hyssop, lavender flowers, comfrey leaves, comfrey root, camomile flowers, valerian. Mix all together. Place in a cloth bag or square of white cloth about four inches square. Tie with a red yarn. Bring a liter and a half of water to boil, not in a metal pan. Add herb bag. Lower heat. Simmer 5-10 minutes. Fill tub with water. Place candles and incense in the room. When the brew is ready add to bath water. Light a pleasing incense and candle and have sea salt in the bath area. Have sabbat oil in the bath area. Hold candle in left hand, make banishing pentagram over the water. Say:

"O water, I exorcise thee with fire in preparation for my rebirth. Be thou purified in the name of Cerridwen."

Do the same with salt, which is earth, incense, which is air, and sabbat oil, which is the holy oil, three drops. Enter water, saying:

"O bless me mother, and make me pure. Cleanse my body, spirit and mind. Make me worthy to be your kind. So mote it be."

Meditate on candle while in the bath. Do mental and emotional cleansing. Use once a month. This is going to the full. Do not use on dark of Moon.

RITUAL BATH — Short Version:

Light incense, take a lit white taper in your left hand, and with the right hand pass incense over the water in a banishing pentagram. Sprinkle three handfuls of salt into the water and three drops of anointing oil, saying:

"O water, I exorcise thee with fire, earth, air, and holy oil which is sacred to the gods. Be thou purified in the name of Aranrhod. O blessed mother of all living, purify and make holy this ritual bath which I am about to take in honor of thee, that I might come before thee in pureness of mind, body, soul and heart. In thy name, Arianrhod, I do ask it."

Make an invoking pentagram over the water with the right index finger, saying:

"So mote it be."

(See Illustration)

SLEEP CIRCLE:

Mentally cast a circle about your sleeping area, envisioning a blue flame marking the circle. Draw a banishing pentagram at your head, each side, feet, and circle the pentagram thus:

(See Illustration)

See it as a blue flame as you draw it. Mentally assure yourself that you are now protected within your circle.

PETITIONING ALTAR:

To open:

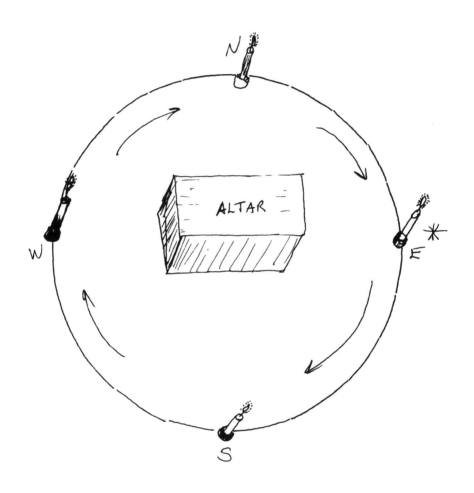

Casting a Circle
o Wicca a

Rhuddlom

Light a taper, make a banishing pentagram with the taper, then
seal. Make an invoking pentagram with the taper, then seal.
Light candle to the goddess, lady. Say:
"My liege, my lady."
Light candle for the god, lord and say:
"Hail, Cerunnos."
Light candle for the petitioner, request. Say:
"Hail, Salamander."
To close:
Make banishing pentagram over each.

WEEKLY CIRCLE:

High priestess prepares ritual bath and bathes, followed by the high
priest, followed by all third levels, all second levels, and other
levels. The high priestess forms the circle and purifies it. The
grove is greeted and purified. Invocation of the mighty one
is given, invocation of the goddess and god is given, all dance
thrice around the altar with the athames. The priestess draws
down the moon,(except on dark of the moon,) while the grove
dances with athames.

SYMBOLIC GREAT RITE:

Priestess holds cup of wine, priest lowers his athame into it saying:
*"As the cup is to the female, so the athame is to the male, and
joined together they be one in truth."*
The priestess gives all a sip and drains the cup. All face north and
say the following:
*"Answer us, o ancient horned one, provender and power are thine.
Hear and answer, gracious goddess, grant us laughter, wit and wine.
Descend on us o thou of blessings, come amongst us, make us glad,
Thou art chief of all creation, why o why should be sad?
Beam on us oh joyous greenwood, banish heavy-hearted hate, Ac-
cept our craft, o greatest mother, let cheerful brightness be
our fate. So mote it be."*
All remove robes and place around the altar. All work magic and
participate in a feast of cakes and wine. All bid farewell to
the mighty one and the priestess closes the circle.

DRAWING DOWN THE MOON — WEEKLY CIRCLE:

After invocation of Mighty Ones and the Goddess and the God,
all join hands holding the athame in the right hand, and part-

ner's wrist with left hand. Circle the altar deosil with a quick walking step three times. Stop. The M iden will now pick up the maiden candle and ring the bell hrice. All will start again to circle slowly except the maiden, and summoner, who will hold the book, and the High Priest and the High Priestess. The High Priest and High Priestess will hold their athame points together upon the waxing moon and the pentacle, and intone:

"IO, IO, IO, IO, Evohe."

They will now put down their athames and face each other, with the High Priestess at the West. The High Priest takes the moon crown and places it upon the High Priestess's head. She assumes the goddess position. The High Priest picks up the pentacle and touches it to her forehead. Right foot, left hand, right hand, left foot, forehead. All invoking pentagram, saying:

"I invoke thee and call upon thee, oh mighty mother of us all, Bring all fruitfulness by stem and by root, by leaf and by bud, by flower and by fruit, I call upon thee by life and by love. Descend into the body of (name), thy priestess and servant, Hear with her ears, speak with her tongue, touch with her hands, and kiss with her lips, That thy servants may be fulfilled."

The High Priest kneels at her feet with the pentacle and says:

"Listen to the words of the Great Mother, who was of old called amongst men by many names."

All here stop circling and listen. The High Priestess speaks, saying:

"All ye assembled at my shrine, mother darkness and divine, All ye assembled in my sight, bow before my spirit bright."

All bow.

as is

"Aphrodite, Arianrhod, lover of the horned god, Mighty queen of witchery and night, I am named of old by men, Artemis and Cerridwen. Summerland's mistress, Gwynned's queen, Ye who would ask of me a rune, or who would ask of me a boon, Meet me in some secret glade, dance my round, in greenwood shade. Work my holy mysteries, ye who are fain to sorcery, I bring ye secrets yet unknown, No more shall ye know misery, who give true worship unto me. Ye who tread my round at night, come all ye equal to the right, In token that

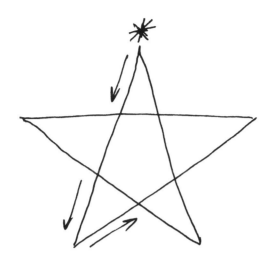

The Earth Invoking
Pentagram

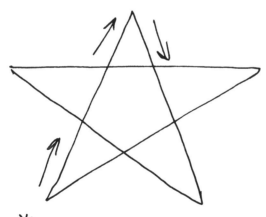

The Earth Banashing
Pentagram

Rhuddlwm

203

ye be truly free, I teach you the mystery of rebirth, work ye my mysteries in mirth, Heart to heart and hand to hand, thou art the wise throughout the land. I bring ye ecstasy on earth, for I am the circle of rebirth, I ask no sacrifice but due bow, no other law but love I know, All things living are mine own, by not but love may I be known. To me they come, to me they go.''

The High Priest stands and salutes with his athame saying with all:

''Bloddwed, Arianrhod, Cerridwen, hail goddess, queen of night, Bloddwed, Arianrhod, Cerridwen, hail goddess, queen of light.''

PAGAN CIRCLE OPENING:

Let all be clean before the gods, being properly prepared. Purify each other with scourge or cord, three, seven, nine, twenty-one, forty times. Give kiss. High Priest lights two white candles and places them on the altar. Then place a white candle on each corner or point of the magic circle. Purify the water and salt. First place one of the athame in water with the right hand and pronounce:

''I exorcise the, oh creature of water, that thou cast out from thee all impurities and uncleanliness and the spirits of phantasms. In the names of Aradia and Cernunnos.''

Touching salt with the athame, pronounce:

''Blessings be upon thee, oh creature of salt. Let all malignity and hindrance pass henceforth and let all good enter in. But ever be mindful that as water purifies the body so does the salt purify the soul. Wherefore do I bless thee in the names of Aradia and Cerunnos, that thou may aid me.''

Then transfer three measures of salt with the tip of the athame into the water and stir in a clockwise direction three times. The athame is now ready and purified.

Draw a nine-foot magic circle, or smaller or larger, as required, with athame, commencing in the east and ending in the east. The circle must be cut in an unbroken line. Then return to the altar facing the north. Take up the water with the right hand, transfer it to your left, go to the east and sprinkle with the fingers in the east, south, west, and north, finish in the east. Return to the altar. Take up the incense and censor in the right hand. Repeat motions, censing circle before returning to the altar.

Celebrants then anoint the opposite sex with water, salt, and the one-two-three triangle and cense likewise. Take your bell in the right hand. Place it in the left hand. Take athame in the right hand and go to the east and salute in the following manner. Athame to lips, straight out above your eye level, back to the lips, then right side down with outstretched arm back to the carry position before the right breast. Cut large, clear pentacle, then pronounce:

"Hear ye, oh mighty ones, dread lords of the Watchtowers of the East, I, (name), priestess and witch, do summon you, and I do petition your presence at this our meeting. Let our circle be guarded and our rites be witnessed."

Strike the bell with the athame once in the east, south, west, and north, finally giving your salute in the east. All present salute. The circle is now perfect.

Dance around the circle, high priestess leading chanting of the ancient call. Dance and chant. Open cirle with the ancient call:

as is

"Eko, Eko, Azurak,
Eko, Eko, Zamilak,
Eko, Eko, Aradia,
Eko, Eko, Cernunnos
Bagabi lacha bachabe
Lamac chai achababe
Kerellyos cahi achababe
Lamac lamac bachalyas
Cabahagy sabalyos
Baryolos
Lagoz athame cahyolas
Samahac et famolas
Hurrah!"

To close or dismiss the circle, with athame go to the east. Salute, then all present salute. Then the celebrant or High   Priestess says:

"Hear ye, oh mighty ones, we thank you for your attendance, and ere ye depart for your lovely realms, we bid you hail and farewell."

All present repeat:

"Hail and farewell."

and point athames high. Repeat at other quarters, south, west, north, and finish in the east.

CASTING THE CIRCLE — WICCA:

The sacred grove of Arianrhod and Gwydion, located between the worlds of the visible and the invisible, is a meeting place of gods and humankind. It is generally nine feet in diameter although it may be of any convenient size. The circle binds the magical power raised within it, and only the Wiccans themselves can release it. The gate is always north or northeast. The altar is always facing north. It's southern edge is aligned with the Watchtowers of the east and west. Beginning in the east with a pole, athame or sword, draw a circle deosil three times, intoning,

"Rama, rama, rama, Tho".

Purification: Starting in the east, sprinkle salt deosil around the circle once, saying:

"With the salt of earth do I purify this sacred grove."

Do the same with the waters of life and sweet air (which is the incense).

ENTERING THE CIRCLE: Cut a gateway with your athame at the northeast and admit all of the opposite sex with a kiss on both cheeks. Each one will give a level password.

First is *" perfect love and perfect knowledge."*

Second, *"All hail be to the breast of the moon, the power of the goddess."*

Third, *"Enjoined together we are one in truth."*

At the meeting of two who are initiated Say:

"Blessed be and Merry meet."

THE PURIFICATION:

This is the purification: the pentagram followed by an ankh, drawn on the forehead with the oil. When all are within, the gateway is sealed. Closing the circle, take the maiden candle deosil around the circle starting in the east, saying:

as is

"Fire race the circle round, let it fade beneath the ground. By the holy flame the circle disappears and can be seen no more. All things are as they were since the beginning of time. So mote it be."

Anyone who breaks the circle during the rites must perform the banishing process, recast, repurify, the entire circle, and reinvoke the mighty ones. Anyone wishing to leave the circle during the rites must cut an X with their athames and then reseal it. And this also applies when they re-enter. Always remember, the circle is there until it is ritually dissolved. However, if it is unproperly broken, there will be a leak of power, and this is not good if magic is being worked.

THE RUNE DANCE CHANT:

as is

> "Canu, Canu, Durionnos, Canu
> D'awnsio, d'awnsio, Arwaen y ros
> Y 'ngo levni'r bel levad dlos
> Lapus ydymni
> Pawb o honom sytyn llon
> Hebungofid don ei fron
> Canu, D'awnsio, aryton
> Dedwyt ydmni"

> "Singing, singing through the night, dancing, dancing with our might, Where ye moon ye moor doth light, happy ever we. One and all of merry mein, without sorrow are we seen, Singing, dancing on ye green, gladsome ever we."

THE CIRCLE DANCE CHANT:

as is

> "Darksome night and shining moon, east then south then west then north,
> Hearken to ye witches' rune, here we come to call thee forth.
> Earth and water, air and fire, wand and pentacle and sword,
> Hearken ye unto my desire, hearken ye unto my word.
> Cup and censor, rod and knife, power of the witches' blade,
> Waken all ye unto life, come ye as the charm is made.
> Queen of heaven, queen of hell, horned hunter of the night,
> Lend thy power to the spell, work my will be magic rite.
> By all the powers of land and sea, by all the might of moon and sun.
> As I do will so mote it be, chant the spell and be it done."

INVOCATION TO THE HORNED GOD:

"By the flame that burneth bright, oh horned one,
We call thy name into the night, oh ancient one,
Thee we invoke by the moonlit sea,
By the standing stone and the twisted tree.
The we invoke, we are together thine owm,
By the nameless shore forgotten and alone,
Come with a round of the dance is trod,

Horn and hoof of the goat-foot god,
By the moonlit meadow on dusky hill,
When the hotted wood is hushed and still,
Come to the charm of the chanted prayer,
As the moon bewitches the midnight air,
Invoke thy powers that potent bide,
In shining stream and secret tide,
In fiery flame, by starlit pale,
In shadowy host that rides the gale,
And by the ferndrakes fairy haunted,
Of forests wild and woods enchanted,
Come, oh come to the heartbeat's drum,
Come to us who gather below
When the rude white moon is climbling slow,
Through the stars to the heaven's height,
We hear thy hooves on the winds of night,
As black tree branches shake and sigh,
By joy and terror we know thee nigh.
We speak this spell by power unlocks
At solstice, sabbat and equinox"

FERTILITY RITUAL:
Within the circle the High Priestess draws the invoking pentagram upon the naked man with the wand. The High Priest does the same with the woman. The couple now join hands and leap over the flaming cauldron thrice. The High Priestess then holds forth the rod and the woman steps over it. It is advisable that this be done on a night when the woman is in her fertile period. It should be done just before the closing of the circle so that the couple can go directly home to perform the Great Rite.

SAINING: (Presenting the child and naming it)
The parents may bring the child to be named before the Mighty Ones. This suffices for the first degree. When the child reaches thirteen second degree will be conferred if it is so desired by the child to continue in the craft and they have done the work. The child is presented to the High Priestess and Priest by the parents. An invoking pentagram is drawn on the forehead with the anointing oil by the priestess and priest, then with water, then with salt. An invoking pentagram is made be-

208

fore the child (or over an infant) with the candle and incense.
The High Priestess then presents the child or infant to the goddess:

"My Lady Arianrhod, I present to thee, (name)."

They bow. The High Priest presents the child to the god.

"My Lord Hu, I present to thee (name)."

They bow. Both High Priestess and High Priest now take the infant to the four quarters, saying at each:

"Mighty Ones of the east (south, west, north), we present to thee (name)."

All bow.

To test the child to see if it is a changeling, suspend a lead bead attached to the green cord above the child. If it swings in a widdershins circle the child is of fairy blood and must be trained properly, because it has the power.

BLESSINGS OF THE WATCHTOWERS:

The High Priest holds out his hands to the east and says:

"Oh, great sun, source of light and wisdom, may thy lifegiving rays shine forth to enlighten thy creatures, and nourish that which is reborn. That by the call of the wild owl in the night we may rejoice in thy return at dawning."

South:

"Oh, golden lights of the flaming one, thou art the glowing eyes of a thousand cats, the spotted serpent who is sacred to the goddess of retribution, quicken that which is reborn, that strength may banish weakness."

West:

"Oh, sacred moon, fertilize the blessed earth with thy rays of silver, that new life which stirs within the womb of the great mother may burst forth in ever increasing abundance."

North:

"Oh, mighty Hu, consort of Arianrhod, and great horned god of the witches, on thy sacred horns do we place our most grievous afflictions. Toss them to the four winds of the world that they may be as dust beneath thy cloven hoofs. Ride the mighty north winds to the Summerlands where thou art guardian of all who await rebirth among us."

OBSERVANCE OF THE SUNRISE:

Face east, light incense but not candles, hold a glass of cold, pure water in your hands in front of you and say:

"Hail to thee o Lugh, thou art adored by me when thy beauty is

before mine eyes and when thy shining rays fall upon my body, that goes forth in peace and thy bode and my heart is glad. Thy foes are cast down. The never-resting stars sing hymns of praise unto thee. The guardians of the east, the south, the west and the north praise thee. Thou risest and thou shinest upon the face of the Mother. Thou who art crowned Lord of Light, make thou glorious my shining form. Make thou strong my soul. Thou art worshipped in peace, Lord of the gods. Thou art exalted by reason of thy wondrous works. Blessed be thy sacred light."

FULL MOON FESTIVAL (ESBAT):

The High Priestess casts the circle and purifies it. The candles are lit. All enter and are greeted in turn. All are asked the passwords, all are anointed on the forehead. The High Priest, High Priestess, Maiden and Candlebearer assume their proper positions, west, east, south, and north. All the grove face east and say:

"All hail thee, o guardian of the watchtower of the east. Thou art lord within the realms of Lugh. Golden bright and wise as the owl, join the children of Diana within the sacred grove."

The grove faces the south. All say:

"All hail to thee, o guardian of the watchtower of the south. Thou art lord within the realm of the serpent. Fiery bright and quick as the cat, join the children of Diana within the sacred grove."

The grove faces the west. All say:

"All hail to thee, o guardian of the watchtower of the west. Thou art lord within the realm of the Lady. Silver bright and triple starred, join the children of Diana within the sacred grove."

The grove faces the north. All say:

"All hail thee, o guardian of the watchtower of the north. Thou art lord within the realm of the horned one. Shining bright, swift as the wind, join the children of Diana within the sacred grove."

The Maiden rings the ritual bell three times and replaces it upon the altar. The High Priest and High Priestess step in front of the altar and place their athame blades upon the moon pentacle and give and invocation. The moon crown is consecrated if it is to be worn, and all assume their former position. The High Priestess gives the charge of the Goddess. This

210

is followed by the response of the High Priest. The High Priestess proceeds to consecrate the salt.

High Priestess:

"Blessed be ye salt of earth, sacred for to keep her way, Sprinkle round about ye hearth, keep ye spirits at their bay."

The High Priestess now censes the circle, east, west, south and north. Say at each watchtower:

"Fragrance of ye air doth rise, sweet thy goddess and thy god, Wondrous scent, seek ye the skies, blessed be ye wand and rod."

The High Priestess strikes the ground three times with the rod, and then holds the wand aloft while the High Priest censes it. The High Priestess raises the bowl of water and says:

"Blessed be ye water cool, life from birth and life to tomb, Gather round ye sacred pool, bless ye lady's fruitful womb."

The High Priestess sprinkles a few drops of water in front of the altar. The Candlebearer takes a taper, candle from the altar, and lights it with the elf fire, or he may light it from one of the altar candles. He hands the lit taper to the High Priest. The High Priestess places the blade of her athame in the flame while the High Priest says:

"Blessed be ye fire bright, light of gods and light of light, Quick ye flames, dance in the night, blessed be ye sacred knife."

The High Priest now proceeds to the east watchtower with the taper and says:

"The children of light greet thee with light."

He continues around the watchtowers, east, south, west and north, he hands the taper to the Maiden who returns it to the altar. The High Priestess places the chalice of wine upon the moon pentacle and dips the blade of the athame into it slightly, saying:

"Blessed be the fruit of the vine, in Diana's name we shall drink and make merry."

The grove says: *"Blessed be."*

The High Priestess and the Maiden hold the plate of cakes between them and the High Priestess says:

"Here the Sabbat cakes of corn, baked upon the hearth, Blessed be Diana's feast, dance and join in mirth."

The High Priestess and the Maiden have just consecrated the cakes. The High Priestess and Maiden hold the bowl of honey between them while the High Priestess says:

211

"Here we bring honey sweet, gathered from the sacred grove, Danzio, danzio, little bees, keep to your hives and do not roam."

The grove says:

"Blessed be."

The High Priestess now offers a sip of wine to the High Priest. He in turn offers a sip of wine to her. The chalice is then passed around the circle, beginning with the Maiden. Following this the circle dance is performed. It may be with joined hands or single file. If it is single file the High Priestess leads the dance, with the High Priest at the end. All silently make a wish upon the moon and then sing, to the tune of "London Bridge:"

"Dance the full moon round and round, round and round, round and round, Let the moon shine on the ground, for our Lady."

"Lift your feet up from the ground, from the ground, from the ground, As we dance the moon around, for our Lady."

Repeat the dance and song until exhausted, and then all fall to the ground, like in the nursery rhyme, all fall down, at a signal from the High Priestess. Have cakes and wine in the circle, sitting on the ground. When finished with these and all magic, the High Priest will give the watchtowers release:

"We thank thee, o guardian of the watchtower of the east (south, west, north), for having joined with Diana's children within the sacred grove. May we depart in peace, love and harmony until we shall meet again."

The grove says:

"So mote it be."

The High Priest continues around the circle in this fashion. The Maiden extinguishes the watchtower candles as each guardian is released. All will now depart the circle except the High Priestess, who remains to extinguish the altar candles, left to right, and then takes the Maiden's candle and walks deosil around the circle once, saying:

"By the hold flame this circle disappears to be found no more. All things are as they were from the beginning of time."

The salt is scattered, the four winds are sprinkled upon the threshold. Leftover cakes are crumbled and put out for the birds.

THE SUN (SABBAT) FESTIVALS:

The festivals are a time of worship. We return energy to the universe

212

during a festival. They are celebrations, thanksgivings for what we have or hope to receive.

The Festivals of the Year:

Samhain — October 31. The festival of the dead. The God presides. At this time the mighty dead can return to earth to be with us. It's symbol is happiness. It is the death of the year at which we look forward to the sun's rebirth at Yule. A black altar cloth should be used, embroidered with constellation symbols.

Yule — December 22, approximation. The rebirth of the sun god. We greet the beginning of the new year.

Olimelc — This is Candlemas, also called Imbolc — February 2. The festival of the flame. We prepare light so that our goddess may find her way out of the darkness and return to us. We bid farewell to the horned god.

Spring Equinox — March 20 or thereabouts. The festival of The Lady. The goddess presides. We welcome the goddess as Bloduewedd and bless her coming fertility.

Beltane — April 30. The festival of fertility. Summer begins. It is the time for planting, and we dance to ensure fertility.

Midsummer — June 22. We dance and make merry in thanks for the crops that are growing. We are of the trees.

Lugnasad, also known as Lammas — July 31. The festival of the crops. The Goddess presides, as we celebrate in preparation of the harvest.

Autumn Equinox — September 22 or thereabouts. The harvest festival.

Festivals in Irish: Samhain — October 31 — ruled by the male aspect, female aspect rests. Also known as Hallowmas or Samhain. Beginning of the Wiccan year. Time when the two worlds draw closest together, dead and living. Feast of the horned god. Waning aspect of the year.

Yule — An Fheill Shlinnen

Candlemas — Imbolg

Spring Equinox — Cothadthrath

May Eve — Beltuinn

Midsummer Eve — Grainstad

August Eve — Lugnasadh

Fall Equinox — Cothadthrath.

BASIC SABBAT RITUAL:

The High Priest or Maiden shall set up the altar and cauldron, light the candles and the incense. During the spring and summer the High Priestess will cast the circle, during the autumn and winter the High Priest. All are admitted. Invoke the Mighty Ones. After each invocation the High Priestess or Maiden will knock thrice upon the ground with a rod and all will say:

"So mote it be."

The High Priest always invokes the Mighty Ones.

Drawing down the moon at Full moon: The High Priest will now kneel before the cauldron, the High Priestess will hold the horn helmet to his head, and he will cast into it glowing charcoal, the handful of magical catalyst. The High Priestess will say:

> *"Out of the north, oh mighty of days, kneel in front of the cauldron blaze, Join the goddess, thy lady above, Join the children of laughter and love."*

He crosses his hands in the god position, holding the athame in one hand and the wand in the other. He stands and says:

"Answer us, oh ancient horned one, provender and power are thine. Hear and answer gracious goddess, grant us laughter, wit and wine. Descend on us, oh thou, of blessings, come among us, make us glad. Since thou are chief of all creation, why, oh why should we be sad? Beam on us, on joyous Bacchus, banish heavy-hearted hate. Accept our craft, oh Great Mother, let cheerful brightness be our fate. So mote it be."

SAMHAIN SABBAT:

After the invocation of the Mighty Ones the High Priest will face north and raise his athame. He will then make an invoking pentagram and intone slowly:

"Io, Evohe,
Hearken unto me all ye mighty dead
Ye who were of merry mein
We bid thee come forth and join us on this holy night
> *Io, Evohe."*

The grove then says:
'Io, Evohe,
Blessed be,
Io, Evohe."

After the honey is consecrated the High Priest blesses the dead, saying:

214

> *"Oh, mighty Hu of the Summerlands,*
> *Guardian of our beloved dead and keeper of souls,*
> *We pour forth our love upon those who are in thy keeping.*
> *Blessed be all those who have gone before us into thy realm.*
> *So mote it be."*

Coven:

"So mote it be."

Any form of divination and necromancing can be worked after this. After the feast the High Priest gives leave of souls. All face north and make the banishing pentagram and hold up their athames in salute. The Priest says:

"Blessed to thee, oh spirits of the Summerland, We thank thee for having joined with us at this holy sabbat, May we depart in peace, love and harmony until again we meet, Guard us, thy children, until thou art reborn again in love, Blessed be, Io evohe, blessed be."

Grove:

"Io evohe, blessed be, Io evohe, blessed be."

SAMHAIN VARIATION ON CIRCLE RITES:

The moon invocation and charge are omitted.

Evocation of the dead (to be given following the invocation of the watchtowers). The High Priest faces the north, raising his athame, and makes the sign of the invoking pentagram, saying:

"I O I O I O Evohe"

"Hearken unto me, all ye spirits who walk the Hallow's night. Ye who are of merry mein, we bid come forth. Speak to us of things forbidden and unknown. If ye be worthy, then may ye join us in this sacred grove of Pan!"

"I O I O I O I O Evohe."

Grove:

"Blessed be. I O Evohe. Blessed be. Blessing of the dead and graveyards may be done in the graveyard. If done in circle, the blessing is given following consecration of the honey."

Grove:

"O Pan of the Summerland, guardian of our beloved dead and keeper of souls, we pour forth our love upon those who are in thy keeping. Blessed be all those that have preceded us into thy realm. Blessed be the resting place of their bones. May they be kept from the thief who lurks in the tomb. May all those who are not bones or dust beyond their time be returned to thee by the fire of purification. So mote it be."

Following the blessing of the dead, the Grove joins in performing

215

acts of necromancy, such as automatic writing (not ouija board), crystal gazing, tarot, trance, the spirit ring, and others. A member should be appointed to take notes of the proceedings.

Leave of Souls:

This is the form following necromancy. All members face north. All make the sign of the banishing pentagram in the air with their athames and say:

"Blessed be thee, o spirits of the Summerland, We thank thee for having joined with us the Sabbats of Pan. May ye depart in peace, love and harmony until we meet again. Guide the children of the Wicca until thou art reborn in love. Blessed be. I O Evohe. Blessed Be."

Special projects for All Hallows would be: carve pumpkins and gourds, prepare pumpkin seeds for roasting and eating or for necklaces, make new brooms, visit and old graveyard and pay hommage to the dead, make an effigy of Old Jack.

The Dumb Supper:

This is merely the usual grove feast taken in silence with a place set for the spirit of a deceased loved one.

Dance of the Dead:

This is a circle dance performed thusly. The High Priest leads the dance with his arms crossed upon his chest. The High Priestess is the last in line. Each person places his or her left hand on the shoulder of the person in front and lets the right arm hang by his or her side. It is a shuffling sort of dance performed deosil as they all intone:

"I O I O I O I O Evohe, I O I O I O I O Evohe."

"Spirits of the dead we raise, join us by the cauldron blaze, Elves and gnomes and goblins all, heed the witches' Samhain call."

This is repeated over and over until all are weary and stop at the signal from the High Priest. It is not needful to fall to the ground with this dance.

The High priest then intones:

"O great god, 'tis by your hand, near the lovely Summerlands, That we part from earthly strife, and await some future life. Bless our loved one sleeping here, bless the soul we hold so dear, End of the life we'll meet and each life must be more sweet."

FESTIVAL OF LIGHTS:

December 13 We welcome the Great Mother in her role as Goddess of Winter as she comes riding through the sky from the frozen north in her silver crescent chariot which is drawn by eight white horses. She is robed in furs and carries sprigs of holly and mistletoe. During the day or evening of the 13th decorate the home with colored lights, garlands, greens, or whatever symbols of the season suits you. Before midnight the witches assemble at the grove. Each brings something to eat. Red and green candles should be lit around the covensite, grovesite, or covenstead, four white candles at the four watchtowers of the circle, and red or green candles on the altar. Sprigs of holly, mistletoe, and boughs of fir and evergreen are placed around and on the altar. A pine or balsam incense is burned. The pine tree is sacred to Pan.

The High Priestess casts the circle and she and the High Priest enter it. The High Priestess stands in the west, holding the rod. The High Priest stands in the northern gateway and greets the members with a kiss as they enter. As all face north the High Priest lights the cauldron fire. The High Priest stands in the east. The High Priestess circles around three times with the rod and all intone:

"Ceridwen, Ceridwen, Ceridwen.
Ceridwen, Ceridwen, Ceridwen.
Ceridwen, Ceridwen, Ceridwen."

The Maid takes the rod from the High Priestess and lays it at the foot of the altar. The High Priestess assumes the pentacle position in front of the cauldron facing north and gives the invocation:

"We bid thee welcome, o gracious Goddess,
Heed the light that beckons thee.
As thy crescent rides from the northlands,
Over the frozen land and sea."

"Heark unto the song we sing thee,
Here the bough and holly grow,
Now the ancient Horned One rises,
Greets his Queen of winter snow.
Bless the season, First Lady,
As the cauldron fires burn,
Do aid the great god in its force,
As the wheel begins to turn."

All members now join hands within the circle and begin to dance deosil with the High Priest in the lead and the High Priestess at the end. Now join hands. They sing as they go, to the tune of "Here we go round the mulberry bush." All:

"Here we go dance the circle round,
Round and round, round and round,
Here we dance the circle round,
With the Lord and Lady.

Lift your feet up off the ground,
Round and round, round and round,
Lift your feet up off the ground,
For the Lord and Lady.''

Repeat this one faster and faster until all collapse in a heap at the signal from the High Priest.

Close the circle, toast the God and Goddess with Wassail, sing pagan carols, and feast.

Some pagan carols: "Wassail, Wassail," "Deck the Halls," "The Boar's Head Carol," and "Good King Wenceslas," and others of that source. If there is any magic on the agenda insert it here.

YULE SABBAT:

December 21 — ruled by the male aspect — Winter Solstice Following *"Answer us, oh ancient horned one,''* the High Priest invokes the god:

"Hail to thee, Sir Cernunnos, great god of Arianrhod's children.
Come ye forth from the rays of the newborn sun.
Seek ye the forest of pine.
Join us that we may know of thy birth
Teach ye us the mysteries of the four winds, the pipes and the bow.
Take ye our tribulations upon thy lusty horns.
Toss them to the four winds of the world.
Hear us, oh Cernunnos.
Make merry with us and herald thy presence with the sounds of the horn, The scents of the pine and the bellow of the raging stag.''

Following the honey, all will take a candle and light it from the High Priest's candle. The High Priest will face the east and all will circle slowly around him deosil three times while he says over and over:

"Blessed be the newborn lord of light. Cernunnos is the sun and he is reborn. The children of light greet thee with light.''

Now all in turn place their candles on the Yule wheel, each one saying as he places the candle:

"Blessed be the lord of light. Io evohe, blessed be the newborn sun.''

If possible after the circle the vines and trees are blessed with wine by the High Priest, saying:

"Blessed be ye vine and tree, the newborn sun shall quicken thee.''

Recipe for Wassail:

One gallon of cider

6 cored apples
4 sticks of cinnamon
1/2 tsp. ground mace
1/2 tsp. ground ginger
1/4 tsp. ground allspice
3 whole cloves
1 tsp. ground nutmeg
1/2 cup raw sugar
2 quarts ale

Have everything at room temperature. Put all except the ale into a large kettle and bring it to boil. Boil very slowly until spices are blended and apples are tender. Cover partially, add more cider if necessary When strong strain into mugs about three quarters full. Fill the rest with ale, stir and serve.

YULE VARIATION ON CIRCLE RITES:

The moon invocation and charges are omitted. The special invocation of Pan is recited with the High Priest following, *"Answer us, o ancient . . ."*

High Priest:

"Hail to thee, o Pan, great god of Diana's children. Seek ye the rays of the newborn sun and come forth from thy forest of pine. Join us in the sacred grove that we may know thy pleasure. Teach us the mysteries of the four winds, the pines, and the bough, and when the season of mis-fortune has befallen us, take thou our tribulations upon thy lusty horns and toss them to the four winds of the four watchtowers. Let them become as dust beneath thy cloven hoofs. Here us, o Pan, ride the great north wind, join us in the sacred grove and let us make merry. Herald thy presence with the scent of the pine and the sound of the racing stag. I O Evohe, Blessed be, I O Evohe."

Following the consecration of the honey, the High Priest and all the grove face east as the High Priest recites the blessing of the newborn sun.

High Priest:

"Blessed be thee, o Lord of Light, Lucifer is the sun and Rah glorifies him. Praise be the newborn sun who has been released from the night mother's gentle arms. The Children of Light greet thee with light."

The Yule log is now lit with neat fire or elf fire, if there be a hearth. If there is no hearth the log is set with 13 candles and the members light one candle each, beginning with the High Priest who lights the

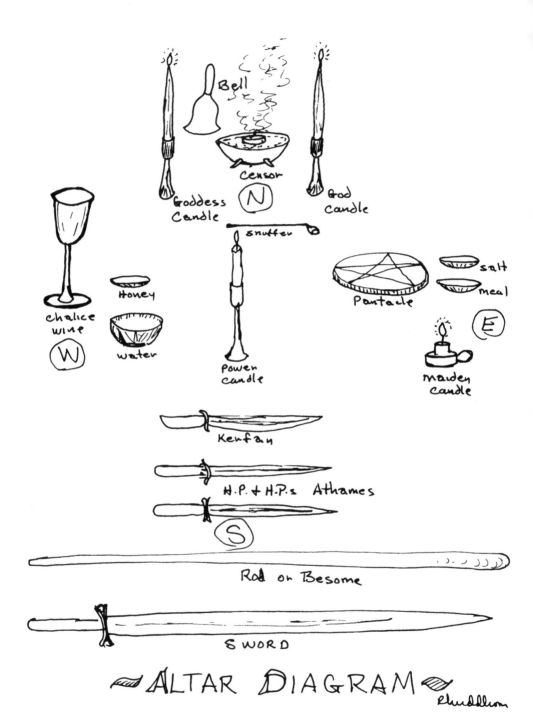

Bell

Censor

N

Goddess Candle

God Candle

snuffer

chalice wine

W

Honey

water

Power candle

Pantacle

salt

meal

E

maiden candle

Kenfan

H.P. & H.P.s Athames

S

Rod or Besome

SWORD

ALTAR DIAGRAM

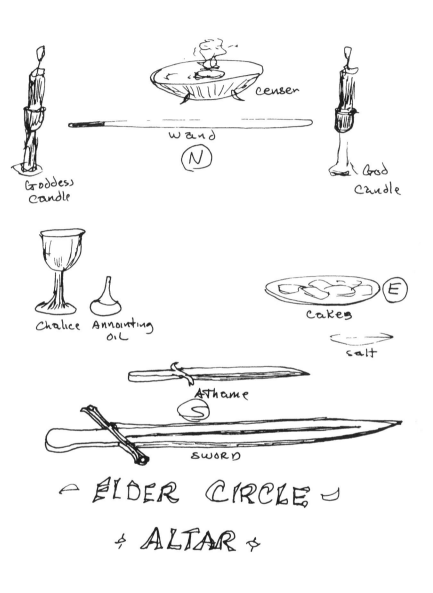

censer

wand

(N)

Goddess
Candle

God
Candle

Chalice   Annointing
Oil

Cakes   (E)

salt

Athame

(S)

SWORD

ELDER CIRCLE

ALTAR

candle on the right, and the High Priestess, who lights the first candle on the left. The others follow in their turn. When the candles all are lit the grove together shouts:

"I O Evohe, Blessed be the newborn sun."

All now join hands and dance the witches' wheel dance deosil around the cauldron, singing to the tune of Good King Wenceslas:

"Here we spin the wheel around, at the Winter Solstice
While the log burns brightly down, steal a mistletoe kiss,
Hail the newborn sun's return from the mother's bower,
We will give the wheel a turn, raising Wiccan power."

The dance may be continued until all are weary. The feast of cakes and wassail follows. The log is allowed to burn itself out or the candles to burn down completely. Upon leaving the circle a blessing of vines and trees with wine is performed, the High Priest in the lead, sprinkling the bushes and saying:

"Blessed be ye vine (tree, or bush). The newborn sun shall quicken thee again. The grove repeats this after him."

CIRCLE OF ELDERS:
December 23

All of the third level or degree shall assemble to adore the sacred goddess. All shall take the ritual bath and come naked into the circle. The High Priestess will draw the circle around all present and then purify it with salt and water and incense. (See Illustration) She will then invoke the Mighty Ones, saying at each point:

"Thus do I summon, stir and call thee up, oh Mighty Ones of the East (South, West, North) to witness our rites and guard this circle."

All will salute and say:

"So mote it be."

She will now anoint the High Priest with a banishing pentagram on the forehead with oil and then touch him on the forehead, chest and genitals with the wand. He will do the same with her. This is the purification. He will then purify all women and she all men. All will now kneel facing north, their athames on the ground in front of them, the blades turned toward the north. The High Priest will invoke the secret goddess. At each mention of her name all will bend low to kiss their athames.

"(Secret name), divine goddess, mother who doth generate all things and brings forth ever anew the sun, which thou hast given to the nations, guardian of sky and sea, and of all powers and all gods, through thy influence all nature is hushed and sinks into sleep. Thou indeed

art rightly called queen of heaven and mother of all living.

"Thou art the source and strength of all people and all gods. Without thee nothing can be born or made perfect. Thou art mighty, Queen of the Gods. Goddess, I adore thee as divine. I invoke thy name, (Secret Name). Vouchsafe to grant that which I ask of thee. So shall I return thanks to thee with the faith that is thy due. So mote it be."

Now all turn their athames toward them so that the blade faces them. All the women will hold up their arms as in pentagram position and repeat after the High Priest the calling down of the moon into the High Priestess:

"Above the cliff, beneath the vale, among the flowers, who but I sets the cool head of flame with incense smoke that roars for blood in a pool from the paradise where poets walk. Ruthless in red, threatening doom, that puts to death, who but I peeked from the unhewn dome and arch of every home, on every hill, of every high, for every head of every home."

All the men then assume the god position and repeat the drawing down of the horned god into the High Priest:

"I am the stag of seven times. Over the flooded world I am borne by the winds. I descend in tears like dew. I lie glittering. I fly aloft like the griffin to my nest on the cliffs. I bloom amongst the loveliest of flowers. I am both the oak and the lightning that blasts it. I am bold in the company of men, I teach the counselors their wisdom. I inspire the poets. I rove the hills like a revening boar, I roar like the winter sea. I return again like the receding wave. Who but I can unfold the secrets of the unhewn dolmen?"

The High Priest or High Priestess is bound

All will now dance to raise the power within themselves and store it. At the command to stop, all will stop dancing and sit around the circle, point their athames at the bound High Priest or High Priestess, and shoot the power into them. When the power has been released, the King of Queen, High Priest or High Priestess, whoever is bound, will say this invocation:

"Hail, (secret name of the Goddess and the God), from thy horned plenty pour forth thy store of love. I lowly bend before thee. I adore thee to the inward loving sacrifice. Thy foot is to my lips, my prayer aborne upon the rising incense smoke. When other gods have fallen thy shrine I'll still adore. Then spend thine ancient love, oh mighty one. Descend to aid me, who, without thee am forlorn."

Untie the High Priest or High Priestess..Now the grace is said and

Cakes and wine are now blessed. If any new third degrees are at the elder circle, visioning is taught to them, and also the grand cone is explained. Magic is now done.

The circle is closed in the usual way but using the names of the Goddess and God at the north:

"Oh, mighty ones of the East (South, West, North), we thank they for having attended and ere ye depart for your lovely realms we bid thee hail and farewell."

All repeat: *"Hail and farewell."*

BELTANE SABBAT:

All should dress brightly and gayly. All should wear flowers and greenery in their hair and clothes. A pole about eight feet high is raised, decorated by everyone prior to the right with ribbons, greenery and flowers. It may be also be circled with thirteen candles or torches. A wreath or archway of branches and leaves, preferably birch, large enough to step through, should be fashioned near the Beltane pole, from the living branches of a tree if possible. A glass ball or black mirror should be wreathed in leaves and flowers and placed nearby. Several cups of herbal incense may be placed about the ritual area and lit. All at the ritual should bring along refreshments (cakes are traditional) for the feasting afterwards. If the rite is done outdoors all should carry torches. If indoors, candles should be held.

The altar should be set in the East and arranged as usual. Five candles should be placed on or about it. As all stand facing west, women with men if possible, the woman chosen to be priestess shall take the wand in her hands and, holding it over her head in salute, shall say: Friends, light the branch you hold, for here we celebrate the sacred night of Beltane and the flowering forth of the woods and meadows. The man chosen to be the priest then takes the wand similarly and says:

"We here do call and bid our goddess to be with us. She, once called the Lady of May, the goddess of things wild, of trees, of skies, of waters, be with us here. Blessed be."

All say:

"Blessed be." The Priestess may take the wand and place it in her sash or belt or near the pole. The Priest, or one chosen by him, shall place a crown of flowers on the head of the Priestess. The Priestess, or one chosen by here, shall place a mask or garland of leaves on the head of the Priest. The Priestess and the Priest lead the others into the circle about the Beltane pole. The procession circles it once clockwise and all place their candles or torches to the outside. All should

stand in a circle about the pole, linked by hands, man to woman, or hands about each others' waists. All should begin moving clockwise, or deosil, as the Priestess slowly chants:

"Here we gather once again, let the sleeper wake, May the old ones now return, let the sleeper wake, Once more let stream and field be pure, let the sleeper wake, Force spreading, peace returning, let the sleeper wake. May the Lady's touch be on the land once more, let the sleeper wake, Blessed be."

All say:

"Blessed be, blessed be, blessed be."

BELTANE VARIATION ON CIRCLE RITES:

April 30 Following the lighting of the Watchtower candles the High Priest will light the Beltane cauldron fire exactly at midnight before the circle has been cast. All members will face the cauldron fire as it is lit, and when the flames leap up they will shout.

All:

"Io evohe, Io evohe, Io evohe, blessed be."

To the watchtower invocations add the words:

"Blessed be the Queen of the May."

Consecration of the Water and the Wine:

"Here we bring new water, here we bring old wine,
For to worship great Diana, as the moon doth shine.
Sing reign of a fair maid with gold upon her toe,
Open ye the north door and let the springtime go.
Sing reign of a fair maid with gold upon her chin,
Open ye the south door and let the summer in.
Sing levez du, levez du, ye water and ye wine,
Hail to fair Diana, whose crescent moon doth shine."

Consecration of Meal and Salt:

"Here the dish of meal we bring, here the salt of earth,
Dance we in the Beltane ring, scatter these upon the hearth.
Fairy queen steals through the night, silver wings aglow with dew,
Blossoms deck her gown of white, deryonos canu, deryonos canu."

Following the consecration of salt and meal offer a few grains of each to the four watchtowers. Following consecration of the honey, the High Priest will perform the blessings of the four watchtowers.

East:

as at spring.

South:

As at spring.

225

West:

"O sacred moon of the Goddess, fertilize the blessed earth with thy silvery white rays that new life which has been born of our mother may wax abundant and sustain the life of all living things. Let the Queen of Heaven, our Lady Diana, ride forth to meet us upon thy crescent chariot. Blessed be the mother of all living!"

North:

"O mighty Pan! Great and courageous god of the Wicca, consort of our blessed Lady and father of all creature, upon thy sacred horns do we place our most grievous afflictions. Toss them to the four winds of the four watchtowers that they may become as dust beneath thy cloven hoofs. Hail thy reign in the Summerland where thou art guardian of the souls who await rebirth among us. Blessed be the father of all living!"

Follow this with the Wiccan prayer of the May Eve. The entire grove, facing west, arms crossed upon their chests, repeat:

"Blessed Lady, Mother dear, listen to our humble prayer, As the springtime flowers bloom, come forth from your silvery moon. Bless your children who pray in need, grant the wish and bless the deed, From your horn of plenty pour all the gifts you have in store. So mote it be."

During the Beltane rite a maypole may be constructed.

The Maypole:

Construct a maypole of any heighth. The top of the pole is sacred to Pan. The ribbons should be no more than 13 in number and may be grove colors or rainbow colors. The Maypole is danced deosil with the dancers weaving in and out so that the ribbons are plaited, braided down the pole. Morris dance music generally accompanies the Maypole Dance, which is often performed at sunrise or high noon. This is not necessary, however.

The Riding Pole:

The staff or riding pole may be used for fertility May dance around the fields, particularly the garden. This is done astride the pole, hobbyhorse fashion. Ribbons may be tied to the top of the pole, or it may be garlanded with spring flowers. Garlands of flowers may be fashioned for the May rituals. These are generally tied with white ribbons. A garland of flowers can be used to outline the circle. A daisy chain is very traditional. Female Wicca should wear flowers or wreaths in their hair. At Beltane it is customary to place clothing upon a tree to honor the Lady.

Daisy Chain Dance:

A daisy chain is made, which should be about 18 feet in length. The High Priestess leads the chain dance, followed by the Maiden and summoner. The High Priest holds the end of the chain. The dance weaves in and out among the trees, bushes, and over the fields.

Beltane Tree Dance:

All grove members form a circle and join hands around an old tree. The dancers skip deosil, singing:

"Here we go gathering nuts in May, nuts in May, nuts in May, Here we go gathering nuts in May, all on a Sabbat morning.

On Beltane it is also customary to give May baskets to children and friends. The baskets contain flowers, good things to eat, and surprise gifts.

SPRING EQUINOX VARIATION ON CIRCLE RITES:

Consecration of the water and the wine:

"Here we bring new water, here we bring old wine, For to worship Diana as the moon doth shine. Sing reign of a fair maiden with gold upon her chin, Open ye the east door, and let springtide in. Sing levez du, levez du, ye water and ye wine, Hail to fair Diana, whose crescent moon doth shine.

Consecration of the meal and salt:

"Here the dish of meal with bring, here the salt of earth, Scatter these to the winds of spring, blessed be the greenwood's birth. Fairy queen steals through the night, silver wings aglow with dew, Bears the child of love's delight, drwy y nos, canu, drwy y nos, canu."

Consecration of the seeds:

"Mother of all, o Lady fair, bless these seeds with life and love, Give to them a beauty rare, filled with fragrance from above. When the moist warm soil of spring, when new buds are on the tree, Go the seeds for nurturing, dearest Mother, blessed be thee."

Following the consecration of the honey the High Priest will perform the blessing of the four watchtowers.

East:

"O great Lugh, source of eternal light and wisdom, may the life-giving rays shine forth to lighten thy creatures and nourish that which is reborn, that by the call of the wild owl in the night we may rejoice in thy return at dawning."

South:

"O golden lights of the flaming one, thou art of the glowing eyes

of a thousand cats, sacred to the goddess of retribution, quicken that which is reborn, that strength may banish weakness.''

West:

''O sacred moon of the Goddess, fertilize the blessed earth with thy silvery rays, that new life, which stirs within the womb of our mother, may burst forth in ever increasing abundance to sustain the life of all living things. May the queen of heaven, our Lady Diana, ride forth to meet us upon thy crescent chariot. Blessed be the mother of all living.''

North:

''O mighty Pan, great and courageous god of the Wicca, consort to our blessed Lady and father to all creatures, upon thy sacred horns do we place our most grievous afflictions, toss them to the four winds of the four watchtowers, that they may become as dust beneath thy cloven hooves. Ride the mighty north wind to the Summerland where thou art guardian of the souls who wait rebirth among us. Blessed be the father of all living.

All the grove members must now take the flower petals and scatter them deosil around the circle, following the High Priestess as they go, and saying:

''Life from light to earth to earth, Scatter ye blossoms thy Lady's way Here ye fruits of the Goddess rebirth Canu, Canu wdmni!''

''One and all of merry mein With our blossoms of the spring Without sorrow are we seen Canu, Canu, ddwydymni!''

The seeds are now to be planted at the full moon of April.

MIDSUMMERS MEET SABBAT

All observe silence. The High Priest commences to beat with his wand or pole upon the ground, basing it on the heart rhythm. He ceases the beat and speaks:

''We are met to oversee the passing of the god and a most solemn ceremony to care the alterations of the annual state, thus to mirror our inner state to find that strange balance of ourselves between the gods of light and darkness. We shall see our god pass from his growth and glory to yet more potent depths. One god, two aspects, and the passage shown between within the fires of our solar selves. The dark self balanced by the light, and then the lord of all light is dead himself. And born, reborn in summer fire, to dominate, control our deathly self. For be warned, this is the end of mystery, sacred and profane, we are part and partners. Let this then our merry ritual make this plain and so distinguish pleasure and pain.''

228

The High Priest pauses, shows the three sigils:
"These are the weapons of poor Robin's death. "
All bow.

"He was born, he reigned, he has worked wonders, his tree was the holly, his tree was the oak, he is the weapons of his death, reeds were his arrows of desire, holly was his spear, oak his conquering club of light, yet by his weapons he died. He turns to face the assembly. Who killed Cock Robin?"

The Maiden replies:
"I say Bran's sparrow."
The High Priest:
"Who sees him die?"
All reply:
"We see him die."
High Priest:
"Who catches his blood?"
All reply:
"We catch his blood."
The High Priest:

"O Lady as we pray, hear our prayer, that as we hope he will receive deliverance, we will receive deliverance. We pray for this deliverance. Finally, the fire is kindled and all walk in solemn procession with lit candles. After eight circles the horned man, garbed in mask and antlers, passes through the flames and is now on the other side, where the Maiden dribbles him with water and wine."

High Priest:
"Between fire and water he passes for our sake, make we pass through fire and water for his sake."
All pass through the flames and are blessed.

High Priest:
"Unto our Lady we offer prayer and praise, entreating that as Robin has passed this way, we will also have the courage to pass from life to death to the realm beyond. We pray we know thy eternal rest within thine own eternal light."

All extinguish the candles to symbolize death. Only the flames of the bonfire light the proceedings.

High Priest:
"Let light perpetually shine here as it does on our departed God who dwells now in the land of Summer. Deliver us, o Lady, through the death of Robin from the terror of our own death. Give us the im-

mortality of constant belief that we may dwell in the land of summer as dwellers in light, eating your sweet apples of bounteous love."

The High Priest commands all to kneel, saying:

"Peace and be still, and the island of apples be received of the dead, attended by the gods of old, and with them be in rest."

Meditation follows until the High Priest says:

"Rise, light bearers, rise. Light pours forth from the horn of plenty. Be blessed. The time of rebirth draws nigh. The gates of the unseen swing open. Be blessed."

The Maiden serves red wine and bread from the platter. She says:

"Drink this wine in token of his blood, shed for her. Eat the flesh of the God, eat of his strength and power."

All reply after they:

"We have eaten of our God, taken his blood, we are with him, he dwells within us."

Each passes again through the flame and is blessed as before. The horned man passes once more through the fire to the other side. The Maiden greets him with a kiss.

The Maiden says:

"Hail Arthur, reborn from the Isle of Apples. Greetings, Arthur, once and future king, Salutations, Arthur, lord of life and mystery of mysteries."

The horned man draws his sword from the earth.

The Priest asks:

"Who killed Cock Robin?"

All reply:

"We did."

GREAT RITE MAGICK:

Prepare yourself with a ritual bath together with your partner, and accumulation the balance of all the elements needed to accomplish your task. Both of you should absorb the universal light to capacity. Cast the circle properly and purify it with all four of the elements. Invoke the mighty ones and tell each of the intent. The male calls down the Goddess into the woman, the woman calls down the God into the man. Keep the emotion of love for each other growing within you. Consecrate the wine and kneel before the altar and repeat the spell, in rhyme, which you intend to accomplish. Drink the wine, sharing. At the end repeat the spell, simultaneously envisioning the act accomplished. Keep the emotion of love strongly growing within each of you. Begin the invocation of the Great Rite. Use the correct mixture of incense. Before you couple, anoint each other's genitals with anointing oil. When the sacred pillar is erected in full, gently begin the coupling, male on top of female. Keep in your minds the spell already accomplished and hold this constantly in your minds. Work so that the orgasms will be together or simultaneous. Both should say:

"So mote it be,"

at orgasm, and then blank the mind to release the spell. Have cakes and wine and properly close the circle. This is a very powerful magic and should be used cautiously.

THE GREAT RITE

Cast and purify the circle. Invoke the Mighty Ones. Draw down the moon into the female, draw down the God into the male. The man kneels at the woman's feet and holds her at the thighs, looking up at her, and says:

"Thou who at noon of night doth reign, Queen of the starry realm above, Not unto Thee may we attain, Unless Thine image be of love. By Amon rays silver shaft of power, By green leaf breaking from the bud, By seed that springeth into flower, By life that courseth in the blood, By rushing wind and leaping flame, By flowing water in green earth, Pour to us the wine of our desire, From out of Thy cauldron of rebirth."

He begins then to remove her robe and stands facing her:

" Here may we see in visions clear The secret strange and veiled at length, The wondrous twin mounds rear, Erect in beauty and in strength."

He kisses her breasts and kneels again:

"Altar of mysteries manifold
The sacred circle's central point
Thus do I sign thee as of old,
With kisses of my lips anoint"

He kisses her genitals:

"Open for me the secret way
The path of intelligence.
He removes his robe.
Between the gates of night and day,
Beyond the bounds of time and sense.

He lies on the ground and pulls her gently down to him and they couple. Each gives a secret name to the other during his or her orgasm. This is so that they will never be forgotten.

RITUAL OF SELF DEFENSE:

Cast a simple circle and purify it. Invoke the Mighty Ones thus:

"O Mighty Ones of the East (South, West, North), protect me from all evil that may come from the East (South, West, North), return the evil to its source in the names of Arianrhod and Cernunnos."

Now light the black candle, white, blue or white, and carry it widdershins for at least fifteen minutes, saying over and over:

"To bane, to bane, begain, begain, Thrice take ye back from whence ye came." Stop and completely blank your mind by staring at the blue part of the flame. Snuff out the candle and get rid of it. Take a bath of purification, and meditate on peace and calm.

PSYCHIC DEVELOPMENT:

For basic psychic development, do this for at least two days:

Relax yourself, burn soft incense, and lie down in silence. Beginning with your toes, feel them with your mind until they begin to tingle. Work up your body slowly, feeling every inch of it, forget nothing. It is of great good if you fall asleep during this. This is basically meditation/ relaxation.

THE SPOKEN WORLD:

There is great power in the spoken word. Always speak in rhyme pause to let the spoken word become even more powerful with raised emotion. Never go back on your word to a Wiccan or anyone else.

AID TO CONCENTRATION-MEDITATION:

Draw the symbol of the element in the proper color upon a piece of white paper. Concentrate upon that symbol. Then shut your eyes. Visualize the symbol. Do this until you can hold this visualization for one full minute. This helps to develop power in concentration. Do each day for five minutes. For the element ether symbolize the black oval. For the element air symbolize the blue circle. For the element water symbolize the silver crescent moon. For the element fire symbolize the red triangle. For the element earth symbolize the green square.

THE SACRED PENTAGRAM:

Draw a pentagram. Inside of the top triangle write rhyw, sex, below it. The right top of pentagram write hun. Under it, self. The right bottom pentagram, write nwyd, under it, passion. The left bottom pentagram, balchder, under it, pride. The top left pentagram, write gallu, under it, power. Over the top part of the pentagram write Arianrhod, the mother, the head. Right top, Arianrhod, the initiator, the chest. Write bottom, Blonewydd, the love goddess, the genitals. Left bottom, Blonewydd, the wisdom goddess, the hands. Right top, Ceridwen, the hag, the feet.

232

THE MOONS:

"Pray to the moon when she is round,
Good luck to you will abound,
What you search for will be found,
In sea, or air, or solid ground.
The new moon rises with the sun,
It's waxing light at midday hour,
Full moon at sunset hour,
Waning half at midnight.

INCANTATIONS:

An Old Invocation — in song form:

"Oh, do not tell the priest of our art,
for they will call it sin,
For we shall be in the woods all night,
a conjuring summer in.
And bring ye good news by word of mouth,
for woman, cattle and corn,
For the sun is coming up from the south,
with oak and ash and thorn."

CHANTS (IN IRISH)

"A righ negiles nag reine
A righ nan rula runach
Agad fein tha fios ar fuima
A dag mheinnich nan dula"
"Oh king of the moon, light of the sea,
Oh king of the stars, mysterious
Yourself aware of our needs
Oh, merciful god of nature."
"Failt or fein a ghellach ur
Aillegan ivil nan neul
Failt or fein aghallach ur
Aillegan cumh nan neamh"
"Hail to thee oh new moon,
Precious beacon of the clouds,
Hail to thee oh new moon,
Precious lady of the heavens."

CHANTS — IN IRISH

"Dia dha mo chaim
Dia dha mo chaiarait
Dia dha mo chainn

Dia dha mo smuain"
"God be my unfolding
God be my circle
God be my words
God be my thoughts."
"Carmich mi a nochd
Eadar eelr ages earc
Eadar run do reachd
Agus dearc mo dhoille"
"Bear me by night
amid the pastures and the herds
Amid the mysterious of the laws
My unseeing eyes."
"Com nadh tri mo dhuil
Com nadh tri mo run
Cona nadh tri mo shuil
Agus mo ghlum gun chlaen
Mo glun gun chloioan"
"Make three eight my hope
Make three eight my lovemaking
Make three eight my eye
And my knee from stumbling,
My knee from stumbling."

GREAT BEL

"The eye of the great god
The eye of the god of glory
The eye of the king of hosts
The eye of the king of life
Shining upon us through time and tide
Shining upon us gently and without stint
Glory be to thee oh splendid sun
Glory be to thee oh sun face of the god of light"

WASSAIL

Recipe for Wassail

One gallon of apple cider
4 sticks cinnamon
3 whole cloves
1/2 tsp. ground ginger

Six apples, cored
1/2 tsp. ground mace
1/2 cup sugar
1 tsp. grated nutmeg

1/4 tsp. ground allspice or 4 whole allspice berries
2 quarts or more of good ale

SABBAT CAKES:

These are recipes for Sabbat cakes.:

Mix together:

1 tsp. honey, 3/4 cup shortening, 1/2 cup brown sugar (or raw sugar), 1 tsp. white wine.

Add:

1 1/2 cups flour, 1/4 tsp. baking soda, 1/2 tsp. salt, 1 1/4 cups oatmeal.

Add:

Cinnamon, cloves, ginger, pinch of mandrake root. Combine well, adding water if necessary. Cut into small crescent shapes, bake at 350 degrees approximately 15 minutes.

MAGICK OIL:

Use a glass pot and a glass stirrer:

Mix:

Olive oil, musk oil, saffron oil, balm of gilead extract, patchouli oil, wood betonay.

Heat slowly to a boil. Bottle and use.

ALTAR OIL, WELSH:

Olive oil, 1 part. 1/8 part of oil of myrrh, 1/8 part of oil of cinnamon, 1/8 part oil of galangal.

CERNUNNOS PERFUME, WELSH:

1/3 patchouli oil, 1/3 cedarwood oil, 1/3 pine oil. 1 drop of vanilla oil, 1 drop of jasmine oil, one drop ilangilang oil, 1 drop cloves oil, 1 drop essence of rose, 1 drop geranium oil.

The following can be added instead of the one drops:

5 parts musk, 5 parts civet, 1 part cassia, 1 part ambergris, 1 part patchouli. The oil should be kept in a well-stoppered, dark vial or flask.

SABBAT OIL, WELSH:

Steep the following in 16 ounces of grain alcohol for one full day when the moon is waxing:

Poplar leaves (balm of gilead), cinquefoil, saffron, lemon verbena or vervain.

Strain the alcohol through muslin and add to two cups purified vegetable oil. Then add 1/8 ounce of Cernunnos purfume.

SABBAT OIL, CELTIC:

3/4 cup of oil (pure vegetable or olive), 1/8 ounce oil of cinnamon, 1/8 ounce musk. Mix. Let sit in sunlight or warm place seven days. Shake daily.

ANNOINTING OIL:

When you anoint, place a daub of the oil on the soles of your feet, the perinnum, wrist, temples, and behind each knee. Chant the following invocation:

"Emen Hetan! Emen Hetan! I am thine and thou art mine. I have nothing not of thine. In the name of Ceridwen. Behold, (own name), thy servant anointing him/herself. I should some-day be great like Thee. So mote it be."

MULSA:

This is a Yuletide malt wine. Make it by adding honey, cloves, nutmeg, allspice, and stick cinnamon to hot wine.

THIS IS THE END OF THIS VERSION OF "THE UNICORN"

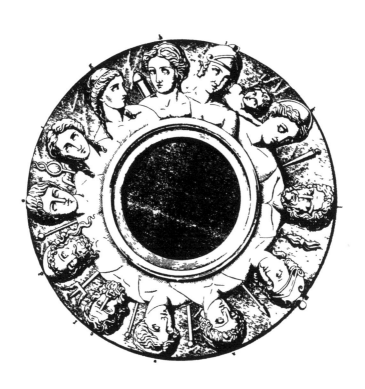

George Bain.

CHAPTER 13

KNOWLEDGE, LOVE AND POWER

The Welsh Triads and a Teaching Story

The Y Tylwyth Teg view is that nothing is totally bad or totally good; it is only our actions that carry meaning. Everything is perfect; everything is seeking a balance. But everything is also Maya - illusion. Everything is also changing and everything can be described by the sound of I.A.O.

THE WELSH TRIADS

1. There were three names given to the Isle of Prydain:
   Before it was inhabited, it was called the Sea-girt Green space; later it was called the Honey Island. After the people were formed into a commonwealth by Prydain, the son of Aedd the Great, it was denominated The Isle of Brydain. And no one has any right to it but the tribe of the Cymmry, for they first took possession; and before this time were no persons living in it, but it was full of bears, wolves, crocodiles and bison.

2. There were three primary divisions of the Isle of Prydain:
   Cambria, Lloegria, and Alban; and the rank of sovereignty belongs to each of the three. Under a monarchy and voice of the country they are governed according to the regulations of Prydain, the son of Aedd the Great; and to the nation of the Cymmry belongs the right of establishing the monarchy by the voice of the country and the people, according to rank and primeval right. Under the protection of such regulation, royalty ought to exist in every country in the isle of Prydain, and every royalty ought to be under the protection of the voice of the country. Therefore it is said: *"A country is more powerful than a lord."*

3. There are three pillars of the social state in the Island of Prydain:
   The voice of the Country, Royalty, and Judicature, according to the regulation of Prydain, the son of Aedd the Great.

4. There are three pillars of the nation of the Island of Prydain:
   The first was Hu the Mighty, who brought the nation of the Cambrians first to the Island of Prydain; and they came from the Summer Country, which is also called Defrobani, the Summer-land; and they came over the hazy sea to the Island of Prydain, and to Amorica, where they settled. The second was Prydain the son of Aedd the Great, who first organized a social state of sovereignty in Britain; for before that time there was no justice but what was done by favor, nor any law, except that of superior force. The third was Dyvnwal Moelmud, for he first made arrangements respecting the laws, maxims, customs, and privileges of the country and tribe. And on account of these reasons, they were called the three pillars of the nation of the Cymmry.

5. There were three social tribes on the Island of Prydain:
   The first was the tribe of Cymmry, who came to the Isle of Prydain with Hu the Mighty, because he would not possess a country and lands by fighting and pursuit, by justice and tranquility. The second was a tribe of Lloegrians, who came from Gascony, and they were descended from the tribe of the Cymmry. The third were the Brythons, who came from Armorica, and who were descended from the tribe of the Cymmry. These were called the three peaceful tribes because they came by mutual consent and tranquility; and these tribes were descended from the primitive tribe of the Cymmry, and they had all three the same language and speech.

6. There were three refuge seeking tribes that came to the Island of Prydain and they came under the peace and permission of the tribe of the Cymmry, without arms and without opposition:
   The first was a tribe of Caledonians in the north. The second was the Irish tribe, who dwelled in the highlands of Scotland. The third were the people of Galedin, who came in naked vessels to the Island of Wight, when their country was drowned, where they had land granted them by the tribe of Cymmry. They had no privilege of claim in the Island of Prydain, but they had land and protection assigned to them under certain limitations; and it was stipulated that they should not possess the rank of native Cymmry until the ninth of their lineal descendants.

7. There were three invading tribes that came to the Island of Prydain and who never departed from it:

The first were the Coranians, they came from the country of Pwyl. The second were the Irish Picts, who came to Alban by the North Sea. The third were the Saxons. The Coranians were settled about the River Humber, and the shore of the German Ocean, and the Irish Picts are in Alban about the shore of the Sea of Denmark. The Coranians and the Saxons united, and by violence and conquest brought the Lloegri-Aloegrians into confederacy with them; and subsequently took the crown of the monarchy from the tribe of the Cymmry. And there remained none of the Lloegrians that did not become Saxons, except those that are found in Cornwall, and the Commot of Carnoban in Deria and Bernicia in this period. In this manner the benevolent tribe of the Cymmry, who preserved both their country and their language, lost the sovereignty of the Island of Prydain on account of the treachery of the refuge-seeking tribes, and the pillage of the three invading tribes.

8. There were three invading tribes that came to the Island of Prydain, and who subsequently left it:

The first was the Scandinavians, who came here under Urb, with the mighty host, and had taken away from the island the flower of the tribe of the Cymmry. He took away with him 63,000 effective men, and steeds of war. At the end of the third age, the Cymmry drove the Scandinavians over the sea into Germany. The second were the troups of Ganval the Irishman, that came into north Wales and settled there for twenty-nine years, until they were driven into the sea by Caswallon, the son of Belli and the grandson of Minogan. The third were the Caesarians, or Romans, who continued by violence on this island more than 400 years, when they returned to Italy to oppose the fierce contention of the black invasion; and they did not return again to the Island of Prydain. Because the Cymmry marched with them, none were left on the island but women, and little children under nine years of age.

9. There were three treacherous invasions of the Island of Prydain:

The first were the Red Irishmen from Ireland, who came to Alban; the second were the Scandinavians; and the third were the Saxons. These last came to this island in peace and by the permission of the tribe of the Cymmry, and in the protection of the

Goddess and her truth, as well as in the protection of the country and of the tribe; and by treachery and mischief they opposed the tribe of the Cymmry, and were able to wrest from them sovereign power of the Island of Prydain, and they mutually confederated themselves in Lloegria and Alban, where they still reside. This happened in the age of Vortigern.

10. There were three disappearances by loss in the Isle of Prydain:

The first were Gavran and his men, who went in search of the green islands of the floods, and were never heard of again. The second were Merddin, the bard of Emrys, and his nine attendant bards, who went to sea in a house of glass, and the place where they went is unknown. The third was Madog, the son of Owain, king of North Wales, who went to sea with 300 persons in 10 ships, but the place to which they went is unknown.

11. There were three oppressions that came upon the Island of Prydain, but which were brought to a termination:

First the oppression of the Horse of Malaen, which is called the Oppression of the first of May; second, was the oppression of the Dragon of Prydain; the oppression of the half-apparent man. That is, the first was from beyond the seas; the second was from the madness of the country and the nation under the presence of the violence and lawlessness of princes; but Dyvnwal Moelmud destroyed it, by forming just regulations between society and society, prince and neighboring prince, and country and neighboring country; and the third was in the town of Belli the son of Manogan, which was a treacherous conspiracy but he extinguished it.

12. There were three frightful plagues on the Island of Prydain:

First the plague that arose from the corpses of the Irishmen who were slaughtered in Manuba, after they had oppressed northern Wales for the space of twenty-nine years. Second, the infection of the Yellow Plague of Rhoss, on account of the corpses which were slain there, and if anyone went within reach of the effluvia he died immediately. The third was the sickness of the bloody sweat, on account of the corn having been destroyed by wet weather in the time of the Norman invasion by William the Bastard.

13. There were three awful events in the Island of Prydain:

The first was a bursting of the lake of floods, and the rushing of an inundation over all the lands, until all persons were destroyed, except Dwyvan and Dwyvach, who escaped in an open vessel; and from them the Island of Prydain was peopled. The second was a trembling of the fiery torrent, until the earth was rent to the abyss, and the greatest part of all life was destroyed. The third was the hot summer, when the trees and plants took fire by the burning heat of the sun, and many people and animals, various kinds of birds, vermin, trees and plants, were entirely destroyed.

14. There were three combined expeditions that went from the Island of Prydain:

The first was that which went with Ur, the son of Erin, the Bellipotent of Scandinavia; and he came to this island in the time of Gadial the son of Erin, to solicit aid, under a condition that should not obtain from every principle fortress, a greater number than he shall bring to it. To the first fortress he only came himself with a servant Mathata Vawr, and from there he obtained two, from the second four, from the third eight, the next sixteen, and thus in like proportion from every other fortress, until that in the last the number could not be procurred throughout the whole island. He took with him 63,000, and he could not obtain a greater number of effective men in all the island, and none but children and old men were left behind. And Ur, the son of Erin the Bellipotent was the most complete levier that ever existed. It was through inadvertancy that the tribe of the Cymmry gave him this permission under irrevocable stipulation; and in consequence of this, the Coranians found an opportunity to make an easy invasion of this Island. Of the men who went, none ever returned, nor any of their progeny, or descendants. They went on a warlike expedition as far as the Sea of Greece, and remaining there in the land of Galas and Avena unto this day, they have become Greeks. The second combined expedition was conducted by Caswallawn the son of Belli, the grandson of Manogan, and Gwenwyn and Gwanar, the sons of Lliaws, the son of Nwyvre and Arianrhod, the daughter of Belli, their mother. Their origin was from the border declivity of Galedin and Saluria, and from the combined tribes of the Boulognese; and their numbers were three score and 1,000. They marched, with their Uncle Caswallawn, after the Caesarians, unto the land of the Gauls of Armorica, who were descended from the primitive stock of the Cymmry. And none of them nor of their progeny, returned to this island. For they settled in Gascony among the Caesarians, where they are at present; and it was in revenge of this expedition that the Caesarians came first into this island. The third combined expedition was marched out of this island by Elen Bellipotent and Cynan, her brother, lord of Meiradog, to Armorica, where they obtained lands, power and sovereignty by the Emperor Maximus for supporting him against the Romans. These men were from the land of Meiriadog, Saluria, and from the land of Gwyr and Gorwennyd; and none of them returned again, but settled there in Ystre Gyvaelwg, where they formed a commonwealth. On account of this expedition, the tribe of Cymmry became so deficient in armed men, that the Irish Picts invaded them; and therefore Vortigern was forced to invite the Saxons to expel the invasion. And the Saxons, observing the weakness of the Cymmry, treacherously turned their arms against them, and by combining with the Irish Picts and other traitors, they took possession of the land of the Cymmry, and also their privileges and their crown. These three combined expeditions are called the Three Mighty Presumptions on the tribe of Cymmry, and also the three Silver Armies, because they took away from the island all gold and silver they could obtain by deceit, artifice, and injustice, besides what they acquired by right and consent. They are also called the three unwise armaments, because they weakened the island so much, that an opportunity was given for the three mighty invasions; namely the Coranians, the Caesarians, and the Saxons.

15. There were three mighty invasions of the Island of Prydain that united in the one, and by this means the invaders took from the Cymmry their rank, their crown and their lands:

    The first was that of the Coranians, who united with the Caesarians until they became one. The second of the three were the Caesarians. The third were the Saxons, who united with the two others against the Cymmry. And the Goddess permitted this for the purpose of chastising the Cymmry for their three mighty presumptions, because they were carried into effect by injustice.

16. There were three primary tribes of the Cymmry:

    The Gwenitians, or the Silerians; the Ordovices including both the north Walians and Powysians; and the tribe of Pendaran of Dyved, including the people of Pembrokeshire, Gower, and Cardiganshire. To each of these belongs a classical dialect of the Welsh language.

17. There were three monarchs by the verdict of the Island of Prydain:

    The first was Caswallawn, the son of Lludd, son of Belli, son of Manogan; the second of Caradog, son of Bran, son of Llyr, son of LLediath; and the third was Owain, the son of Maximus. That is, sovereignty was conferred upon them by the verdict of the country and the nation, when they were not elders.

18. There were three holy families in the Island of Prydain:

First the family of Bran the Blessed, the son of Llyr, Llediath; for Bran was the first who brought the faith of the Goddess to this island from Atlantis, where he was imprisoned through the treachery of Boadicea, the daughter of Mandubratius, the son of Lludd. The second was the family of Cynedda Wledig, who first gave land and privilege to the Goddess and the saints in the Island of Prydain. The third was Brychan of Brecknocashire, who educated his children and grandchildren in learning and generosity, that they might be able to share the faith in the Goddess with the Cymmry, where they were without faith.

19. There were three benignant guests of the Island of Prydain:

David ab Hern, Padarn, and Teilaw. They were so called because they went as guests into the houses of the nobles, the yeomen, the native and the bondman, without accepting either gift or reward, food or drink; but they taught the faith in the Goddess to everyone without pay, or thanks, and to the poor and the destitute they gave of their gold and their silver, their clothes and their provisions.

20. There were three treacherous meetings on the Island of Prydain:

First the meeting of Mandubratius, the son of LLudd, and the traitors with him, who gave place for the landing of the Romans on the narrow green point, and not more; and the consequences of which was, the gaining of the Isle by the Romans. The second was the meeting of the Cambrian nobles and Saxon claimants upon Salisbury plain, where the plot of the long knives took place through the treachery of Vortigern, whereby his council, in league with the Saxons, nearly all the Cymmry nobility were slain. Third, the meeting of Medrawd and Iddawg corn Prydain with their men of Nanhwynian, where they entered into a conspiracy against Arthur, and by this means strengthened the Saxon cause on the Island of Prydain.

21. The three errant traitors of the Island of Prydain:

First, Mandubratius, son of Lludd, son of Belli the Great, who invited Julius Caesar and the Romans into this island, and caused the invasion of the Romans. That is, he and his men gave themselves as guides for the Romans and received a treasure of gold and silver from them every year. In consequence of this, the men of this island were compelled to pay 3,000 pieces of silver every year as a tribute to the Romans until the time of Owain the son of Maximus, who refused to pay the tribute. And under pretense of being content, the Romans drew from the Island of Prydain the most effective men who were capable of becoming warriors, and marched them to Aravia and other far countries, from which they never returned. The Romans who were in Prydain went into Italy, and left only women and little children behind them; and, therefore, the Prydainians were so weakened, that they were not able to oppose invasion and conquest for want of men and strength. The second was Vortigern, who murdered Constantine the Blessed, seized the crown of the island by violence and lawlessness, first invited the Saxons into the island as his defenders, married Alis Ronwen, the daughter of Hengist, and gave the crown of Prydain to the son he had by her, whose name was Gotta; and on this account, the kings of London were called children of Alis. Thus, on account of Vortigern, the Cymmry lost their lands, their rank and their crown in Lloegria. The third was Medrawd the son of Llew, the son of Cynvarch: for when Arthur left the government of the Island of Prydain in his custody, whilst he marched against the Roman Emperor, Medrawd took the crown from Arthur by usurpsion and seduction; and in order to keep it, he confederated with the Saxons; and, on this account, the Cymmry lost the crown of LLoegria and the sovereignty of the Island of Prydain.

22. The three secret treasons of the Island of Prydain:

First, the betraying of Caradog, son of Bran, by Boadicea, daughter of Mandubratius, the son of Lludd, and delivering him up a captive to the Romans. Second, the betraying of Arthur by Iddawg Corn Prydain, who divulged his designs. And third, the betraying of Prince Llewellyn, son of Grufudd, by Madog Min. By these three treacheries the Cymmry were completely subdued; and nothing but treachery could have overcome them.

23. The three heroic sovereigns of the Island of Prydain:

Cunobelinus, Caradog, the son of Bran, and Arthur; because they conquered their enemies, and could not be overcome but by treachery and by plotting.

24. The three primary battled princes of the Island of Prydain:

Caswallawn the son of Belli, Gweirydd the son of Cunobelinus, and Caradog, the son of Bran, son of Llyr Llediaith.

25. The three accomplished princes of the Island of Prydain:
    Rhun, the son of Maelgwn; Owain, the son of Urien; and Rhuvon the Fair, son of Dewrath Wledig.

26. There were three plebian princes in the Island of Prydain:
    Gwrgai, son of Gwrien in the north; Cadavael, son of Cynvedw in north Wales; and Hyvaidd, the tall son of St. Bleiddan, in Glenmorgan. That is to say, sovereignty was granted them on account of their heroic actions, and virtuous qualities.

27. The three banded families of the Island of Prydain:
    The family of Caswallawn with the long hand; the family of Rhiwallon, son of Urien; and the family of Belyn of Lleyn. They were so called, because they were not subjected to either head, or sovereign as it respected the ranks of their families and power, but owed submission only to the voice of the country and the nation.

28. The three golden banded ones of the Island of Prydain:
    Rhiwallon with the broom hair; Rhun, the son of Maelgwn; and Cadwaladyr the Blessed. That is, they were permitted to wear golden bands about their arms, their necks, and their knees, and with these were granted the privilege of royalty in every country and dominion in the Island of Prydain.

29. The three battle knights of the sovereign of the Island of Prydain:
    Caradog with the brawny arms; Llyr, the Bellipotent, and Mael, the son of Manwaed, of Arllechwedd. And with reference to these, Arthur composed the following lines: *"These are my three battle knights, Mael the Tall, and Llyr the Bellipotent, and Caradog the Pillar of the Cymmry."* That is to say, they were the bravest heros of all battle knights, and therefore royalty was granted them, and what they wished of power; and their courtesy was such, that they would do nothing but what was judicious and right, in whatever country they came.

30. The three generous princes of the Island of Prydain:
    Rhydderch the generous, son of Tudwall Tudclud; Mordav the generous, son of Servan; and Nudd the Generous, son of Senyllt. Their courteous dispositions were such, that they did not fail to grant anything whatever to any person who solicited it of them, if they had it in their possession, or could obtain it by a gift, loan, or present, whether the applicants were friends or foes, relatives or strangers.

31. The three bloodstained ones of the Island of Prydain:

Arthur, Morgan the Greatly Courteous, and Rhun, the son of Belli. When they marched to war, no one would stay at home, so greatly were they beloved; and in every war and battle, they were victorious, where there were neither treachery, nor ambush. Hence rose the proverb: *"There were three heroes who obtained men wherever they marched: Arthur, Morgan the Greatly Courteous, and Rhun the son of Belli; and there were three armies who obtained soldiers wherever they marched; the soldiers of Arthur, the soldiers of Morgan the Greatly Courteous, and the troups of Rhun, the son of Belli."*

32. The three resolute-minded ovates of the Island of Prydain:

Greidiawl the Resolute-Minded Ovate, Envael the son of Adran, and Trystan, the son of Tallwch; for they had the privilege of going wherever they wished in the Island of Prydain without opposition, unless they went unlawfully.

33. The three obstructors of slaughter of the Island of Prydain:

Grudnew, Henben, and Eidnew. Their principle was, not to retreat from battle and conflict, but upon their biers, after they were unable to move either hand or foot.

34. The three conventional monarchs of the Island of Prydain:

First, Prydain, son of Aedd the Great, when there was established discriminating sovereignty over the Island of Prydain, and its adjacent islands; second, Caradog, the son of Bran, when he was elected generalissimo of all the islands of Prydain to oppose the incursions of the Romans; and Olwain, the son of Ambrosius, when the Cymmry resumed the sovereigned the sovereignty from the Roman emperor according to the rights of the nation. These were called the three conventional sovereigns, because they were raised to the dignity by the conventions of the country and the bordering country, within all the limits of the nation of the Cymmry, by holding a convention in every district, Commot and the Hundred in the Island of Prydain and its adjacent islands.

35. The three blessed princes of the Island of Prydain:

First, Bran the Blessed, the son of Llyr Llediaith, who first brought the faith of the Goddess to the Cymmry where he had been seven years as a hostage for his son Caradog whom the Romans put in prison after being betrayed through the enticement, deceit and defrauding of Boadicea. Second, Lleirwg, son of Coel son of St.Cyllin, and called LLeuver the Great, who built the first temple in Llandav, which was the first on the Island of Prydain, and who gave the privilege of the country and tribe, with civil, and ecclesiastical rites to those who professed faith and knowledge of the Goddess. The third was Cadwaladyr the Blessed, who gave protection, when it was within his lands and within all his possessions, to those who fled from the infidel and lawless Saxons who wished to murder them.

36. Three system formers of royalty of the Island of Prydain:

Prydain the son of Aedd the Great, Dyvnwal Moelmud, and Bran the son of Llyr Llediaith. That is, their systems were the best systems of royalty, royalty being of the Island of Prydain, and they were judged superior to all of the systems which were formed on the Island of Prydain.

37. The three disgraceful drunkards on the Island of Prydain:

First, Ceraint, the drunken king of Siluria, who in drunkenness burned all the corn far and near over all the country, so that a famine for bread arose. Second, Vortigern, who in his drink gave the Island of Thanet to Horsa that he might commit adultery with Rowena his daughter, and who also gave a claim to the son that he had by her to the crown of Lloegria; and added to these treachery and plotting against the Cymmry. Third, the drunken Seithynin, son of Seithyn Saida, king of Dimetia, who in his drunkenness left the sea over the hundred of Gwaelod so that all the houses and land which were there, were lost; where before that event 16 fortified towns were reckoned there, superior to all the towns and fortifications in the Cymmry, with the exception of Caerllion upon Usk. The hundred of Gwaelod was a dominion of Gwydnaw Garanihir, king of Cardigan. This event happened in the time of Ambrosius. The people who escaped from the inundation landed in Ardudwy, in the country of Arban, in the mountains of Snowdon, and other places, which had not been inhabited before that period.

38. The three humble princes of the Island of Prydain:

Manawyda son of Lleir Lliediaith, after Bran the son of Llyr, his brother, was carried into captivity; Llywarch the Aged, son of Elidir, Llydanwyn; and Gwgon the hero, the son of Eleuver with the Mighty Retinue. These three were bards; and after they had attached themselves to song, they sought not for dominion and royalty, but no one could debar them from it. On this account, they were called the three humble princes of the Island of Prydain.

39. The three chiefs of Deira and Bernicia:

Gall, the son of Dysgyvedog, Difedel the son of Dysgyvedog; and Ysgavnnel the son of Dysgyvedog. These three were the sons of bards, and after they had attached themselves to song, the sovereignty, the sovereignty of Deira and Berniciawere bestowed upon them.

40. The three bards of the Island of Prydain who hinged spears with blood:

Tristvardd, son of Urien Rheged; Dygynnelw, the bard of Olwain, son of Urien; and Avanverddig, bard of Cedwallen, son of Cedvan. These three were sons of bards, and they could not be separated.

41. The three supreme servants of the Island of Prydain:

Caradog, the son of Bran, the son of Llyr Lleidiath; Cawrdav, the son of Caradog with the Brawny Arm; and Olwain, the son of Ambrosius. They were so called because all the men of the Island of Prydain, from the prince to the peasant, became their followers at the need of the country, on account of the invasions and tyranny of the foe. And wherever these three marched to war, there was not a man on the Island of Prydain but who would join their armies, and would not stay at home. And these three were the sons of bards.

42. The three fetter-wearing kings of the Island of Prydain:

Morgan the Greatly Courteous, of Glenmorgan; Elystan Glodrydd, between the Wye and the Severn; and Gwaithvoed, King of Cardigan. They were so called because they wore fetters in all their primary functions of royalty in the Island of Prydain instead of frontlets or crowns.

43. The three frontlet-wearing kings of the Island of Prydain:

Cadell, King of Dinevor; Anarawd, King of Aberfraw; and Mervin, King of Mathravael.They were also called the three frontlet-wearing princes.

44. The three foreign kings of the Island of Prydain:

Gwrddyled of the Conflict; Morien with the beard; and Constantine the Blessed.

45. The three disgraceful traitors who enabled the Saxons to take the crown of Prydain from the Cymmry:

The first was Gwrgigarwlwyd, who after tasting human flesh in the court of Edlfled, the Saxon king, became so fond of it that he would eat no other but human flesh over. In consequence of this he and his men united with Edlfled, king of the Saxons; and he made secret incursions upon the Cymmry, and brought a young male and female whom he daily ate. And all the lawless men of the Cymmry flocked to him and the Saxons, for they obtained their full of prey and spoil taken from the natives of this isle. The second was Medrod, who with his men united with the Saxons, that he might secure the kingdom to himself, against Arthur; and in consequence of that treachery many of the LLoegrins became as Saxons. Third was Aeddan, the traitor of the north, who with his men made submission to the power of the Saxons, so that they might be able to support themselves by confusion and pillage under the protection of the Saxons. On account of these three traitors the Cymmry lost their land and their crown in Lloegria; and if it had not been for such treason, the Saxons could not have gained the island from the Cymmry.

46. The three bards who committed the three beneficial assassinations of the Island of Prydain:

The first was Gall, the son of Dysgyvedawg, who killed the two brown birds of Gwendolleu, the son of Ceidiaw, that had a yoke of gold about him, and that daily devoured two bodies of the Cymmry for their dinner and two for their supper. The second was Ysgavnell, the son of Dysgyvedawg, who killed Edlfled, King of Lloegria, who required every night two noble maids of the Cymmry nation, and violated them, and every morning he killed and devoured them. The third was Difedel, the son of Dysgyvedawg, who killed Gwrgi Garwlylwyd, that had married Edlfled's sister, and committed treachery and murder in conjunction with Edlfled upon the Cymmry. And this Gwrgi killed a Cymmry male and female every day and devoured them, and on Saturday he killed two males and two females, that he might not kill on Sunday. And these three persons, who performed these beneficial assassinations, were bards.

47. The three infamous assassinations of the Island of Prydain:

The assassination of Aneurin of flowing muse and monarch of the bards, by Eiddin the son of Einygan; the assassination of Avaon, son of Taliesin, by Llawgad Trwm Bargawd; and the assassination of Urien, the son of Cynvarch, by Llovan Llaw Dino. They were the three bards who were assasinated by these three men.

There are 140 Triads; the remaining can be found in other works by Rhuddlwm Gawr.

251

THE TRIADS OF THE MOUNTAIN

There are over 500 "Mountain Triads", these are a sample:

1. Snow on the Mountain: the world is spiritual.
   The teacher and the taught together produce the teaching.
2. Snow on the Mountain: the maiden is happy.
   Service to humanity is not only a way of correct living; it is a means of preserving and transmitting more knowledge.
3. Snow on the Mountain: bright is the sun.
   Information can be in fragments, knowledge is not.
4. Snow on the Mountain: wide is the ocean.
   The way may be by looking into a drop of water; it also can be looking into the universe.
5. Snow on the Mountain: the way is hard.
   No matter where the truth is, your teacher can help you find it; if he applies only one method to everyone, he is not a teacher.
6. Snow on the Mountain: great is the sky.
   Pass from time and space to timelessness and spacelessness, to other worlds and other dimensions. There is our origin.
7. Snow on the Mountain: easy is the way.
   Talk not of the eightfold path, or of the twelve virtues, or of the thirteen treasures; talk instead of "the way" and the attaining. All else is secondary.
8. Snow on the Mountain: the way is clear.
   You cannot destroy us if you are against us, but you can make things difficult for us even if you think you are helping.
9. Snow on the Mountain: knowledge is peace.
   Truth manifests only in understanding.
10. Snow on the Mountain: love is good.
    If you follow a stream, realize that it leads to the ocean. Do not mistake the stream for the ocean.

A TEACHING STORY

One day a new seeker came to class and was describing how a certain false pagan teacher was describing exercises for her followers. *"The woman is obviously a fraud. She asks her students to have an intense sexual experience while thinking of nothing. It is an easy thing to say, but everyone knows it is impossible to think of nothing while you are having sex!"*

I asked her, *"Why have you come to this class?"*

"To point out the deception of this woman and also to discuss spirituality and wicca.," she answered.

I asked, *"Not just to gain support for your decision that this woman is an imposter?"*

"No, I already know this."

"Not to show those of us who are sitting here that you know more than most people?"

"No. In fact, I want you to teach me!"

"Very well. The best guidance I can give you is: have an intense orgasm while thinking of nothing."

She immediately left our group, convinced I was a fraud.

But a new member who had just walked in and only heard me say, *"The best guidance I can give you is: have an intense orgasm while thinking of nothing,"* was very impressed.

"To think of nothing; what a wonderful concept," he said to himself.

And he left after the class having heard nothing to contradict the idea of sex and thinking of nothing. The following day one of my students called me up and asked me which of the two seekers had been correct, the one who left thinking me a fraud or the one that had left with a new teaching.

"Neither; they both still have to learn that their greed is a veil and a barrier. Their answer is not in one idea, one visit or one easy solution. Only by continuous contact with a teacher does the seeker absorb, little by little, knowledge that accumulates into an understanding of truth. Thus does a seeker become an initiate."

Becoming a seeker of the way is to put away imagined truth, preconceptions, conditioning, and to face your real self. Seeking truth with your teacher is the first stage toward finding it. Then comes the realization that this truth is also seeking the seeker. The third stage is when the seeker realizes he is aquiring knowledge in a range beyond 'seeking and finding' or 'being sought.'

Y Tylwyth Teg is a religious "Way" for those who have lost faith in organized religion.

Y Twlwyth Teg is a ultimate "Way" for those who wish to find peace and trust.

Y Twlwyth Teg is an answer to the Quest for truth.

For more information contact:

Rhuddlwm Gawr

Y Twlwyth Teg

P.O. Box 674884,

Marietta, GA 30006-0006

e-mail camgroup@tylwythteg.com

(The editors)

Appendix No. 1

(The following laws have appeared in several versions.)
but they are as valid today as a thousand years ago.

The laws of the Cymmry.

1. The law was created and ordained of old by the gods.
2. The law was created for the Cymmry to advise and help in their troubles.
3. The Cymmry must give due worship to the gods and obey their will, which was ordained, for it was created for the good of the Cymmry as the worship of the Cymmry is good for the gods, for the gods love the Cymmry.
4. As a man loveth a woman by merging with her, so the Cymmry should love the gods by merging with them.
5. It is necessary that the circle which is the temple of the god should be truly cast thrice and be purified that it may be a fit place for the gods to enter.
6. And all the Cymmry must be properly prepared and purified before entry into the presence of the gods.
7. With love and worship in their hearts they shall raise power from their bodies to give power to the gods, as has been taught of old.
8. For in this way only may the Cymmry commune with the gods, for the gods cannot help the Cymmry without their help.
9. And the high priestess shall rule her coven as a representative of the goddess in the summer.
10. And the high priest shall rule the coven as a representative of the god in the winter.
11. And the high priestess or high priest shall choose their companion, if he or she be of sufficient rank to be the high priest/ess.

12. For as the god himself kissed her feet, laying his power at the feet of the goddess, because of her youth and beauty, her sweetness and kindness, her wisdom and justice, her humility, gentleness and generosity, so he shared his power with her.

13. The high priestess should ever mind that all power comes from him. It is to be shared and to be used wisely and justly.

14. And the greatest virtue of a high priestess or high priest is that they recognize that youth is necessary to the representative of the god/dess.

15. So they will gracefully retire in favor of a younger man or woman if the grove so decides in council.

16. For the true high priest/ess must realize that the graceful surrendering of the pride of place is one of the greatest virtues.

17. And that thereby will they return to that pride of place in another life with greater power and beauty.

18. In the old days when the Cymmry wandered far we were free to worship in all the greatest temples, but in these days we must celebrate the sacred mysteries in secret.

19. So be it ordained that none but the Cymmry may see our mysteries, for our enemies are many, and the torture loosens the tongue.

20. So be it ordained that no grove shall know where the next grove abide or who is a member save only the priestess, priest and candlebearer.

21. And there shall be no communication between them save by the candlebearer, the messenger of the gods.

22. And only if it be safe may the groves meet in some safe place for the great festivals.

23. And while there, none may say whence they came or give their true names.

24. To this end if any be tortured or in agony they may not tell if they do not know.

25. So be it ordained that no one shall tell anyone not of the craft who be of Cymmry or give any names or where they abide or tell anything which can betray any of us to our foes.

26. Nor may he tell what the family be, or the grove, or where the meetings be.

27. And if any break these laws, even under torture, byddo'r melltith o dduwies arnat ti.

28. Let each high priest and high priestess govern their grove with justice and love with the help and advice of the elders, always heeding the advice of the messenger of the gods as he comes.

29. They will hear all complaints of all brothers and strive to settle all differences amongst them.

30. But it must be recognized that there will ever be people who will strive to force others to do as they will.

31. These are not necessarily evil, and they may oft have good ideas which should be talked over in council.

32. But if they will not agree with their brothers and sisters, or if they say I will not work under this high priestess or high priest, it has ever been the old law to be convenient to the family and to avoid disputes.

33. Any of the second level may claim to found a new grove because they live over a league from the grove or are about to do so.

34. Anyone of the second level living with a family wishing to form a new grove shall tell the elders of their intentions and straightaway avoid their dwelling and remove to a new place.

35. Members of the old grove may join the new one when it is formed, but if they do they must ever leave and avoid the old grove.

36. The elders of the old and new groves should meet in peace and love to decide the new boundaries.

37. Those of the Cymmry who live outside of the families may join either but not both. Though all may meet for the festivals if the elders agree, and if it be truly in peace and love.

38. But splitting the Grove often means strife. For this reason, these laws were made of old. Any who disregard them, byddo'r melltith o dduwies arnat ti. So be it ordained.

39. If you keep a book, let it be in your own hand of writ. Let brother and sister copy what they will, but

never let the book out of your hands and never keep the writings of another. For an it be in their hand or writ, they may be taken and arraigned.

40. Let each guard the writings and destroy them whenever danger threatens.

41. Learn as much as you can by rote and when danger is past rewrite your book an it be safe.

42. For this reason if any Cymmry die, destroy the book if they have not been able to, for if it is found it is clear proof against them, and our oppressors know well ye may not be a witch alone. For all their kin and friends be in danger of torture, so destroy everything unnecessary.

43. If your book be found on you 'tis clear proof against you alone and you may be arraigned.

44. If you are arraigned, keep all thoughts of the craft from your mind. If the torture be too great to bear say, "I will confess, I cannot bear this torture. What do you want me to say?" If they try to make you talk of the family do not.

45. But if they try to make you speak of impossibilities such as flying through the air, consorting with their Christian devil, or sacrificing children, or eating human flesh, to obtain relief from the torture say, *"I dreamed an evil dream. I was beside myself. I was crazed."*

46. Not all magistrates are bad. An there be any excuse they may show mercy.

47. If ye have confessed ought do not afterwards say you babbled under the torture, say you do not know what you said. If you are condemned fear not, the family is powerful. They will help you escape if you stand steadfast.

48. But if you betray ought, there is no hope for you in this life or that to come.

49. Be sure, if steadfast you go to death, drugs will reach you and You will feel naught. You go but to death and what lies beyond, the ecstasy of the goddess.

50. To avoid discovery, let the working tools be as ordinary things that any may have in their house.

51. Let the pentacles be of wax that may be broken at once or melted.
52. Have no sword unless your level allows.
53. Have no names or signs on anything. Write them on in ink immediately before consecrating them, and wash them off immediately afterwards. By the color of the hilt tell which is which, the athame black, the kerfan white.
54. Ever remember that ye are the hidden children of the goddess so never do anything to disgrace her.
55. Never boast, never threaten, never say that you would wish ill of anyone.
56. If any person not in the magic circle speak of the Cymmry, say 'speak not to me of such, it frightens me, 'tis evil to speak of it.'
57. For this reason Christians have their spies everywhere. These speak as if they were well affected towards us, as if they would come to our meeting saying, *"My mother used to go to worship the old ones. I would that I could go myself.'* To such as these ever deny any knowledge.
58. But to others say, *'"Tis foolish talk of witches flying through the air. To do so they must be light as thistledown. And men say that all witches must be bleary-eyed old crones. So what pleasure can there be in a witch meeting such as folks talk of, "'* and say *"many wise men who know, say there are no such creatures."*

59. Ever make it a jest and at some future time perhaps the persecution may end and we may worship our gods in safety. Let us all pray for that happy day, and may the gods preserve the craft.
60. May the blessings of the Great Spirit be on all who keep these laws which are ordained.
61. If any of the craft have any appanage, Let all guard it and help to keep it clear and good for the craft, and let all justly guard all monies of the craft.
62. And if any brother or sister truly wrought it, 'tis right they have their pay, an it be just. An this be not taking money for the art, but for good and honest work.

63. And even the Christians say, *"The laborer is worthy of his hire,"* but if any brother work willingly for the good of the Craft without pay, it is to their greatest honor. So be it ordained.

64. If there be any quarrels or disputes among the brethren the high priest or high priestess will straightaway convene the elders and inquire into the matter. And they shall hear both sides, first alone, then together, and then they shall decide justly, not favoring one side or the other, ever recognizing there be people who can never work under others, but also there be people who cannot rule justly. To those who must ever be leader, there is this answer. Void the grove; seek another or make a grove of your own, taking with you who will go. To those who cannot rule justly the answer be, those who cannot bear your rule will leave you.

65. For none will meet with those with whom they are at variance.

66. So an either cannot agree get thee hence, for the Craft must ever survive. So be it ordained.

67. In the olden days when we used The Power we could use the art against any who ill-treated the brotherhood, but in these evil days we must not do so. So be it ordained.

68. For our enemies are everywhere and have devised a burning pit of everlasting fire into which they say all are cast except for a very few who are released by their priests, spells and masses; and this be chiefly by giving monies and rich gifts to receive the favour of their god who is ever in need of money.

69. But as our gods need our aid to make fertility for the family and crops, so is their god ever in need of mans help to search out and destroy us. Their priests ever tell them that any who get our help are damned to this hell forever, so men be mad with the terror of it.

70. But they make men believe that they may escape this hell if they give victims to the tormentors. So for this reason, all be forever spying, thinking, *"an I can catch but one of these witches, I will escape from this fiery pit."*

71. So for this reason we have our hiding places, and men searching long and not finding, say, *"there be none, or if there be, they be in a far country."*

72. But when one of our oppressors die, or even be sick, ever the cry is made, *"This be the work of witches,"* and the hunt is on again. And though they slay ten of their own to one of us, still they care not. They have countless thousands while we are few indeed, so be it ordained.

73. That this law shall ever help us in our plight, no one, however great an injury or injustice they receive may use the art in any way to do ill or harm to any, but they may after great consultation with all, use the art to restrain the Christians from harming us or others, but only to let or restrain them and never to punish.

74. To this end some will say, *"Such a one is a mighty searcher out and a persecutor of old women, whom they deem to be a Cymmry. And none hath done him harm so that it be proved that they cannot or more truly there be none."*

75. For all know full well that so many of our people have died because one had a grudge against them or were persecuted because they had money or goods to seize, or because they have none to bribe the searchers, and many have died because they were scolding old women, so much that now men say that only old women are witches, and this be to our advantage and turn suspicion away from us.

76. In England and Scotland 'tis now many years since a witch hath died the death. But misuse of the power may raise the persecution again, so never break this law, no matter how much you are tempted, and never consent to it being broken in the least. If you know it is being broken you must work strongly against it, and any high priestess who consents to its breach must immediately be forbidden. And any high priest or high priestess who consents to its breach must immediately be deposed of for, tis the blood of the Family they endanger.

77. Do good an it be safe and only if it be safe, and strictly hold to the old laws.

261

78. Never accept money for the use of the art, for money ever smeareth the taker. 'Tis sorcerers and conjurers and the priests of the Christians who ever accept money for the use of their art, and they sell dwale and evil love spells and portents so to let man escape from their sins. Do not as these. If you accept no money you will be free from temptation to use the art in evil causes.

79. All may use the art for their own advantage or to the advantage of the Craft only if you are sure that you harm none, but ever let the Grove decide this at length. Only if all be satisfied that none be harmed may the art be used. If it is not possible to achieve your ends one way, perchance the aim can be achieved by acting in another way so as to harm none. If any of you break this law, dyddo'r meltith o ddeuwies arnat ti. So be it ordained.

80. 'Tis judged lawful if any of the Craft need a house or land and none will sell to incline the owner's mind so as to be willing to sell, providing it harmeth him not in any way, and that full price is paid without haggling.

81. Never bargain or cheapen anything whilst you live by the art. So be it ordained.

82. Tis the old law and the most important of all laws, that no one may do anything that will endanger any of the craft, or bring them in contact with the law of the land or the persecutors.

83. In any dispute between those of the Cymmry, no one may invoke any laws but those of the craft, or any tribunal but that of the Priest, Priestess and Elders of the Cymmry.

84. It is not forbidden to say as Christians do, *"there be witchcraft in the lands,"* because our oppressors of old make it heresy not be believe in witchcraft, so a crime to deny it, which thereby puts you under suspicion. But ever say, *"I know not of it here. Perchance there may be, but afar off. I know not where."* But ever speak of those old crones consorting with the Christian devil and riding through the air, but ever

say, *"But how may many men ride through the air and be not as light as thistledown?"*

85. But if any cast suspicion on any of the Family or speak of any real meeting place or where they abide, byddo'r melltith o dduwies arnat ti. So be it ordained.

86. Let the Craft keep books with the names of all herbs which are good for men and all cures so all may learn. But keep another book with all bills and apices and let only the elders that are trustworthy people have this knowledge. So be it ordained.

87. For any who speak of any real meeting place where any abide, byddo'r melltith o dduwies arnat di.

88. Remember the art is a secret of the gods and only may be used in earnest and never for show, pride or vainglory.

89. Magicians and Christians may taunt us, saying: *"You have no power. You have no power. Do magic before my eyes and then only will I believe you,"* seeking to cause you to betray our art before them.

90. Heed them not, for the art ꞌ noly and may only be used in need, and the curse of the gods be upon any who break this law. So be it ordained.

91. It ever be the way with women, and with men also, that they ever seek new love, nor should we reprove them for this, but it may be found that this a disadvantage to the Craft, that so many a time it hath happened that a high priest or high priestess, impelled by love, have departed with their love, that is, they have left the Family and the grove. Now if any wish to resign they may do so in full coven or full grove, and this resignation is valid. But if they should run off without resigning, who may know if they may not return within a space of thirteen moons. So the law is, if they return within the space of thirteen moons, then shall they be taken back and all shall be as before.

92. If a high priestess leaves, her maiden shall act as deputy high priestess for as long as she is away. If she returns not within thirteen moons then shall the deputy become a true high priestess, unless there be

good reason to the contrary. If someone else is elected high priestess the deputy shall resume as maiden to the new high priestess. The one who has done the work shall reap the reward.

93. It hath been found that practicing the Art does cause a fondness between the aspirant and the tutor, and it the cause of better results that this be so. But if for any reason this is undesirable it can easily be avoided by both persons from the onset firmly resolving in their minds that if any such thing ensues it shall be that of brother and sister or parent and child, and it is for this reason that a man be taught only by a woman and a woman only by a man. Women and women and men and men should not attempt these practices together. Upon any who do so byddo'r melltith o dduwies arnat ti. So be it ordained.

94. Order and discipline must be kept. The high priestess or high priest may and should punish all faults. To this end, all the craft must receive their correction willingly. The culprits, all properly prepared, should be told, kneeling, of his fault, and their sentence pronounced. Punishment should be to recast the circle or something of the device of the high priestess or high priest. It should be followed by purification by each member or something of this nature.

95. The culprit must acknowledge the justice by kneeling and kissing the hand of the high priestess or high priest or whoever is sitting punishment, and also thanking for the punishment received. So be it ordained.

Appendix 2

Sacred Words
IAO. OUE

The secret and sacred name of Don, the transendental god/dess of the Cymmry.

O-A-O-U-E-I-Y

or

IAO. UAI

or

IAO. OUAI

This word is hidden in its revelation.

I = 3 = eaglet.

A = 1 = lapwing.

O = 5 = cormorant.

----

9 = the levels of initiation.

I.N.R.I. = word of power.

Ignis natura renovata integra. The fire of nature renews and refreshes.

R.O.T.A.S. = tarot.

A = the Fool.

O = the Devil.

T = the Hanged Man.

A.O.M. Adytum Operis Magni.

The voice of threefold utterance:

Plennydd — Arawn — Gwron.

O   A   I

The Spiritual Path of the Ancients
The following teaching outline is the first step on a seeker's
way to the first level of Y Tylwyth Teg.
  Introductory Class:
    Orientation
    Background of the Craft, Philosophy and Traditions:
      Gardnerian, Alexandrian, Celtic traditional,
      eclectic paganism, neopaganism, or others.
    Y Tylwyth Teg:
      Background, philosophy and leaders
    Meetings, day, time, etc.
    Assignments:
      Obtain a notebook for temporary Book of Shadows
      Read handouts
      Buy a notebook, take notes
      Buy The Quest, and read other assigned reading
  materials
First Class:
Statement of purpose, Story of Y Tylwyth Teg, breath-
ing and awareness, dream analysis, being quiet, keep a
dream journal and bring it to class, grounding, center-
ing and ungrounding.
Given: Thirteen Precepts
Introduction to Y Tylwyth Teg
Three Night Ritual
Blue fire visualization for circle work
Second Class
What is religion? What is Y Tylwyth Teg philosophy?
What is Y Tylwyth Teg cosmology? Duality form of
religion. What is the Great Spirit? Gwlad Yr Hav--
Summerland. Reincarnation and karma
  Given: Salt circle
         Wiccan Rede
         Meditation on the planes
  Read: The Quest, Chapter 1
  Read: Lesson 1

Third Class
Description of planes, universal laws, ethics--threefold return, cross and circle, what is a circle? arc and spiral? invocation of Pentacle

Given: Cingulum ritual
Robe ritual
Insignia
The laws 1-4,
Meditation on the planes.

Read: The Quest, Chapter 2

Fourth Class:
Tribal attire, tribal symbols, witches' pyramid, color symbols, consecration of ritual tools, psychic development, discussion of precognition, clairvoyance, clairaudience, empathy, ESP, aura sensing.

Given: Ritual purification bath
Basic candle ritual,
The laws 5-8
Psychic exercises

Read: The Quest, Chapter 3

Fifth Class:
What is ritual, altar construction, watchtowers, four elements, elementals, devas, and Pan, casting a circle, purpose, opening/closing, casting boundaries, ritual sealing

Given: Sleep circle
Guided meditation
The laws 9-12

Read: The Quest, Chapter 4
Read: Lesson 2

Sixth Class:
Triad of God/Goddess, Welsh triads, moon trinity, triads of wisdom

Given: Guided meditation
The Quest, Chapter 5
The laws 13-16,
Triad of mystery

Seventh Class:
Balance, Sabbat and Esbat festivals, Sabbat oil and cakes, Sabbat wine, the hidden children of the Goddess

Given: Guided meditation

The Quest, Chapter 6
The laws 17-20

Eighth Class:
Greater and lesser mysteries, Mabinogian, Taliesin
Given :The laws 21-24
The Quest, Chapter 7
meditation
Lesson 3 and Exam

Ninth Class:
Pagan songs and stories, celtic folklore, nudity and purpose, psychic healing, healing powers of colors and gems, charging
Given: The laws 25-28
The Quest, Chapter 8
meditation
protective robe visualization

Tenth Class:
Tree offering and blessing, garden blessing, natural foods and diet, herbs and natural healing, cosmic power sources, odic energy, sacred trees.
Given: The laws 29-32
The Quest
Chapter 9
meditation

Eleventh Class:
Secret keys, astronomy and astrology, magic squares, cycles, power nodes, gemstones, sacred wells and ley lines, and standing stones.
Given: The laws 33-33
The Quest
Chapter 10
meditation
rune dances

Twelfth Class:
The power of will, the power of imagination, the power of secrecy, the power of knowledge, raising of power in circle, intonation, third eye visualization.
Given: The laws 37-40
The Quest, Chapter 11
meditation

Lesson 4
Homework: To write a thesis on your beliefs.
Thirteenth Class:
Sexual energy, Tantra, sex magic, mystic exercises, candles, incense, fragrant oils.
   Given: The laws 41-44
         The Quest, Chapter 12
         Meditation
Fourteenth Class:
Dancing, mantras, fasting
   Given: The laws 45-48
         The Quest, Chapter 13
         Meditation
         Homework: Attraction spell
Fifteenth Class:
Hypnosis, resolving conflicts, the Druids, the search for perfection
   Given: The laws 49-52
         Meditation
         Homework: Protective spell
Sixteenth Class:
Tarot, evocation, invocation
   Given: The laws 53-56
         Meditation
         Homework: Create a Saturn ritual. Make a gift for the temple with your own hand.
Seventeenth Class:
Cataclysms, economic and social upheavals, cycles of nature, survival, spiritual retreats, Camelot of the woods.
   Given: The laws 57-60
         Meditation
         Homework: Jupiter ritual.
Eighteenth Class:
The naming, initiation, the ordeal, absorption of evil by the power or compassion.
   Given: The laws 61-65
         Meditation
         Homework: Perform a Mercury ritual.
Nineteenth Class:
Kabala, making talismans, the thirteen treasures

Given: The laws 66-69
    Meditation
    Homework: Do a Uranus ritual.

Twentieth Class:
Kabala, making talismans, Tuatha de Danann
  Given: The laws 70-73
    Meditation
    Homework: Mars ritual.

Twenty-first Class:
Kabala, pentagram rituals, Children of Don
  Given: The laws 74-77
    Meditation
    Homework: Neptune ritual.

Twenty-second Class:
Tarot, pentagram rituals, Hu Gadarn, Children of Llyr
  Given: The laws 78-81
    Meditation

Twenty-third Class:
Karot, hexagram ritual, the Grail
  Given: The laws 82-85
    Meditation

Twenty-fourth Class:
Tarot, hexagram rituals, dreams and symbolism
  Given: The laws 86-89
    Meditation

Twenty-fifth Class:
Tarot, consecration, leadership behavior
  Given: The laws 90-93
    Meditation
    Requirement: Your first Book of Shadows must be submitted for examination.

Twenty-sixth Class:
Divination, which is dousing, crystal; begin copying The Owl.
  Given: The laws, 94-97
    Meditation

Twenty-seventh Class:
Divination, dousing, pendulum. Continue copying The Owl.
  Given: The laws, 98-101
    Meditation

Twenty-eighth Class

Divination, scrying, mirror; copying The Owl.
  Given: The laws, 102-105
    Meditation

Twenty-ninth Class:

Divination, scrying, crystal ball; copying The Owl.
  Given: The laws 106-109
    Meditation

Thirtieth Class:

Psychometry, copy The Owl.
  Given: The laws 110-113
    Meditation

Thirty-first Class:

Psychometry, copy The Owl, herbs and healing
  Given: The laws 114-117
    Meditation

Thirty-second Class:

Begin astrological chart, copy The Owl, herbs and healing
  Given: The laws 118-121
    Meditation

Thirty-third Class:

The Quest, copy The Owl, herbs and healing
  Given: The laws 122-125
    Meditation

Thirty-fourth Class:

Copy The Owl, Atlantis, Mu, and Lemuria
  Given: The laws 126-129
    Meditation

Thirty-fifth Class:

Copy The Owl, Atlantis, Masadia
Given: The laws 130-133
    Meditation

Thirty-sixth Class:

Copy The Owl, Atlantis, demonstration of the 26 requirements
  Given: The laws 134-137
    Meditation

Thirty-seventh Class:

Copy The Owl, Atlantis, demonstration of the 26 requirements

Given: The laws 138-141
    Meditation
Thirty-eighth Class:
Copy The Owl, astral projection, demonstration of the
26 requirements
    Given: The laws 142-145
    Meditation
Thirty-ninth Class:
Copy The Owl, astral projection
    Given: The laws 146-149
    Meditation
Fortieth Class:
Copy The Owl, regression
    Given: The laws 150-153
    Meditation
Forty-first Class:
Copy The Owl, regression
    Given: The laws 154-157
    Meditation
Forty-second Class:
Copy The Owl, telekinesis, cloud dissolving
    Given: The laws 158-161
    Meditation
Forty-third Class:
Copy The Owl, telekinesis, cloud dissolving
    Given: The laws 162-165
    Meditation
Forty-fourth Class:
Copy The Owl, telepathy
    Given: The laws 166-169
    Meditation
Forty-fifth Class:
Copy The Owl, telepathy
    Given: The oaths
    Meditation
Forty-sixth Class:
Copy The Owl, automatic writing
    Given: The oaths
    Meditation
Forty-seventh Class:

The I Ching, copy The Owl
  Given: The triads
     Meditation
Forty-eighth Class:
Copy The Owl
  Given: The triads
     Meditation
Forty-ninth Class:
The adoption, copy The Owl
  Given: The triads
     Meditation
Fiftieth Class through the Fifty-second Class:
Initiation weekend. This time is taken up by initiation rituals, overnight rituals, and reading of student work.

Appendix 4
The neophyte must demonstrate the following at the end of nine months:

1. Ritual bath and purpose.
2. Casting the circle with diagram.
3. Entering a circle with diagram.
4. Invocation of the Mighty Ones.
5. Invocation of the Goddess.
6. Invocation of the Horned God.
7. Bidding farewell to the Mighty Ones.
8. Prepare a diagram of the altar.
9. Perform a weekly Esbat as an acting Priest or Priestess.
10. Perform a full moon ritual as an acting priest or priestess.
11. Consecration of tools.
12. Preparation of cords, cinguluum, and robes.
13. Demonstrate the invoking and banishing pentagram.
14. Demonstrate the salute.
15. Three-night ritual and purpose.
16. Drawing down the moon.
17. Wiccan Rede, long and short version.
18. Meditation and purpose.
19. Anointing and purpose.
20. Nudity and purpose.
21. Reading auras.
22. Know the colors of candles and purposes.
23. Know the twelve astrological signs and general characteristics.
24. Demonstrate psychometry.
25. Know the names and characteristics of the elements and elementals.
26. Start The Owl, workbook, or the Book of Shadows.

Appendix 5

All seekers of Level 0 must first register with Y Tylwyth Teg before beginning their work toward initiation with:

Y Tylwyth Teg of Georgia

P.O. Box 4196

Athens, Georgia 30605

Completion of an application will satisfy this requirement.

Each seeker must the accomplish the following:

1. One year and one day of individual instruction and completion of the correspondence course prescribed by Y Tylwyth Teg in Georgia. (The one year and one day of qualification time can be satisfied by either one year and one day of personal instruction or one year and one day of correspondence course participation.)
2. Completion of The Quest.
3. Copying The Owl.
4. Request to be Named, and be Named.

With the completion of the above requirements the seeker will then qualify to be Adopted to Level 1. Each teacher and guide is responsible for the instructions of his or her students. If any claims that they are of the Welsh tradition of Y Tylwyth Teg and claim to be able to initiate you, and they are not registered with Y Tylwyth Teg of Georgia, they are not telling the truth. Please contact us concerning such people.

The seeker must demonstrate the following at the end of one year and one day: completion of copying The Owl, which is checked by an elder; aura sensing, which is checked by an elder; knowledge of colors; numerology and astrology, complete a horoscope chart on a person not known to the seeker; divination by Tarot cards and palmistry; and psychometry using a blind study.

Appendix 6

The Thirteen Treasures

I.   The Book of Arawn, The Cauldron of Cerridwen symbolizes the cauldron and the circle, water and Scorpio.

II. The Book of Plenydd symbolizes the Thurible, Incense and the bell. This is the Basket of Gwydino Guerenhaer, which is Air, Gemini.

III. The Book of Tuatha de Danann. The Wand, the Ring, the Lamps. Volume I and II of The Ring of Luned, Air and Aries.

IV. The Book of Triads. The Cup. Volume I and II of The Horn of Bryan Galead, Water, Cancer.

V.   The Book of Hajarel Fehm; Maen Leog. The Altar, the Stone and the Temple. It is the Whetstone of Tudwall Tudclud as the center.

VI. The Book of the Radiant Brow. This is the robe of the Priest and the Priestess. Also the Cord. The Mantle of Tegan Eurvron. It is Water, Pisces.

VII. The Book of Y Tylwyth Teg. This is the Sword. It is also the Sword of Rhyddrech Hael. Dyrnwyn, Fire, Aquarius.

VIII. The book of Gwydion. This is Oil. The garment of Pedarn Veisrudd.

IX. The Rites and Rituals of Cymmry. This is Pentacle and Talisman. They symbolize the Platter of Rhegynydd Ysgolhaig. This is Earth, Capricorn.

X.   The Book of Speel. The Athame. It symbolizes the Knife of Llawfrodded Frachawg. Air, Libra.

XI. The Book of Donn. Robe of priest, the Scourge. They represent the mantle of Arthur, Fire, Leo.

XII. The Book of Migrations. The Platter. This represents the Pan of Rhegnydd Ysgolhaig. This is Earth, Virgo.

XIII. The Book of Gwron. This is the Staff and the Broom. It represents the Chariot of Morgan Mwyvawr, Fire, Sagittarius.

The Owl, which is our Book of Shadows, or the work-book. It is represented by the Chess Board of Gwendolyn, which represents the Thirteen Treasures in its entirety.

Appendix 7

The Structure of Y Tylwyth Teg

Level	Description	Training	Duration
0	L and F awenydd (seeker)	1 year	1 day
	First Circle: Cylch yr Abred (Circle of Courses) Class / Ovate		
1	Gwiddon (witch / ovate)	1 year	1 day
2	Offeriad / es (priest / priestess / ovate)	1 year	1 day
3	Dysgawderdos (teacher / disciple / ovate)	1 year	1 day
	Second Circle: Cylch y Gwynfyd (Circle of Blessedness) Class / Beirdd Cylch Cyfrin (Mystic Circle of Bards)		
4	Mynechdid cana (historical bard)	2 years	2 days
5	Cawr clewr (lecturer / bard)	2 years	2 days
6	Hebryngyet fileollamh (learned bard)	2 years	2 days
	Third Circle: Cylch Cyfrin (Circle of Infinity) Class / Derwddes y Cylch Cyfrin (Mystic Circle of Druids)		
7	Tywysog / es aikas derwddes (learned druid)	3 years	3 days
8	Credadun anruth leader of the families (believer of the noble strain)	3 years	3 days
9	Cyfrin Arwenydd (secret leader, enlightened one	3 years	3 days

19 years 19 days total
Cycle of the moon and cycle of humanity

Appendix 8
LEVEL REQUIREMENTS AND TRAINING OUTLINE

Level 0

Awnydd

Meaning: Seeker - a pagan neophyte

ADMISSION REQUIREMENTS:

One must make the following commitments: to work with your teacher, have a desire to learn, be willing to work hard, perform a three-night ritual, learn the Wiccan Rede, learn a salt circle, learn a self-blessing, be consecrated, take an oath of secrecy and dedication, and be 15 years of age at least.

TRAINING:

1. Learn the three columns and the three circles.
2. Complete a one-year dream diary.
3. Complete the required readings.
4. Attend and complete the thirteen treasures, the required thirteen lessons of instruction.
5. Attend all festivals and perform rituals as directed by your elders.
6. Begin preliminary study in meditation, sexual energy and symbolism, astrology, reincarnation, natural healing, karma, survival, psychic development, natural magic, consciousness raising, psychic music, Celtic folklore and religious symbolism, the duality of the god and the goddess, philosophy and ethics, history of the old religion and the Celts, survey of ancient and modern Wicca (witchcraft), divination, valley herbs.

DURATION OF TRAINING: One year and a day minimum.

RAISING REQUIREMENTS:

1. Show dedication and commitment.
2. Show extraordinary talent.
3. Spend a year and a day in training.
4. Request naming and be named.
5. Complete your quest.
6. Complete the introductory course of instruction and achieve satisfactory results on all tests.
7. Produce a written and oral report of your experiences and progress.
8. Turn in and discuss your dream journal.

9. Make a formal request for adoption.
10. Know and accept the ethics of the tribe.
11. Be adopted.

RESPONSIBILITIES:
1. Begin to live the ethical system.
2. Study and understand the philosophy of the tribe.
3. Know the basic cosmology of the tribe.
4. Attend all possible rituals.
5. Learn the ritual year and festival year.
6. Offer service to the tribe.
7. Become an active member of the clan.
8. Attend all classes.
9. Read the required texts.
10. Prepare the proper tools.
11. Prepare your robe and cord.
12. Understand the meaning and obligation of initiation.
13. Know the gods' and goddesses' names.
14. Learn the basic rituals.
15. Learn the basic occult sciences.

CIRCLE ONE *"Cylch yr Abred"*
Circle of Courses
Class — Ovate
Level 1 — Gwiddon (Witch)
"Welsh Wise One"

ADMISSION REQUIREMENTS:
1. You must be named, go on your quest, and be adopted, no exceptions.
2. You must spend one year and a day as an "awenydd" (seeker), no exceptions.
3. You must show dedication and commitment.
4. You must be 18 years of age.

TRAINING COURSES:
1. You must learn the meaning of "liberty — equality — unity".
2. You must learn the meaning of *"the raven"*.
3. You must learn to deal with material things.
4. You must learn to follow others whose knowledge is greater than yours.
5. Begin your basic studies:
   a. Holistic health of body, mind and spirit.

b. Begin basic psychic development:
   Divination and Tarot
   Divination of the I Ching
   Divination with Runes
   Divination with Crystals
   Dousing
   Clairvoyance and Clairaudience
   Hypnosis and Psychic Healing
   c. Begin basic magical studies: natural magic, ceremonial magic, ritual magic, talismatic magic
   d. Herbs and Oils
   e. Contemporary Religions: Christianity, Islam, Buddhism, and others.
   f. Celtic Mythology and Spirituality
   g. Celtic Philosophy and Metaphysics
   h. Philosophy and Today's World
   i. Celtic Ritual and Drama
   j. Survival
   k. Physical and Biological Sciences
   l. The Dance
   m. Raising Consciousness — Mystical States

DURATION OF TRAINING:

One year and a day minimum
"Raising" (initiation) requirements:
   1. Achieve satisfactory results in tests, written and oral.
   2. Produce a written and oral report of your progress and experiences.
   3. Teach a class of awennddiath (seekers).
   4. Ask for raising to level 2.
   5. Show extraordinary talent.
   6. Show dedication and commitment.
   7. Turn in and discuss your second dream journal.

Class — Ovate Level 2

Offeriades

Priest / Priestess

ADMISSION REQUIREMENTS:

   1. Spend one year and one day at level one or show extraordinary talent.

TRAINING:

   1. The seeker must understand and control the inner self, and

unite that self with the conscious mind. Must learn the Dragon ritual, learn the level 2 symbolism and begin the inward journey.

2. Skill development and basic studies.
3. Continue the dream journal.
4. Teaching a class.
5. Assisting Level 1 members.
6. Choose your second specialty.
7. Study the use of drugs and misuse of drugs.
8. Emotion, its meaning and control.
   a. Study of the two types of consciousness, inward and outward.
   b. Study of the false paths.
      (1.) Thinking or talking about work instead of doing it.
      (2.) Starry-eyed syndrome.
      (3.) False Messiah syndrome.
      (4.) Personal salvation syndrome.
      (5.) Sunday-go-to-Meeting syndrome.
      (6.) Hump the guru syndrome.
   c. Study emotional center problems.
      (1.) Aimlessness.
      (2.) Self Pity.
      (3.) Self Hatred.
      (4.) Overdependence.
      (5.) Will to dominate.
      (6.) Will to pleasure.
   d. Ego Problems
      (1.) Lower self and persona problems.
      (2.) Persona and ego.
      (3.) Higher self and ego problems.
      (4.) The group mind.
      (5.) How to control ego.
   e. Indentify with the water goddess.
   f. Identify and study the sex drive and discuss sexual problems.
   g. Dionysian experience versus Christian repression.

DURATION OF TRAINING:
One year and one day of Level 2 training.

RAISING REQUIREMENTS:

1. Achieve satisfactory results on tests.
2. Produce a written and oral report of your experience and progress.
3. Discuss experiences of Level 1.
4. Ask for Level 3 initiation.
5. The seeker must take the subliminal mind.
6. The seeker must contact the inner self.
7. The seeker must know divination.
8. The seeker must isolate and control the ego.
9. The seeker must become of one with water.

RESPONSIBILITIES:

1. Attend all possible rituals.
2. You must conquer the spirit.

Class — Ovate

Level 3 — *"Dysgawder/dos"* (The High Priest/ess)

ADMISSION REQUIREMENTS:

Spend one year and one day at Level 2 or show extraordinary ability.

TRAINING:

1. You must learn the meaning of secrecy — obedience — fidelity, industry — honesty — diligence, faithfulness — duty and justice.
2. You must develop and discover control over your own true will and learn to direct your life transformations.
3. Study and understand your initiation.
4. Know the meaning of air.
5. Know the will.
    > The will to pleasure
    > The will to pain
    > The will to power
    > The will to meaning
    > The will to self-transcendence
6. Control of will. Magickal use of will.
7. Construct and use talismans of air.
8. Control of karma.
9. Learn the use of sex drive to transcend the self. Primal energy, orgone energy, life force, kundalini.
10. Understanding control of violence.
11. Use of inward drama to act out balance.
12. Study of the goddess of air.

13. Use of magic and sound. Contact exercises.
14. Know humility.
15. Work air rituals.
16. Establish your own true will with that of the Goddess.
17. Master the astral light.
18. Master the magical use of sound.
19. Learn the minor keys.
20. Know the minor wards of power.
21. Study the basic Cabala.
22. Become the element air.
23. Study the use of magical condensers.
24. Study the use of the wand.
25. Conjure the devas of air.
26. Demonstrate knowledge of your karma.
27. Study goddess forms.
28. Continue advanced study and skill development.
29. Assist circles of courses members in their work.
30. Spend at least one month living with your teacher.
31. Teach a class in your specialty on a continuing basis.
32. Continue to perform the usual duties.
33. Intensive practice in your specialty.
34. Help to run local activities of your Y Tylwyth Teg grove.
35. Lead and advise one grove.

DURATION OF TRAINING:
One year and one day of Level 3 training.
RAISING REQUIREMENTS:
1. Achieve satisfactory results on tests.
2. Produce a written and oral report of your experiences and progress.
3. Discuss experiences in Level 2 (self-evaluation).
4. Ask for Level 4 initiation.
5. Be ordained.
6. Produce a thesis on your specialty.
7. Train at least one qualified successor for your grove.

CIRCLE TWO
"Cylch yr Cwynfed" (Circle of Blessedness)
Class — Bard (Mystic Bards) (beirdd cylch cyfrin)
Level 4 — Mynechdid Cana (Historical Bard)
        One of the mystic circle of bards

ADMISSION REQUIREMENTS:
Spend two years and two days in Level 3 or show extraordinary talent
TRAINING:
1. Learn the meaning of study and application, bravery, devotedness, patriotism, protect the oppressed, devoting yourself to the honor and interest of your country and tribe.
2. Continue studying basics.
3. Produce a thesis tying together all your studies.
4. Assist second circle members.
5. Practice your specialty professionally.
6. Supervise activities of several groves.
7. Helping to run Y Tylwyth Teg regional activities.
8. Continue to grow.
9. The seeker must know that that which is rational shall free the transformed body/mind/spirit from every oppression of matter.
10. Study the initiations of fire.
11. Know the ancient mystery philosophies.
12. Have knowledge and control of the intellect.
    a. Control visualization
    b. Control meditations
    c. Develop time shapes
    d. Develop awareness of process
    e. Know the gods of fire
    f. Study illusion
    g. Meditate on forms
    h. Meditate without forms
13. Develop the soul.
14. To move free within the systems of philosophy of the ancient mysteries.
15. Continue the extraction of the auric egg.
16. To free the mind/soul for the oppression of matter.
17. Learn Greek, Hebrew, Egyptian and Roman philosophies.
18. Learn the secret symbol of fire.
19. To know and identify with eternal matter.
20. Free the "great lord Pan who is within".
21. Know the alchemy of truth.

DURATION OF TRAINING:
Two years and two days minimum.

RAISING REQUIREMENTS:
1. Train at least two qualified successors for your groves.
2. Produce satisfactory results in tests.
3. Discuss experiences in Level 3.
4. Produce a written and oral report of your experiences and progress.
5. Produce a thesis of your specialty.
6. Continue basic studies.
7. Request advancement.

Class — Bard
Level 5 — Cawr Clewr (Lecturer Bard)
ADMISSION REQUIREMENTS:
Spend two years and two days as Level 4 of show extraordinary talent.
TRAINING:
1. Learn the meaning of:
   Toleration, liberality against fanaticism and persecution, political and religious.
   Education and enlightenment against error.
   Barbarism and ignorance.
   Devoting your head and heart and mind.
2. Be honest, true, reliable and sincere.
3. Be true unto mankind.
4. Be sincere in all things.
5. Be ernest in your duties.
6. Learn the slogan "Let us begin to rise toward the stars".
7. Continue to seek training.
8. Write or produce a thesis that ties together your studies.
9. Assist first circle members.
10. Practice your second specialty professionally.
11. Supervise the activities of the regional Y Tylwyth Teg staff.
12. Continue to grow.
13. Study the following levels of Masonry:
    a. Grand Master Architect
    b. Loyal Arch of Solomon
    c. Grand Elect Perfect and Sublime Mason
    d. Knight of the East of the Sword
    e. Prince of Jerusalem
    f. Knight of East and West
    g. Knight of Rose Croix

h. Grand Pontiff

14. Study the Myfferian archeaology of Wales (Book).

DURATION OF TRAINING:

Spend two years and two days at Level 5.

RAISING REQUIREMENTS:

1. Train two qualified successors for your groves.
2. Produce and write a report of your progress.
3. Complete a written and oral examination.
4. Request advancement.
5. Read the Nine-Level Way.

Class — Bard

Level 6

Hebryngyet Filebeirdd Ollamh *"Learned Bard"*

ADMISSION REQUIREMENTS:

Spend two years and two days as Level 5 or show extraordinary talent.

TRAINING:

1. Reflect and meditate on the symbols and learn the secret Welsh knowledge.
2. Seek and ye shall find.
3. Learn knowledge and truth forever.
4. Teach truth.
5. Learn fidelity to your obligations.
6. Constancy and perseverance.
7. Vow to crusade against ignorance, intolerance, fanaticism, uncharitableness, and error.
8. Learn, love, peace, charity, and toleration.
9. Your slogan is "Human knowledge is but an imperfect reflection of the infinite."
10. Continue advanced study.
11. Write or produce a thesis that ties together your studies.
12. Assist 4th level members.
13. Practice your third specialty professionally.
14. Supervise the activities of a national staff.
15. Continue to grow.
16. Complete all requirements according to Y Tylwyth Teg tradition.

DURATION OF STUDY:

Spend two years and two days at Level 6.

RAISING REQUIREMENTS:
1. Train two qualified successors as your regional leaders.
2. Produce a written and oral report of your progress.
3. Request advancement.
4. Complete a written and oral examination.

It is not allowed to discuss the Third Circle, Cylch y Cyfrin with those who are not initiates.

Appendix 9

Requirements for copying of the *"Thirteen Treasures"*.

1. Seeker — must copy The Owl before initiation.

1st Level — must copy the book of Rites and Rituals and the book of Tuatha de Danann, Volumes 1 and 2.

2nd Level — must copy the books of Gwron, the book of Hajarelfehm, the book of Radiant Brow.

3rd Level — must copy the book of Plenyedd, the book of Spiel, and the book of Gwydion.

3rd Level — must begin copying the book of Guidion, the book of Migrations, the Book of Triads Volumes 1 and 2, the Book of Don, the Book of Arawn, the Book of Taliesen.

4th Level — must complete copying of the Thirteen Treasures.

5th Level — must copy the secret manuscript, The Nine-Level Way.

6th Level — must copy the secret manuscript, Oral Traditions and Chronology of Knowledge.

7th Level — must copy the manuscripts The Mystic Circle and Cylch yr Abred.

8th Level — must copy the secret manuscripts Cylch yr Cwynfyd and Cylch yr Ceugant.

0-595-23125-X